Ecopolitics

SUNY Series in Environmental Philosophy and Ethics

J. Baird Callicott and John van Buren, editors

Ecopolitics
Redefining the Polis

GERARD KUPERUS

Cover image: The side of a tide pool showing sea stars (*Dermasterias*), sea anemones (*Anthopleura*), and sea sponges in Santa Cruz, California (2007) by Brocken Inaglory. Wikicommons

Published by State University of New York Press, Albany

© 2023 State University of New York

All rights reserved

Printed in the United States of America

No part of this book may be used or reproduced in any manner without written permission. No part of this book may be stored in a retrieval system or transmitted in any form or by any means including electronic, electrostatic, magnetic tape, mechanical, photocopying, recording, or otherwise without the prior permission in writing of the publisher.

For information, contact State University of New York Press, Albany, NY
www.sunypress.edu

Library of Congress Cataloging-in-Publication Data

Name: Kuperus, Gerard, author.
Title: Ecopolitics : redefining the polis / Gerard Kuperus.
Description: Albany : State University of New York Press, [2023] | Series: SUNY series in environmental philosophy and ethics | Includes bibliographical references and index.
Identifiers: LCCN 2022053662 | ISBN 9781438494258 (hardcover : alk. paper) | ISBN 9781438494272 (ebook)
Subjects: LCSH: Political ecology. | Green movement. | Environmental policy—Social aspects.
Classification: LCC JA75.8 .K86 2023 | DDC 304.2—dc23/eng/20230228
LC record available at https://lccn.loc.gov/2022053662

10 9 8 7 6 5 4 3 2 1

Contents

Acknowledgments		vii
Introduction: Ecopolitics beyond the Human World		1
Chapter 1	Salmon Politics and Latour's Gaia	37
Chapter 2	Crossing Borders: On Rats, Mice, and Other Decolonizing Packs	63
Chapter 3	Chimpanzee Politics: Towards Empathy	87
Chapter 4	From the Tidepool to Human Migration: The Biological Roots of Politics	113
Chapter 5	Human and Other Ants: Decentralized Ecopolitics	131
Conclusion: Ecopolitics as a Decentralized Basis for a New Future		161
Notes		193
Bibliography		213
Index		219

Acknowledgments

Collaboration is the key to ecopolitics, and this book itself can be seen as the result of such a politics. Many people, non-human animals, and places have been involved directly or indirectly in the processes that ultimately led to this book. Different interactions with animals, such as rats, cats, salmon, bears, ants, and deer, told in short stories throughout the book, have greatly informed my thinking and feeling. Likewise, many places have been significant in shaping the thoughts and relationships that are expressed here: the USF Campus, our home in San Anselmo, Sitka (Alaska), Aroma Café in San Rafael, the canals and the public library (OBA) in Amsterdam, the Oostvaardersplassen, the Marker Wadden, and the Marconi Center.

Many have heard earlier versions of papers that eventually formed the chapters of this book. The feedback I received after presenting works in progress has in particular been extremely valuable. Earlier versions of the chapter on ants were presented at the Werkgroep Dieren Ethiek and the Radical Philosophy Association (RPA). Different parts of the chapter on tidepools were presented at the Pacific Association for the Continental Tradition (PACT), the International Steinbeck Association, and at my National Endowment for the Humanities (NEH) Lecture at the University of San Francisco (USF). Parts of the mice and rats chapter were discussed at PACT and a philosophy and environment workshop in Leuven. Parts on Zen Buddhism were presented at meetings of the Comparative and Continental Philosophy Circle (CCPC). The first chapter on salmon took its initial shape during the seminar I gave at the Sitka Institute. I am deeply grateful to all the people who were part of these societies of thinkers, and who listened, read, commented, suggested, or rolled their eyes.

Besides the many colleagues who provided feedback at and outside of these meetings, my great inspiration are my students! Their enthusiasm, along with the raised eyebrows when bringing in my ideas, assisted me in writing this book, more so than they are aware. Thank you all! Students who have helped me as research assistants: Isabella Britt, Zachary Clausen, Maya Lawton, Savannah Perry, Mahtop Ranjber, and Garrett Starr. Many thanks for fixing my English and for providing honest feedback when I needed it. You are all an inspiration and a hope for a future to come!

I also want to thank the National Endowment for the Humanities (NEH) for the yearlong research support, the Faculty Development Fund at the University of San Francisco, the provost, and College of Arts and Science deans' office for providing a sabbatical which allowed me to complete this manuscript. I am also grateful for the support of the writing retreats made possible by the dean's office.

I would like to thank my colleagues at USF, in particular Kim Carfore, Rafael Dumett, Stephen Friesen, David Kim, Sam Mickey, Marjolein Oele, Amanda Paris, Tanu Sankalia, Ron Sundstrom, Jackie Taylor, and Steve Zavestoski. Collaborators in thinking on the West Coast: Josh Hayes, Brian Treanor, and Jason Wirth have all been extremely generous in helping me become a better thinker in and through this place. I would also like to thank Chuck Miller of the Sitka Clan of the Tlingit People, who generously welcomed me in Sitka and shared Raven stories. Finally, Tom Thorpe for always telling me I am wrong because "that ain't politics!" Thank you all for pushing me along (and against me)! At SUNY I would like to thank Michael Rinella, Susan Geraghty, the series editors Baird Callicott and John van Buren, as well as the three anonymous reviewers who provided constructive feedback!

An earlier version of chapter 1 was published in *Environmental Philosophy*. Some parts of chapter 4 have been previously published in a very different format in *Thinking in the West*.

Last but not least, I want to thank my own *oikos,* my family consisting of Lars, Imma, and Marjolein. Thank you for letting me navigate the complex politics of the household!

Introduction

Ecopolitics beyond the Human World

> Now I would like to think of the possibility of a new humanities.
>
> —Gary Snyder, *A Place in Space*, 127

During a global pandemic, while humans are battling tiny microbes, a group of orcas convenes off the coast of Portugal and Spain. After their meeting, the orcas start their campaign against humans by ramming the stern (rear) of boats. They cause substantial damage to rudders while some crew members face injuries due to the impact of the collision. Several boats must be towed back to land after losing the ability to steer. One boat sinks. The aggression towards boats baffles scientists, to say the least. Orcas may seem curious and playful, but their aggressive hunting strategies earn them the name killer whales. Yet, none of that can possibly explain this sudden vandalism. Humans, or their boats, have never been a target. Some aboriginal cultures address the truce between humans and orcas, indicating indeed a long-lasting peaceful relationship. For example, Haida and Tlingit cultures (in the Pacific Northwest) regard the orca (or Blackfish) as the representation of the force of nature. In the well-known story of Natsilane, it is made clear that humans are not the target of orcas. The story tells how Blackfish, the orca, kills the jealous brother of Natsilane. After this act of violence, Natsilane and Blackfish agree that the latter will never again hurt any human beings. While the story might be fiction, it is true that attacks on humans are virtually nonexistent—that is until now.

Why have the orcas in the North Atlantic broken their truce? One possible explanation may be stress, as they are an endangered species. Perhaps an orca has been hit by a ship. Perhaps, indeed, a council of orcas decided to collectively harass the root of their distress: humans.

"What do you mean by a council of orcas?" the reader may ask. I suggest we find a political reality at work in orcas as well as in the relationship between humans and orcas, even if the trigger was indeed stress (a feeling not unfamiliar to human political players). In this book, I argue that non-human societies do have a lot in common with human political societies. Or, more accurately, I show how our political societies have a lot in common with earlier life-forms.

This argument implies a reassessment of both human and non-human collectives in which *logos* becomes less of a defining characteristic. The distinction between animals with and without reason or speech has been a crucial aspect in the history of Western thinking. As is evident in the *De Anima,* Aristotle in many ways makes a sharp distinction between animals that have *logos* and those that do not. *Logos* is our *capacity*. Likewise, he calls humans the political animal, suggesting politics is *our* realm. Etymologically, politics is tied to the *polis,* the city, or the country of which one can be a citizen. Sometimes *polis* is translated as "community" and *politika* as "social." Thus, it seems that etymologically politics is tied to humans. Nevertheless, Aristotle's own writing casts doubts on the exclusive political status of humans when he states the following: "The social (Πολιτικὰ / politika) animals are those which have some one common activity (ἔργον / ergon); and this is not true of all the gregarious (ἀγελαῖα / agelaia) animals. Examples of social animals are man, bees, wasps, ants, cranes. Some of them live under a ruler, some have no ruler; examples: cranes and bees live under a ruler, ants and innumerable others do not."[1] The passage suggests that politics for Aristotle, at least in this passage, is defined as a community that collectively engages in a common activity, with or without a ruler. Using this definition, different animals could be considered as political, of which Aristotle only provides a few examples. Interestingly, today we call insects such as ants and bees *social*, whereas Aristotle uses the word *political*.

The difference between society and politics—and likewise between the social and the political—is not always clear. Politics typically involves structures of governance and power, whereas society refers to structures beyond the political that involve class, gender, race, education, and so forth. Thinkers such as Rousseau, Marx, Kropotkin, Foucault, or Bookchin have in different ways shown that political structures and techniques (or technologies) of power are found throughout our social structures. Charbonneau likewise takes politics beyond those who govern and defines it as "the act of managing together."² Political power is then not centralized in a few elected officials. For better or worse, it is found in larger structures. In that regard, we could say that we already live in a politically decentralized world. Economy, class, gender distinctions, and public opinion are all formed through historical, social, cultural, and economic structures of great complexity. The so-called leaders are in service of a system. The same can be said for parental and household structures, as well as education. None of our societal structures could function without a general inclination of people to follow orders, to be part of hierarchies and social structures. As we see in the Women Marches, Black Lives Matter (and earlier the Civil Rights movement), the Dakota Access Pipeline protests, or the #MeToo movements, resistance to governments and existing structures are typically collective endeavors, again falling into structures. How social structures are formed in particular depends on the social, economic, and political contexts in which groups and individuals live. Yet, beyond the particularities, it is a given that we can easily function in these contexts. Moreover, we need it as we could not survive as individuals. The two natural social functions that Kropotkin and others point out are *competition* and *mutual aid*. The latter especially cannot occur without structures. We can wonder if structures of freedom are made possible through the existence of necessary structures. Kant suggests our political structures and restrictions generate the conditions for the possibility of freedom.

When comparing human and non-human animals, the distinction is often made on the grounds that non-human animals merely act out of necessity, whereas humans, even while their society is generated out of necessity, act out of freedom. Thus, it is argued that we can engage freely in politics to think about and pursue "the good life." This raises the question: if in today's society the majority of people are not engaged in politics and do not reflect on or attempt to pursue the good life, then are our lives in any essential way different from those of other social animals?

Nietzsche, for good reasons, refers to humans as herd animals. Marx speaks of alienation from our human essence as social beings. Going back to Ancient Greece: while Plato's political agenda is often difficult to accept at face value, his idea that we all live like prisoners in a cave is not blaming the oppression by rulers, but rather his point is that we ourselves are the cause of our own oppression. Within the Western canon, we encounter the danger of emphasizing individualism. Freedom is often confused with individualism, and we tend to neglect the fact that it is the collective in which we exist that makes individual choices possible in the first place. In this book, I do occasionally engage with Zen Buddhist thinking insofar as it shows us that we are beings in relation to other human beings as well as to the natural world. It is sometimes mistakenly assumed that there is no individuality in Buddhism. However, the point of Zen Buddhism, as I understand it, is rather that individualism always involves the context in which we function. Individuality can only occur within a collective, or ensemble of others, consisting of human and non-human entities.

As already indicated one might be hesitant to call non-human structures political. When I suggest that ants, salmon, or rats are political beings, I can already hear some readers protest: "that ain't politics!" They will argue that politics involves active and conscious participation, making choices that are not driven by necessity and instinct alone, but rather through representation, government, laws, and envisioning a common good. On the basis of such definitions of politics and non-human animals, we can quickly dismiss the very possibility of politics for non-human animals because they do not conceptualize a common good and have no notion of "the good," or "the good life" (as far as we know). Indeed, we typically do not find such political features in non-human animals. Yet, we should be careful about using too high a standard here, a prejudice sometimes called anthropofabulation. If we apply the same strict criterion to human beings, most will fail to truly function "politically." Just like animals, humans typically, indeed, do not think about "the good." How many people explicitly participate in a collective endeavor that aims at the good? Can we even agree on what we mean by "the good?" How many people manage to act freely? How many are well-informed? Interestingly, our contemporary human ways of living have moved away from the stricter definitions of politics. Along similar lines, organizational models we find in non-human animals are often considered purely necessary, in which it is assumed that freedom is impossible. Thus, it is suggested that they are not engaged in politics defined as such. After all, we suggest that animals behave most of all instinctually. If they have a goal, even a collective goal, they are not aware of this goal. They do not think teleologically, as opposed to humans.

Against this tendency, I claim that politics is much older than the human species. We have inherited certain traits directly from some species, or as the theory of convergent evolution suggests, species might have developed in similar ways by facing similar challenges and opportunities. In terms of language, *politics* is etymologically rooted in the city, the *polis*, yet we have seen above that already Aristotle uses the word *politika* to describe animal societies. In this book, I follow and exploit this Aristotelian trace and argue how the chimpanzee colony, the ant colony, packs of rats, schools of fish, or tidepools can be considered "cities." While I am not doubting that we humans are in some ways essentially different from other animals, at a very basic level, we share traits even with fish and ants. In particular, we share traits that make us able and want to collaborate. Species, including ours, can thrive because of that collaboration. Likewise, it is not an exclusively human characteristic to experience feelings for one another. For example, rats and chimpanzees also experience empathy.[3]

There might be a purpose to a *polis*, for example, the mutual benefits that arise from collaboration. Such benefits range from work and education to cultural events. A city, like any society, *ideally* provides food, shelter, safety, health, and education for all. While social contract theories suggest that the move towards society was a human one, animals live together and collaborate for exactly the same reasons we do: mutual benefit. This should not surprise us, since we are also animals. All animals, and in fact all living beings, need some level of collaboration in order to live, survive, and/or reproduce. The ant colony can consist of tens of thousands of individuals who—just like most humans—would not even know how to survive on their own. They build cities consisting of networks of tunnels and chambers, as well as engage in a sophisticated division of labor. Salmon can only reproduce through massive collective movements, and chimpanzee colonies function through complex social and, as De Waal argues, political dynamics.

Aristotle speaks about some animals as being involved in one common activity, whereas according to Kropotkin all species and organisms rely on what he calls "mutual aid." A species that is not in some fundamental way drawn towards collaboration is bound to go extinct quickly. Even solitary species of animals will need to procreate and raise their offspring. Most species of animals spend the majority of their lives in groups. Groups need to make decisions, and we all know how difficult that is. Deciding which restaurant to go to with a small group can be a monumental task if all individual tastes, dietary restrictions, economic backgrounds, and quirks of all the members of the group are to be taken into account. The decisions most animals have to make as a group are perhaps less complicated than those of humans, yet the point is that collective decisions are made and that different animal communities use a variety of mechanisms to make them. We might be able to learn something from studying the dynamics of a variety of animal communities.

The endeavor at the center of this book is to regard the collective or ensemble of non-human animals as political. Returning to the issue of relating the social and the political, we find that these words are often used in conjunction. For example, when we speak of political societies, the social contract is often the founding principle of the political unity. It is on the basis of this idea of an agreement that we find that a society indeed becomes political. Definitions of politics include some combination of elements such as laws, policies, leadership, government, and representative power. Our social abilities seem to either be a prerequisite for political unity, or our sociability is brought out when we function within a political body. When we speak of social animals, we are hesitant at best to describe, for example, a colony of ants as a political unity. It is argued that they do not deal with laws or governance, and/or that their association is not a free one. Others suggest we cannot speak of a political community if all the members of the colony are daughters of the mother queen. We tend to be good at creating exclusive definitions.

Aristotle's loose use of the words *politika* and *polei* to describe non-human animals, in the passage cited above, is heavily criticized by Hobbes in the *Leviathan*. This should not come as a surprise since it conflicts with Hobbes's idea that the commonwealth is artificial (yet necessary). Other animals live in natural unities that do not escape the realm of necessity, while our commonwealth is created by humans. The idea that other animals are social and political, collectively engaged in a common activity, does not rhyme with Hobbes's chaotic and violent version of the state of nature in which we are all beasts with only one goal: to preserve our existence. Mutual aid or collective work is not a possibility in the imagined world of the war of all against all.

The classical social contract theories (Grotius, Hobbes, Rousseau, and Locke) all regard the contract as an imagined one, which mostly means that no one signed the contract. Furthermore, the step into society is explicitly a thought experiment and not a historical event. In the imagined state of nature, we could supposedly do whatever we wanted. Regardless of whether they give it a positive or negative spin, all social contract theorists use the state of nature in their theories. It marks a rift between the pre-political society and the political one, a move in which we supposedly alienated some of our natural rights in order to obtain civil ones. It is no coincidence that this discourse of states of nature and social contracts arises in a time of colonialism. "Savage barbarians" who supposedly lack foresight and organizational skills are moved into civilization. The aboriginal scholar Yunkaporta objects to such characterizations of Indigenous cultures by writing that if Paleolithic lifestyles were so basic and primitive, how did humans evolve with trillions of potential neural connections in the brain, of which we now use only a small fraction? What kinds of sophisticated lifestyles would be needed to evolve such a massive brain over hundreds of thousands of years? What kind of nutritional abundance would be needed to develop such an organ, made mostly of fat? How does the narrative of harsh survival in a hostile landscape align with this fact? If our prehistoric lives were so violent, hard, and savage, how could we have evolved to have such soft skin, limited strength, and delicate parts?[4]

These are some excellent questions that drive us towards the following hypothesis: we have been political (arguably much more political than we currently are) for hundreds of thousands of years.

After Darwin and Nietzsche the social contract theory has been revisited repeatedly, in terms of justice (Rawls), racism (Mills), sexism (Pateman), and nature (Serres). Yet, should we not revise (or reject) the social contract theory from a more radical post-Darwinian, postcolonial, and post-Nietzschean standpoint? The social contract theory obscures what we inherited from other life-forms. Biologically we inherited our natural tendencies to be social, to be drawn to groups, to compete, to collaborate, to be drawn to hierarchies. Historically, we forget the long Indigenous history of political communities, and even prior to that humans lived together with Neanderthals. While the classical social contract theories were given shape within a European Christian context, we are living within the idea of that contract in a secular and global world. As Mills points out, the social (or racial) contract is not just a thought experiment; it is real in the way we live together. Slavery, genocide, and the stealing of Native American land lie at the basis of our political reality. As part of the postcolonial perspective, we also have to consider the influence of Christianity. Even while the separation of church and state is at the center of political developments in the early modern period, the idea that humans evolved from other life-forms is entirely absent in the social contract theories that originated in that same time period (even while in that same period the idea of different lineages of human races, some more closely related to apes, was informing social political discourses). The story of how our social and political lives evolved is laid out in the respective theories. All those stories start from scratch, the famous (or infamous) state of nature.

In this book, I am revisiting the social contract by imagining a political and social world long before humans emerged. I am proposing to go back at least 100 to 168 million years in time when ants already lived on the earth. An even more radical approach would be to go back close to a billion years and include sponges and fungi. While not quite going that deep into the past, I will consider how the tidepool forms a society as well. By exploring different non-human societies, I suggest that we should get rid of the idea of the social contract altogether, while acknowledging that its specter will keep haunting us.

This project involves different animal communities. Needless to say, it would be foolish to say that humans are similar to fungi, ants, or even chimpanzees. How their communities function and what they are capable of as a society is different from human societies. Yet, we do find certain shared characteristics in all forms of life. First and foremost, the need to collaborate is universal. My argument is that we humans inherited social traits from at least some of these animals and that it has been a mistake to overlook this evolutionary aspect of our social and political being. Chimpanzee colonies form political units; rats share the important social feeling of empathy; fish and birds collectively migrate; ants work together in a decentralized social order. None of this could happen without an instinctual drive to be part of a group. Understanding the drive towards a collective and recognizing how we humans are also determined through similar drives are essential to, first of all, understanding ourselves. Such an understanding does not have to lead to resignation of our instincts and feelings. Quite the opposite: to understand ourselves as creatures driven by social impulses, along with selfish ones, could lead us to a political society in which freedom can finally be pursued.

As already mentioned, Kropotkin describes politics as "mutual aid." This is a collaboration, or a working together, in which individual members provide and receive assistance to and from the group. As we will see in chapter 4, for Kropotkin, mutual aid leads to ethics and a sense of justice in the animal world. Justice occurs when members of an animal community that steal or in other ways act selfishly at the expense of other members are punished by the group. Many will accuse Kropotkin of anthropomorphizing the animal world, yet the real problem might be that we fail or refuse to acknowledge that the natural world is full of political relationships. The criterion for politics as mutual aid is simply that the members collectively work towards a common objective and, in doing so, follow certain standards. I suggest that even while the purpose is unknown or not explicit, maintaining the group collectively is the most important determining factor in suggesting that a community is engaged in politics. The composition of the group does not need to be the same all the time because the size, shape, and duration of a group can vary between different species as well as within the same species at different times. Yet, what determines the group (in all its varieties) as political, is cooperation or mutual aid. Collaboration is "taking part in" or "co-working." It requires involvement. When looking at salmon or ants, it could be suggested that they "participate" involuntarily in the group activities since it is their only chance at survival; and instead of making a choice, they simply follow a basic drive or instinct. I have suggested already that this classic distinction between necessity and freedom is problematic. Social contract theorists, from Grotius and Hobbes to Rawls, agree that no one explicitly or voluntarily agreed to the social contract. Even while we supposedly "give up" natural rights, the theory immediately involves an assumption of human "passivity" because we are born into a situation in which we are already subjects of the contract, and therefore subject to its rules. While conceptually the social contract indicates a subjection and passivity, in reality, we cannot be inactive. The same is true for non-human animal collaboration which is active and much more than an involuntary or passive involvement. As the Actor Network Theory (ANT) of Latour suggests, we are engaged in networks of actors. With that he is reconsidering who and what can be an agent. Along similar lines, I propose to rethink and reformulate the idea of human and non-human animal participation within their respective societies. I suggest that we can find an active engagement that steps beyond the passive-active dichotomy. This will be discussed in greater detail in chapter 1.

Thus, one of the guiding questions is whether non-humans take part, collaborate, and involve themselves in structures that could be called political. Ants constantly make decisions as individuals and moreover, as a whole. Rats have empathy, yet seem to exclude others from their group if exclusion favors the conditions of the group. In other words, their empathy seems to be selective. My suggestion is that similarities between human and non-human animal communities are abundant and that we have similar instincts, feelings, and structures. Therefore, ultimately, this project is a reassessment of our own political drives, needs, goals, and decisions.

The Beginning of Politics

In elementary school, we learn that human communities started as hunter-gatherer groups. How these groups exactly functioned is unclear. A common narrative is that the groups consisted of several families that worked together in their efforts to survive. Some lived in huts; others were more nomadic. The character of these groups changed when agriculture developed. Social contract theorists, while typically emphasizing that their version of human history is speculative, either suggest that we simply had to work together in order to avoid Hobbes's "war of all against all," or that the contract was simply a ruse of the wealthy (or whites, or men) as suggested first by Rousseau. What all social contract theories leave unquestioned is that we humans (and even more: we European humans) created politics. It is never suggested that humans have always already lived in political communities. Against this long-standing viewpoint, I suggest that we have not created politics (as is assumed in what Rancière refers to as "the logic of the *arche*").[5] I argue that we humans have always lived in a world full of politics. Other animals collaborate and are organized in structures. They belong to their community, depend on it, protect it, and are drawn to it.

On what exact basis can I make the outrageous claim that the human species came into existence in a world that was already political? Part of the justification lies in recent archaeological discoveries. Neanderthals are no longer considered to be the skull-smashing brutes they were once perceived to be. As discussed in chapter 3, chimpanzees live in political societies. It does not only seem unlikely, but even irrational to assume that hominids such as the Neanderthal (and the Homo sapiens) did not inherit (and further develop) the political aspects of other great apes. We see that chimpanzee leadership is established not just through an exercise and display of power, but through complex dynamics that involve all members of the colony and in which feelings of empathy are central.

Thus, we first of all stand in a lineage of political creatures that reaches back to other great apes. Yet, there are political structures much older, reaching back to social insects and other animals that live in groups. As Kropotkin, Allee, Ricketts, and De Waal suggest, cooperation or mutual aid is essential for all life.[6] Our tendency to be drawn to groups is a very old animal instinct, even a tendency of all forms of life. While Darwin's theory is often explained (especially by the social Darwinists) in terms of the survival of the fittest, leading to an emphasis on struggle, his theory also emphasizes the need for individuals to work together. Thus, there is struggle *and* there is cooperation. No species can survive without *both* components. Once we recognize that these two forces are at work in all life, non-human communities become much more complex and dynamic. Individual members might be driven towards their own selfish needs, but they are also driven towards one another, among others to assist other members of their community.

It is tricky to make speculations about animal intentions. Even if the intentions of most animals are not consciously aiming at the common good, they might nevertheless serve the common good. If the intention of an animal is a subconscious drive to self-preservation, does this mean that the animal is not political? As mentioned, Hobbes explicitly argues that non-human animal forms of organization are not political. Yet, his *Leviathan* proposes the body politic precisely on the account that human beings are creatures that act out of one impulse: self-interest. The only thing that keeps them from brutally killing one another is the social contract, which constitutes the artificial body. Thus, while human beings are merely matter in motion, and are nothing special as they are driven towards their own self-interest, the Leviathan is special. While I do not agree with Hobbes's assessment of human nature, he does show beautifully how the artificial state is in fact, an organic whole. While lessons are to be taken from this, I want to bring the Leviathan into question at its most fundamental level by first of all simply noticing that other animals can survive without a similar contract. We are the only animals who need a contract, or who have been convinced that we need one. We might possibly be better off without a contract, without an organizational structure in which we have alienated our right to truly participate in governing. In order to rethink our own organization, I propose to understand ourselves as part of a greater organic whole, a greater organizational structure in which we have to find (or retrieve) our proper place.

Human and Non-human Others

This book is written in the context of the disenfranchised in both the human and the non-human realm, framed within what I consider failed human politics. We live in a world of great contrasts. Streets are full of so-called homeless encampments while second (or third) residences are mostly vacant investment properties. Refugees try to cross borders while we vacation effortlessly all over the globe. Meanwhile, wildfires and storms are displacing and disrupting communities, leaving more people without a home. While we could mitigate these issues, we have not, and as long as we continue electing climate change deniers who serve industries rather than people, nothing will change. Even in a best-case scenario, it is very questionable what a "green" government can accomplish. International climate agreements aim at *reducing*, not *stopping* global warming. The latter is what we need while even the first is failing. Our current political reality has turned our actions into reactions to symptoms, failing to address causes. Instead of limiting consumption, we are sold on the idea of green consumption. Instead of reducing greenhouse gasses to stop climate change, we are talking about climate change mitigation (typically only available to wealthy communities). Instead of aiming for a peaceful world in which all humans can thrive, we are building walls and increasing border security. Or to take another example, a 68-million-dollar suicide barrier on the Golden Gate Bridge is supposed to keep people from jumping to their deaths, while the support of mental well-being is failing and underfunded. Walls and barriers are mostly symbolic measures. Fighting causes is not impossible even while the current system calls it exactly that: impossible. It calls one crazy for even imagining something beyond the current system. In fact, the current system seems to deplete our imagination to such a degree that even envisioning anything beyond the current situation is impossible.

Failed human politics has enormous consequences outside of the human realm. We fail when we open up areas from mountains to oceans for mining and oil winning. We fail to meet (or place) caps on carbon emissions. We fail to preserve mountains and forests, and "harvest" them instead. We fail in our fish quota and the standards for industrial farming. In all these examples, failed human politics is in direct relation to non-human politics.[7]

It sometimes seems that in the development of political systems, we have made very little progress, if any. The problems of the Greek democratic *polis* such as corruption, the influence of wealth, political demagogues, and those who lack true knowledge are representative of our problems today. Power seems to corrupt people, which is also confirmed in other political systems such as aristocracies and dictatorships. Our democracies today fail to live up to their name. Considering the long history of failed politics and the lack of true solutions to recurring problems, we could conclude that all human political models are bound to lead to the same negative outcomes.

This attitude, first of all, ignores the fact that political societies have existed much longer than the democracy we find in Ancient Greece. Unfortunately for us and the planet, the ecopolitical wisdom of Indigenous cultures has been largely destroyed. We are just working with 2,500 years of knowledge, and even beyond that we can suggest that the human species has only just started its attempts to figure out our human politics. We are in the developing stages, at best. Our species is, without a doubt, the most dominant species on earth at this time, yet we have existed only for a brief period. If we consider that human political systems are a tiny part of a much longer history of politics, we might find some hope. Ants have lived in collaborative models for 130 million years. Homo sapiens have only been around for 300,000 years, modern humans for around 40,000–50,000 years, and democracy only for 2,500 years. This might seem like a long time, especially if one's country has only been in existence for a few hundred years, but not if you consider that some trees are older than that! We are only at the beginning of learning how to live together successfully. Indeed, Gary Snyder suggests that we should think about "our situation in nothing less than a forty-thousand year time-scale. That is not very long. If we wanted to talk about hominid evolution we would have to work with something like four million years."[8] Challenging the notion of progress, he suggests that there is an indication that our brains have actually become smaller, which he blames on human society, through the loss of "personal direct contact with the natural world."[9] What he then proposes is the possibility of "a new humanities" which "would take the whole long *Homo sapiens* experience into account, and eventually make an effort to include our non-human kin. It would transform itself into a posthuman humanism, which would defend endangered cultures and species alike."[10]

My project follows Snyder's sentiment in which the idea of a new humanities emerges. In a "posthuman humanism" different (endangered) cultures and species are regarded as political. Snyder (and Haraway) speak(s) of non-human "kin." By grasping ourselves within a much larger context, a context that I call political, in which the family—kin—is the original political unity, we can start to make a place for a humanities that saves rather than destroys cultures and species.

In this book, I discuss different individual species, yet we always find that species can never be seen in isolation. In discussing a particular species, I try to understand how they function together and collaborate as communities or societies. While some aspects of non-human communities are extremely fascinating, I am not romanticizing or idealizing their existence. To state it bluntly, being an ant is a brutal existence. Nevertheless, we find that other species are successful at maintaining their species long-term, while we seem to be on track to self-destruction. We humans still have to learn how to live without destroying one another and without destroying the very ability to live in the first place. E. O. Wilson points out that ant colonies always fail and so do human colonies. Some human empires (super-colonies, one could say) might last for a few hundred years, but failure is inevitable. If we examine our own history of wars, genocides, slavery, oppression, and environmental destruction, what are we to conclude from this? Are we bound to fail as individual colonies or as a species? Can we, out of our failures, establish a truly functional human political system? The problem of the human species is that we are acting on a global scale. In his famous piece "Is Humanity Suicidal?" Wilson calls the human species an "environmental abnormality" and blames our intelligence.

Besides Snyder, phenomenological perspectives argue that we should again open our senses and experience the natural world. As we have lost direct contact with our environment, we are also losing direct contact with other humans, partially because communication has moved in virtual directions. Our brains seem to be shrinking further, along with our feelings towards non-human animals and other humans. Elisa Aaltola suggests in her book on empathy and animal ethics that with "the birth of the faceless, consumeristic, information- and market-based society governed by fragmented social spheres, an increasingly optimizing, instrumentalizing, profit-orientated approach to existence and the diminishment of embodied, attentive encounters, we are quickly detaching from the experiential lives of others. This signals a loss of empathy."[11] The loss of experience of the world is a common theme in phenomenology since Husserl. In focusing on feelings such as empathy as part of this loss, our ethical existence is brought into question. Emotions themselves, Aaltola suggests, have become brands. Certain products promise pure bliss; passion itself can be expressed by fashion (Just Do It); hotels guarantee to relax you; and Valentine's Day proves that love can be purchased with flowers, cards, jewelry, and dinners.

It seems that we have largely lost empathy for other human beings, as well as for the non-human world. With Snyder (as well as thinkers such as David Abram), we find that the loss of direct contact with the natural world has diminished our intellectual capacities, whereas Aaltola focuses on diminishing empathy due to the lack of embodied attentive encounters. Both are problems in our increasingly technological worlds, in which humans are often communicating with a person they have never met in person (who might not be the person they claim to be or they might not even be a person at all) while we are oblivious to the others physically closest to us. We pay little to no attention to the food we consume, or to our environment, urban or natural, while whatever is left of our brains is occupied with the junk social media is feeding us.

Situating Ecopolitics

The "disenfranchised" discussed in the previous section are placed within the particular context of our current ecological crisis, the Sixth Great Extinction, anthropogenic climate change, the Anthropocene, Capitalocene, or whatever we want to call the current global crisis in which both humans and non-humans are oppressed, destroyed, suffering, and/or dying. As discussed in the previous section, I indeed emphasize the double nature of the oppression of humans and non-humans alike. Within the last couple of decades, the discipline of "environmental philosophy" has quickly established itself in reaction to the self-induced crisis that we are facing as a species. Nature has always been a predominant theme in philosophy, in both Western and "non-Western" approaches. Indigenous philosophies presumably were established through lessons nature provided. Western approaches have often separated humans from their "environment"—a term that already indicates distinction. We are confronted with the results of this separation. Like no other period in human history we are confronted with and have to address the scale of environmental destruction of which we ourselves are the cause. We have to face the obvious and uncomfortable reality that our way of living destroys the very possibility of living.

Most of the approaches that call for a radical rethinking of ourselves as political beings and members of a political community lie on the fringes or even outside of the field of what is traditionally called philosophy. Remaining true to the very meaning of *philosophia* as a love of wisdom, I am bringing philosophy into conversation with literature, poetry, art, and science, and I am listening to voices in the "environmental humanities" and "science studies" in order to engage collectively in these important questions.

One of the thinkers on the fringes of philosophy is Bruno Latour, who is particularly discussed in the first chapter and is known for presenting us with a different way to think about agency through his Actor Network Theory. By placing human and non-human agents in a network in which (what Latour calls) "actants" are acting and reacting to one another, he provides a different interpretation of what it means to participate. We find, for example, that in scientific research, the object of research—that what is researched—actively participates.

For Latour, the idea that science has access to primary qualities ("the essential ingredients that really make up the world") as opposed to secondary qualities ("that do not refer to what the world is like but only to their cultural and personal imaginations") is refuted.¹² Scientific truths and social constructs or narratives cannot be separated. Science itself presents different imaginations and articulations. Within this multiplicity, all we can do is add more imaginations and articulations. This insight will open up the world in entirely new ways. The world will be enriched through what we imagine and learn to articulate.

What we can learn from this is not so much an application of science to politics, or that science is political, but rather that we consider both the interaction and participation (or collaboration) between different entities and the singularity of every territory as a form of politics. Along similar lines, Donna Haraway in *Staying with the Trouble* writes about "sympoiesis" or symbiotic assemblages. She uses here the idea of sympoiesis as defined by Dempster: "Collectively-producing systems that do not have self-defined spatial or temporal boundaries. Information and control are distributed among components."¹³ Like Snyder, Haraway recognizes the significance of kinship with the non-human world. We are related to non-human beings, including animals, organisms, technology, and inanimate beings, in such a way that we become or make *with*: "Nothing makes itself; nothing is really autopoietic or self-organizing . . . *Sympoiesis* is a word proper to complex, dynamic, responsive, situated, historical systems. It is a word for worlding-with, in company."¹⁴ Everything is organized with others, in company, assembling different entities.

Haraway does not frame her project explicitly as a political one. Politics, typically, uses a discourse of rights, stakeholders, and obligations. Such a language is in itself exclusionary, since it cannot be applied unilaterally to all different entities, or the language is used to explicitly exclude certain entities from rights. We can name some examples of natural entities such as rivers that have rights, but this is rare. Moreover, the language of rights is ultimately limiting: we cannot provide equal rights to all beings, and we ultimately end in a binary opposition between having and not having rights.

I would like to suggest that Harraway's language of assembling and organizing is an alternative political language. In Haraway's words, we become, live with, and are "worlding" in company with all kinds of organisms. If we can say the activity of worlding constitutes a political community, we find that we are living together with beings that can pose a threat to our existence. The political community consists, thus, of both beings with which we can cooperate, and those that can kill us. It is thus not a community of equals, and we would not want to give equal rights to all those with whom we are worlding, if that was even possible.

To provide an example of this we can think of our own bodies: One will take antibiotics without having to wonder about the rights of the poor bacteria that are being killed. However, we also know that the issue is not that straightforward since antibiotics will not make any judgments about which bacteria they will kill. It simply kills all the flora in your "guts," including the millions of good bacteria that are part of the digestive system. Medicine is, then, perhaps insightful in how we are organized with other beings even in our own bodies. In Haraway's language of worlding, we are an assembly with these organisms, a unity in which rights have no place. Outside of our bodies we likewise are co-organized, first of all with other humans but also with the rest of our world. We are worlding with different entities, such as the buildings in which we dwell, the technologies we use, the food we eat, the infrastructure of cities, the soil, air, and water. The whole constitutes a unity in which we all depend on others who build, dwell along, provide and maintain technologies and infrastructure, grow, distribute, prepare, and sell food. The whole also includes non-human animals, including the ones that fertilize the soil and pollinate plants and trees. The whole includes all kinds of organisms, some living in our bodies. Finally, the whole also includes inanimate objects, from the concrete of the sidewalk to the laptop and gadgets, which often seem more animate (and animating) than our next-door neighbors.

Not all of these entities have rights and certainly not equal ones. Yet, that does not mean we should not respect these other beings with which we are worlding. They are part of the assembly that is our world, and we are part of their world. The idea that not all these entities have the same rights might sound problematic as it suggests inequality. One of the principles Isabelle Stengers sets up in her "cosmopolitics" (discussed in some more detail below) is that of "*mise en égalité*," translated as equalization (as opposed to equivalence). Even while we are all tied together, this does not mean that we are all equals. Stengers suggests that the cosmos does not make us all equals in the sense that we cannot use equal measures or interchange positions, but the cosmos sets us all on equal footing. With that, she suggests we can, first of all, think about the common good as a shared world with other species.

In a time in which equal rights, equal treatment, and equal opportunities often inform political discourses, the challenge of equality calls for more clarification. A helpful image is provided by Snyder who describes an ecosystem as "a kind of mandala in which there are multiple relationships that are all-powerful and instructive . . . Although ecosystems can be described as hierarchical in terms of energy flow, from the standpoint of the whole all of its members are equal."[15] From the perspective of the whole, bears, salmon, eagles, and trees are all equal. Relationships within the whole are complex. All members give and take, but not in equal ways, as one species might be the main nutrition of another species. Bears eat salmon, trees are fed by the carcasses of salmon, bears fertilize the forest, salmon find a place to lay and fertilize their eggs in the forest that is maintained by all. The ecosystem could not exist in the way it does without all of its members. This seems to rhyme with Stengers's idea of equalization in which we indeed are not all equals, but at least on equal footing in relation to the common or shared good, which is for her the cosmos, for Snyder (and myself) the *oikos*.

It is indeed the whole to which we have to find a perspective, and I will further suggest that to assume homogeneity would lead to injustices. In order to explain this, I turn briefly to Jean-François Lyotard's philosophy of the "differend," the injustice that occurs exactly in the inability to express or challenge it. His philosophy of "discourses," which is loosely based on the Wittgensteinian notion of the language game, consists of rules and goals. From this philosophy, politics is defined as a whole ensemble of different discourses or games, each with their own rules and goals. Lyotard uses examples of human activities, each framed within its own set of rules, and each striving for its own goal. For example, an academic working in a university encounters different rules and goals than a nurse working in an emergency room, or a stockbroker on Wall Street. While we might be tempted to think about a common goal that ties all these activities together (let's say "advancing humanity"), for Lyotard, a meta-discourse is a dangerous idea to be avoided at all costs. A meta-discourse assumes that somehow we can all agree on a common goal, yet instead of agreement, we will find that one discourse will try to dominate all others. For example, if "the common good" or "advancing humanity" is translated into economic growth and the economic genre takes over—one of Lyotard's justifiable worries—all other goals will be subordinated to this goal. The nurse and doctor, operating within the medical system (hospital and health insurance), will then no longer act and make decisions in pursuit of human health (and the common good) but only on the basis of economic interest. We immediately see ethical problems arise. In fact, for Lyotard, the task of ethics is precisely to make sure that discourses do not dominate others. Some (notably Rancière and Esposito) have suggested Lyotard leaves no room to express injustices, yet for Lyotard, the point is that the inability to communicate should not be dismissed. Instead, we should develop sensitivity towards silence, towards issues that cannot be expressed. I will return to this in the concluding chapter of the book.

When stepping beyond Lyotard, while maintaining his ideas regarding heterogeneous discourses, we can again say that different entities in the world, even in human society, pursue different goals and follow different sets of rules in order to pursue these diverse goals. Salmon swimming up the river, a bear rummaging through garbage, trees competing for light, rats overrunning a farm, insects in our homes, and humans all have conflicting goals and live according to (unwritten) rules. As I will argue through, among others, Kropotkin, many species of animals follow rules and even have a sense of justice to guide them in maintaining their political community. Besides the rules of each separate species, the lives of species in an ecosystem are also intertwined or integrated. Even while one might be the food for the other, they do not impose the rules of their discourse upon that of another species. Lyotard's "differend" does not seem to exist here, yet we could argue that it occurs when we set up new forms of animal living in zoos, labs, or factory farming.[16]

If we regard our society as an ecology, we find a plurality of discourses, each with its own rules and goals. It is the fear that one discourse dominates. In such a situation the goal and rules of one discourse (such as the capitalist economic one) prescribe rules to other discourses. Thus, returning to Snyder's image of the mandala, the suggestion would be that all parts constitute the whole, and from that perspective, they are all equal. The spider and the bear are equally important members of a natural ecosystem, while health care and poetry are equally important members of a social ecology. They bring different strengths, follow completely different rules and goals, yet influence one another, directly or indirectly, within a common home, or *oikos*.

Redefining Home

In my first book, *Ecopolitical Homelessness,* I argued for a retrieval of a sense of place on the basis of which we can redetermine ourselves politically, philosophically, ethically, and practically in a larger ecological unity. I am further building on that idea. Inspired by different animal political communities, I suggest that in order to make progress in our collaborative models, we should first of all study the long history of politics before humanity. The tendency to separate the human from the non-human, and specifically the idea that politics is only found in the human realm, has prevented us from even asking this question. De Waal writes about the dangers of "anthropodenial," the tendency to deny that humans and other animals are alike, leading to a misunderstanding of ourselves.[17] The purpose of my project is not to say that human and non-human animal politics are the same. Instead, the purpose is to discover the origins of our political tendencies by tracing different non-human political models. With that, we can better understand who we are.

I am calling this idea that our political being is rooted in a natural world that is political "ecopolitics," although I could have called it many other names, such as "earth politics," or "cosmopolitics." The latter term is far from new but has recently been given a new meaning. Particularly Isabelle Stengers—with the two-volume work bearing the title *Cosmopolitics*—has attempted to redefine the politics of the cosmos. Traditionally, the term refers to human beings as citizens of the world, and when we speak about a cosmopolitan city today, we refer to a city with great cultural diversity and diverse habitants, representing virtually the whole world. Stengers provides a twist to the idea of cosmopolitics by suggesting that it is a politics of the cosmos, in which we humans are rooted not only in the social and cultural, but moreover in natural ecology. We find ourselves along with non-human participants involved in cosmological procedures. Mickey and Robbert accurately describe Stengers's cosmopolitics as a way "to designate the ongoing procedures and events wherein humans and nonhumans participate in the craft of composing a shared world."[18]

The reason I have chosen ecopolitics, as opposed to cosmopolitics, is that my emphasis is not on the cosmos (or on the earth as such) but on the shared ecology, which can encompass both the natural environment and the human-built environment. Most importantly the term *eco* (or *oeco*)—derived from *oikos*, the home—does first of all capture this idea of the shared home. I have chosen to use the prefix *eco* or *oikos*, as opposed to *cosmos* to avoid connotations to cosmology, and thus questions of origin. Different cultures and religions provide us with different ways to think about the origin of the universe, and those different ways of thinking lead to different ways of relating to and engaging with the world.

Instead of starting with the cosmos and cosmology, I emphasize the idea of the *oikos*, resulting in ecopolitics. It emphasizes a sense of shared dwelling and being at home. It could be suggested that dwelling can occur in different ways and leaves room for different ways of acting. Yet, I emphasize that dwelling is a habitation that emphasizes being in place. Whether we look at the Greek *oikos* or Confucian notions of becoming good, harmony in the household is central. That household extends beyond the family. One is regarded as a being in relationships and as a political being related to the *polis* or empire. This political character of our being should once again extend beyond the human realm so that we indeed truly dwell on the earth. Dwelling does not occur when one destroys one's living conditions or the possibility for other beings to dwell. Living in an enormous house with a guard who keeps those without a home out of sight is not dwelling on the earth. Likewise, destroying the habitat of salmon by building a house on the banks of a river is not dwelling on the earth. In other words, instead of thinking about the cosmos, I suggest starting at the level of the ecosystem, not because it is smaller, but because it starts with a notion of home, *oikos*. I propose to use the word *oikos* as a way to emphasize the cohabitation with one another and with other species, so that we will all consider the earth as a place of dwelling, with others.

The Common Good as Shared Good

The *oikos*, or place of dwelling, is always shared with non-humans. The aim of ecopolitics is to indeed recognize this as the shared good we should all contribute to. This is a radical turn away from politics as we know it. In this discourse, we are typically working with already mentioned rights and obligations, rules, and laws. Politics suggests that we aim at the common good and hope to move from the realm of necessity into the realm of freedom. Maybe non-human communities are different in not conceptualizing the common good, freedom, or rights and rules or laws. Yet, not conceptualizing rules and laws does not imply that non-human societies function without them. When it comes to rules, it is clear that some animals live in strict hierarchies and that individual animals are acting in particular roles that are determined through (unspoken) rules. I suggest, with Haraway, Stengers, and Latour, that we are worlding with non-human entities and thus co-organizing or composing a shared world with these beings.

An ecosystem as a common home in which we "world" is anarchic in the sense that it does not have a central leader. While there are no designs, regulations, and meetings, an ecosystem is highly organized. We could try to follow such a system in the form of social ecology. One way to do this is to, first of all, regard ourselves as part of a natural ecology. In doing so, we find that the ideal of democracy is nonsensical. The ideal only functions so far as we can all agree to certain conditions already set up in dichotomies that make judgments for us, in terms of good and evil (or bad), for or against, even yes or no. Every vote and every political discourse as a whole is already defined in terms of dichotomies in which our voices are already oppressed before a vote is cast. Voting itself (whether one votes or not) plays in the hand of this oppression.

In relation to Kant, Stengers makes the claim that it is a misunderstanding "that politics should aim at allowing a 'cosmos,' a 'good common world' to exist. The idea is precisely to slow down the construction of this common world, to create a space for hesitation regarding what it means to say 'good.'"[19] This is often the problem in everyday politics, which guides and drives conversations towards the goal of consensus. All the more, the idea of consensus itself is taken for granted. We live in a world where one cannot remain in dissensus (the closest we can get to this is "to agree to disagree"). This is directly related to Lyotard's "differend" in which the need to find consensus often leads to injustices. The majority often rules, and the parameters are typically set by the demands of technological economic models, focusing on efficiency and profit. Likewise, legal language is the language of the industrial colonial world, forcing Indigenous voices to become lost and fall victim.

A different critical voice is that of Rancière who criticizes the idea of consensus, or *sensus communis,* and proposes a politics of dissensus. His definition of politics also challenges our common perception of politics as associated with exercising power. He states that "politics is not the exercise of power. Politics ought to be defined in its own terms as a specific mode of action that is enacted by a specific subject and that has its own proper rationality. It is the political relationship that makes it possible to conceive of the subject of politics, not the other way round."[20] His project does not include animal politics (his "specific subject" is human), and in that sense is traditional, but I see the redefinition of politics as "a specific mode of action" and with "its own rationality" opening up the possibility to include other rationalities and modes of actions. Animal colonies, migration, and communication are all modes of action that, I argue, can be considered political. Thus, it is helpful to follow Rancière's emphasis that politics lies in relationships, even though he would not agree to include non-human entities as political subjects.

Rancière certainly recognizes that we are part of the whole and that we are defined through our political context, but the language of subjectivity utilized holds onto the idea of individual autonomy and emphasizes human relationships. How the whole is guided is often puzzling, both in human and non-human politics. As Rancière states, politics is not merely the state, or "living with a view to a good."[21] In his analysis of the difficulties around consensus, Rancière does certainly not establish ecopolitics but opens the door to it. Instead of focusing on subjects, as traditional political theory does, I propose to focus on political relationships, where the whole determines the mode of action of the individual members. Of course, discourses of unity, and especially totality, rightfully have a horrific reputation. Bookchin opposes the wholeness of fascism and totalitarianism that "provide an inexorable finality to the course of human history" to the wholeness of ecology, as a "dynamic *unity of diversity.*"[22] As opposed to totalitarianism, in ecology nothing is permanent, everything changes, and unity thrives on diversity, not on uniformity. In addressing the question of how to avoid the oppression of the whole, I rely here on Lyotard's idea of avoiding the "differend." The problem to tackle is the situation in which we either regard ourselves as the whole, or simply are the oppressing part. We have made the earth into *ours*, even calling this our era. As opposed to this domineering of the earth, I propose a wholeness in the form of a unity that is based on the simple recognition that we are not independent individuals or autonomous subjects: we are beings in political relationships with other human beings (including those who cannot vote, are members of a different state, or are stateless) as well as non-human entities.

It is perhaps impossible to work towards a common good, since (1) many did not agree to it in the first place, and (2) it is undermining our abilities to thrive in terms of living conditions and health. Regarding the first point, we can start with colonialism, which has forced a capitalist image onto most of the globe. The destruction of Indigenous cultures, the obliteration of their languages, and the subsequent need for these cultures to express themselves in a language that does not reflect their cultural values leaves them with nothing to propose or even object to. And in the non-human world, we find a trend in which victims are silenced and not even recognized as victims, since they cannot express themselves. They are not part of the goal (the common good), and as we fail to stop and not recognize their exclusion, we further silence them. The ideal of equalization is not so much aimed at bringing us all into the same political discourse, but to disrupt our discourse in order to let others express themselves in novel and unknown ways, to open up new goals, new common goods, or move beyond such a language entirely. Before developing a new language that expresses and encourages sensitivity towards the idea of the shared *oikos*, we should table the discussions involving decisions that impact human and animal communities. Instead of gathering the votes to open up an area for drilling or mining, we should go for a hike in the area that we are about to destroy.

What Does Ecopolitics Want?

Some will say ecopolitics is suggesting the impossible. In fact, it wants very little: recognizing a common or shared home that is political in its very essence. Within that shared home, there is not one common, but a multiplicity of different goods, which all members can pursue in equal ways. In order to change our political system and include the whole world, we have to first of all change who we are, by—as Latour suggests—learning to articulate and imagine ourselves and our relation to the world in different ways. Perhaps this sounds too ambitious, but we are adaptable beings, as exemplified by Latour's smell training example in which he speaks of training of affectivity. In the example, the nose (or smell) is trained with a kit of samples of different smells. It shows we can learn to smell things we never smelled before. He speaks of an articulation, which means here "being affected by differences."[23] In short, our bodies alongside our brains can be trained in the sense that the differences in smell could not be articulated before and can now be articulated after training, which makes us effectively aware of the differences, creating a richer world in terms of smell. A person having gone through the training can articulate smells that used to be undifferentiated affections.

Ecopolitics wants us to simply learn to look at (and possibly smell) the world differently, by opening up our senses and mind to a different reality that is already there. We are, after all, largely determined by our environment. Looking differently at that environment and letting that environment interact with us differently will lead to radical changes in who we are. By emphasizing the *oikos*, we can construe a politics that places us in the midst of a community of all living beings. This will redetermine who we are as a collective, partially by being differently affected. A different affection or a different sensibility is indeed going to be central in a redefinition of the *polis*, in which feelings such as empathy are encouraged and not suppressed as currently is the case. Collaboration or mutual aid is going to be more significant than struggle and competition. The proposal of ecopolitics argued for in this book is thus asking us to experience the world, one another, and our place in different ways.

Thus, what ecopolitics wants is the opposite of a philosophical thought experiment without any practical implications. I agree with Baird Callicott that environmental philosophy *is* environmental activism.[24] The way we think determines how we act, or do not act. While my proposed ecopolitics is conceptual, what we think and how we think are not "merely" thoughts. Our ideas, how to think about who we are, and how we relate to other beings—human and non-human—determine how we act in relationships with those beings. Conceptual ideas, such as the idea of ecopolitics, thus, have real political consequences.

Ecopolitics does not want a common goal in the form of a common good. We have already seen above that we should recognize a multiplicity of goods. With that, it is fighting the current idea of the common good as one measured and determined through GNP or other economic indexes. In chapter 5, this is phrased as growth for the sake of growth, and it is this mindset that is constantly challenging us and makes us challenge the earth. As discussed above in relation to the refugee crisis and environmental destruction, the "common good" is a "common disaster" for millions of people who live in an apocalyptic world. Today we also find these scenes of disaster and mass evacuations in those parts of the world that are responsible. Yet, the patterns of vulnerability and poverty also repeat on the local level.

The destruction and alteration of the face of the earth is driven by capitalism's value that making money (by manipulating human beings into consuming as much as possible) is more important than preserving the planet, or more accurately, our living conditions. We are typically removed from the victims of our way of living. Similar to Stengers, I argue for a confrontation with the victims of our actions. Instead of speeding past the roadkill, past the person without a home who in our eyes and minds has become something subhuman, we must confront those whom we attempt to avoid. A confrontation will not consist of a simple and quick reduction of guilt by donating to charity, or by assisting another human being (although it is a start). We will have to truly open our eyes and actually acknowledge the victims of our capitalist world, in which a few profit at the expense of others. Recognizing those who suffer, first of all by looking them in the eyes, will be a step in the right direction, as we are now in the presence of the victim. That does not mean that we will not destroy the homes of other creatures, or that we will not kill other creatures, but we will face them in the process. Coming face to face will radically change our relationship, which is not unlike an Indigenous hunter, such as the one described by Nelson, who looks the animal in the eye to thank it for giving its life.[25] Indeed, this relates to Robin Kimmerer's description of the gift economy. She suggests that "something is broken when the food comes on a Styrofoam tray wrapped in slippery plastic, a carcass of a being whose only chance at life was a cramped cage. That is not a gift; it is a theft."[26] She argues that the gift economy creates reciprocity. Gift giver and gift taker both become entangled in a larger web, which is a community. One could say that a gift economy grounds us in a community that gives and expects something in return. It is the community rather than the individual because I am not necessarily returning a gift directly to a particular individual. Rather, I provide something to my community in return. This kind of reciprocal relationship is what ecopolitics wants.[27]

Currently, we often lack an understanding of ourselves as part of society or society as a part of us. The lack of our involvement in politics is a symptom of this issue, as is our lack of connection to non-human and human victims. Perhaps we have some empathy for the person who lost everything because of medical bills, but for most of us, "the alcoholic," or even worse, "the drug addict," is something less than human and should only blame themselves for their actions and situation. Cities such as San Francisco fill up with "homeless camps," and in that sense, the victims are in our presence. If we keep blaming those who are without shelter and if we keep lacking empathy, we will just regard these people as a nuisance. Meanwhile, it does not seem to take much to open our eyes and feelings. Volunteering at a shelter and hearing some of the stories can be a transformative experience. A true confrontation with the disenfranchised can help us reinterpret the source of the problem and can instigate empathy. As discussed earlier, Aaltola suggests that a lack of empathy can be attributed to a lack of meaningful embodied experiences. Being with the disenfranchised is an important step to feed our empathy.

Starting with the experiences of others, we can move to better solutions. Currently, we are incredibly skillful at putting time and resources into solutions that just shift the issues and will always fail to solve the underlying causes. Foucault powerfully analyzes how such failures not only maintain but further strengthen the status quo. We need to fight these structures, but we can only do so by first understanding those structures, and once we do we can start changing ourselves, not only as individuals, but moreover as communities.

We often think that such changes are impossible, while other much more radical changes (such as the way in which technology in the form of social media has reshaped our lives completely) are taken for granted. Revolutionary new ways of being come into existence without actual revolutions. Changes to communities often happen uneventfully. A simple example of a redetermination of a community occurred in the Spring of 2018 at my home institution, the University of San Francisco. On April 30, Public Safety sent out an email with the subject "Coyotes on Campus." The basic message of the email was that the campus is home to two coyotes. After consultation with organizations and experts, and complying with California State law, it was decided that the coyotes are here to stay. The message included a link to the documentary "San Francisco—Still Wild at Heart" on coyotes in the city, along with (naturally) some safety messages. The email itself reflects a radical redetermination of our relationship with coyotes and seeing our campus as a space, or habitat (*oikos*), shared with these wild canines. Co-existence is not only possible but the only viable option. As the email stated, "Lethal removal is ineffective . . . since another coyote will simply take its place, often within weeks." The event was miraculously uneventful. No protests ensued, all people living and working on campus carried on as usual, yet with an awareness (appropriately reawakened by signage) of the coyotes' presence and instruction on how to behave around them. Yet, more importantly, we as a university community now have made explicit the relationship and the values of cohabitation. The email message simply stated the new reality as a fact, the reality in which we live. Recognizing that we live in this reality, we now live with the potential victims of our actions. Thus, relocation or lethal removal is deemed to be "inhumane" as well as ineffective and the campus has been redetermined as a shared habitat. Coyotes do not pay rent or tuition and yet they give. Our cities and campuses are certainly very attractive places for rodents, which are on the menu for coyotes. So, they fit well into the campus ecosystem and make it a better place.[28]

While traditionally only a part of this was seen as political (the administration of the university, public safety, and the processes that led to the California law to protect coyotes), ecopolitics wants to also regard our relationship with the coyotes as political. Even more so, the coyotes themselves form a political community and engage in politics with us and among themselves (evidence is found, among others, in the fact that the removal of coyotes will only lead to a quick replacement). Their society is full of structures and hierarchies we have only limited knowledge of. In providing a place for them, coyotes provide a healthier environment. Only when we approach politics in this way can we collectively find a way forward. The recognition that all human and non-human entities are part of our political community, and that they in their own right are political, can be seen as a rediscovery of kinship or a reconstruction of kin. Within this reconstruction we are part of a larger political unity, the *oikos*: home of all living beings.

Within this recognition of ecopolitics, we no longer see a forest (or campus) as something to be manipulated and used by us, but as an *oikos*, a home that, perhaps in itself, should be seen as something alive or at least as an actant. Similar to considering the earth as a living thing as the Gaia Hypothesis suggests, the *oikos* constitutes a unity, not as a static object, but as something that is constantly becoming and can die. This is what ecopolitics wants. Kimmerer expresses a similar idea when she describes her Native language, Potawatomi, in which natural things are expressed as a verb as opposed to a noun. A bay is not simply a bay, it is being a bay. "Wiikwegamaa—to *be* a bay—releases the water from bondage and lets it live. 'To be a bay' holds the wonder that, for this moment, the living water has decided to shelter itself between these shores, conversing with cedar roots and a flock of baby mergansers. Because it could do otherwise—become a stream or an ocean or a waterfall, and there are verbs for that too."[29] Furthermore "it," the bay, is a personified entity: "In Potawatomi and most other Indigenous languages, we use the same words to address the living world as we use for our family. Because they are our family."[30] Combined with the fact that their list of inanimate objects (expressed as nouns) is a lot smaller than that of ours, she then speaks of "a grammar of animacy" in which rocks, water, fire, mountains, and places are all considered as animate.

One could further suggest that considering an entity such as a bay as "a thing" also commodifies it. David Graeber discusses how the Roman notion of property included slaves exactly on the basis of defining a slave as a thing.[31] The transformation of a person into a thing creates the possibility to own "it." Likewise, to regard a natural entity as a thing, also suggests it is something that can be possessed and exploited directly or indirectly. Vacations can be sold with pictures and descriptions of the bay. It is the unforgettable view that makes the hotel so attractive. A verb would not necessarily avoid the commodification entirely, but the description and the experience would be fundamentally different. You will not buy the view, but you will be provided the opportunity "to converse with the living water that will shelter itself among you." That does sound strange, even tacky, I agree. Yet, our collective task will be to reinvent language to express our relationships with the natural world in different ways. This is what ecopolitics wants. Although we cannot adopt the Potawatomi language for this purpose, we might find some guidance in it, for example by replacing nouns with verbs when we speak about natural entities.

A place, or an *oikos*, as either animate or as an actant or personified entity can be, can change and become, and can die. We can act with it, listen to it, and obtain its knowledge in the hopes that we can indeed live in harmony with it. When "it" is not a thing, ownership is problematized. Perhaps we can see ourselves as one of the caregivers or stewards of a piece of land. Maybe we can reenvision our roles as positive agents or actants along with actants consisting of many different species and entities. Ecopolitics wants to recognize that no one owns a creek. The salmon as well as the rocks are not mine or yours. They do their thing and can never be owned. In sharing an *oikos* with them, we world with them. Returning to the coyotes on my campus, they reconstitute that particular *oikos* as a shared one, and indeed as one that is becoming and changing. Bookchin suggests understanding ecosystems, specifically social ecosystems, holistically. Thus, "social ecology seeks to unravel the forms and patterns of interrelationships that give intelligibility to a community, be it natural or social."[32] Here, we find that ecology bridges "the natural" and "the human" as well as living and nonliving things. It is ultimately about the "dynamic balance of nature."[33] We can object that not all changes are welcome ones. A wildfire is an example of how a forest can act against us. Yet, oftentimes, these acts are not unrelated to our inability to listen to a forest or to be positive players in the dynamic balance of nature. More positively, we can recognize ways in which we can coexist with the forest, managing through control burns, harvesting some trees but not all, not suppressing all fires at all times, and building in some areas but not in high fire danger zones, etc. Again, Bookchin provides an interesting metaphor citing Charles S. Elton: managing the future is "'not like a game of chess—[but] more like steering a boat.' What ecology, both natural and social, can hope to teach us is the way to find the current and understand the direction of the stream."[34] The exact path is not determined as we have to navigate the forces of nature, which cannot be ignored if we want to move forward. In this sense what ecopolitics wants is to become a part of nature as our *oikos*, as humble members who do not simply use everything, but live with and coexist with the other members of the ecopolitical community we are a part of.

Is this unrealistic? Ecopolitics starts by subtly suggesting a new way to envision ourselves. From that we can revise and reinvent our language, develop a different sense of community, a different economy, and so forth.

It surely is not going to happen overnight, and while there is plenty of reason for pessimism, there are reasons for hope. First of all, we do not have much choice: if there is a future for the human species, it will involve a radical change of course. The facts are clear: natural resources are limited, while we use them at an ever-accelerating rate. One can keep denying this, which is exactly what we have been doing. The effects of climate change are already here, no matter how hard we try to deny it. Bookchin provides the following thought: "If we don't do the impossible, we shall be faced with the unthinkable.[35]" With the "unthinkable" he is presumably referring to what he earlier phrased as "an apocalypse that may well end humanity's tenure on the planet."[36] Secondly, and most importantly, different structures already exist and changes are already occurring. Alternative economies without the exchange of money already exist, for example, in the music world.[37] Lastly, in terms of environmental activism, young people are our hope, and their activism is both courageous and inspiring, often starting with individuals who inspire others. They even show that social media can have a positive impact. While some, thus, recognize that we are on a fatal collision course with ourselves, we keep telling the next generation to become successful entrepreneurs, and we keep selling our universities as great investments in their future. Following David Orr, I suggest it is reckless to keep educating our students on how to become successful proprietors and not discuss and discover alternative economies.

Our students are a part of the reimagining. In my classes I do not have to critique capitalism: my students already do it. The next generation is ready for change! With our beliefs in individualism and the pursuit of freedom on an individual basis, we do not need to fall into quietism and a general belief that the die has been cast. When it comes to stopping climate catastrophe, we need both the power of the individual and the power of the group. Indeed, ecopolitics calls for a different perception of politics grounded in a different perception of ourselves. It suggests that we not only have to regard ourselves as part of the natural world; moreover, this world is full of political relationships. Ecopolitics thus wants a new perception of ourselves and of politics, so that we collectively can avoid "the unthinkable."

Learning from Non-human Politics

What are these different political relationships that we can find in the non-human realm? Different living communities function through different systems of governance or political systems. Even while some (most notably great apes such as the chimpanzees discussed in this book) appear to have centralized forms of governance, a leader (typically an alpha male) will quickly be dethroned if they lack the support of the group. Interestingly, care for the weakest members of the colony turns out to be crucial. On the other side of the spectrum, we find decentralized groups of fish and ants. The ant colony is hierarchical, yet without a leader. It seems that a school of fish moves by consensus, somehow agreeing collectively to move in a certain direction at a particular speed. Presumably, fish or ants do not really deliberate. Perhaps the answers are quite simple: one survives and makes it home or not while the group survives. As we will see with ants in chapter 5, the ant colony is, as a whole, quite intelligent and does survive collectively, often in challenging conditions. They can solve complex problems as a community.

In non-human communities, decisions are made collectively through a group intelligence in which typically all members are involved. An individual ant has very limited intelligence, but a colony is smart. Species that seem more hierarchical, such as ants and chimpanzees, use structures in which even the weakest members play a significant role. As Bookchin suggests, the language we use to describe the non-human world (such as "alpha males," "colonies," "queens," and "domination" is often more reflective of our own political and social structures than those of the animals we study. Indeed, De Waal acknowledges that in his earlier (groundbreaking and otherwise revolutionary) work he failed to recognize the true significance of the role of the female members for the colony, in fact suggesting that power in the chimpanzee colony is even less centralized. As the example of the unexplained behavior of the orcas shows, we are often humbled in our lack of knowledge of non-human animals.

In our systems, typically parts of our human collective decision-making are "outsourced" to elected officials. Nevertheless, we are also involved in more direct ways, yet we often fail to recognize those ways as political. Despite my criticism of the lack of true engagement, on a day-to-day basis we make collective decisions in which we are all directly involved. Our commutes by car or public transportation are full of variables, and when we go out for lunch, little is certain. The daily dynamics are run in a nonhierarchical fashion. Once in a while, long lines or delays will occur, but most things work out through collective decision-making. It is here that I also find hope. We are part of an embodied collective. Even when we are walking on the sidewalk ignoring one another, or in the café typing on our phones or laptops with little direct communication, we are still there together. We are drawn to one another, and even when we are alone together and annoyed by others, that togetherness is an indication of our community. This community is extended beyond humans. From the pets that live with us to sounds of birds and squirrels, or the ants and rats that dine on us: whether we like it or not, we are sharing our home.

How do non-human animals share their world? While animals will fight over food if there is not enough, they typically do not take more than their share and do not keep it away from other members. It is not all good and just in the animal world, though. Interestingly, greedy behavior in the animal world, as studies have shown, can occur in zoos but is not a "natural" behavior. Those studies indicate that apes can become rather selfish if there is, ironically, an abundance of food. Likewise, rat behavior can vary in radical ways, again depending on the circumstances. As Kropotkin points out in *Mutual Aid,* animals in areas with an abundance of food rely less on one another, whereas those who live in the most challenging circumstances rely upon one another and display mutual aid.

It seems we humans display similar tendencies. The greed displayed in the wealthy industrial parts of the world is a case in point. Thinking just about food, we find that some communities are left behind hungry or with poor food choices, despite having enough food available overall. Not only do the wealthy nations fail to care for the Third World, but also within the "First World," the disparity between the poor and wealthy is enormous. As we will see, rats, apes, and humans in some cases display empathy, while in others it seems to be nonexistent. Different behaviors displayed in both the human and non-human realm depend on the circumstances, in which the more positive affects and behaviors are encouraged in challenging conditions.

The closeness between human and non-human animal behavior is not incidental: as we inherited all kinds of physical features of our evolutionary predecessors or developed similar traits as our species faced similar challenges to other species, we also inherited or developed similar feelings, behavioral traits, and skills as those other animals. The tendency towards group-being and the attraction to the group is as old as life. What happens when we recognize the engagements of animals with one another in a group as political and regard our political skills as inherited from other animals? Behavior in a chimpanzee colony might be easier to recognize as bearing resemblance to human activities than that of salmon, rats, or ants. Yet, those antlike, fishlike, and ratlike activities are also deeply ingrained in our being. What can we then learn from how these species function together? It can explain certain tendencies we have. Understanding those tendencies can assist us in overcoming certain tendencies, and moreover, help us reorganize ourselves amongst ourselves as well as with other species and the natural world in one shared *oikos*.

Summary of Chapters

More specifically, the first chapter of this book discusses salmon as political beings. Of all the species discussed in this book, this species is arguably the most difficult to regard as political. Yet, we quickly can see them as important in our political decision-making. Whole human communities depend on them, and so do many non-human communities. They are important members of a number of different ecosystems, feeding whales, bears, eagles, and trees. Salmon migrate collectively and after spending years in the ocean, they miraculously find their way back to the place where they were born. In arguing that they are political beings, I draw in particular on the insights of Bruno Latour as well as the Indigenous philosophy of the Tlingit. While the first challenges our ideas of agency, the latter simply regard the salmon as beings that are just like us.

While salmon are admired and loved by many, the opposite is true for mice and rats, the subject of chapter 2. It arguably would have been easier to make the main argument by focusing merely on animals we have a positive relationship with. Yet, including those species we call rodents and pests adds more interesting and more challenging dimensions on how to break down barriers. First of all, we see that the pests are the result of rampant capitalism. Secondly, we see that rats and mice seem incredibly good at breaking down borders, at deterritorializing, unless they have something to protect. While they are—like humans—empathic beings, it turns out that rats in certain circumstances keep other rats out. In fact, they are very much like humans in this regard: when their situation is an advantageous one, protecting that wealth will be more important than helping others, as feelings of empathy seem to disappear, or are overruled by other feelings.

The third chapter further finds strong resemblances with humans in discussing the politics at work in the chimpanzee colony, in which empathy and caring for the weakest members of the colony turn out to be surprisingly important. I draw here mostly on the work of primatologist De Waal and discuss different notions of sympathy and empathy as we find them in Hume among others. This chapter is a more in-depth reflection on how society determines towards whom empathy is experienced and who is excluded, both in non-human and human communities.

Returning then to the water, in chapter 4, I further explore animal politics by looking at some fairly "simple" organisms in the tidepool. Here I use in particular the insights of Steinbeck and Ricketts, the latter influenced by neo-Darwinist biologists who emphasize cooperation over struggle. The tidepool is an example of cooperation, and Ricketts regards it as an "unmasked replica" of human society. Inspired by Zen Buddhism, Jung, and poets such as Jeffers, Steinbeck, and Ricketts offer here an unconventional yet helpful redetermination of the political outside of the human realm as well as in the human realm. The idea of the phalanx, the group mentality, plays a central role, and the question that arises here is if we as individuals can resist being drawn to the group, or alternatively, how we can make sure we are part of the right group.

Chapter 5 leads us to one of the smallest, yet incredibly successful creatures, the ant. Sometimes seen as socialists or communists, ants are organized in a decentralized fashion, making decisions as a group. For that reason, they can be called anarchists. Through the work of Edward Abbey and Peter Kropotkin, I discuss our antlike existence in both positive and negative ways. We work and keep growing our colonies, just like ants, and as ant colonies always fail, so will we. This then leads to the question of whether the anarchistic organization of ants can possibly work in the human realm.

The book concludes by bringing the different animal communities together into ecopolitics—a politics for the future, rooted in our (non-human and human) past. Instead of a social contract, I propose a decentralized political ecology, that is, an ecopolitics that does not consist of a contract but of a multiplicity of ways of relating to other living and non-living beings. We do not need to give up on democracy, just on the one we currently have. Ecopolitics is a true democracy, not run by a majority consisting of people, but by all members of the larger ecological community.

Most chapters, including this introduction start with a short story. The concluding chapter ends with a short story. Telling stories is an essential part of ecopolitics. Throughout the book, I argue that the fact that we have never recognized politics in the animal realm does not mean it doesn't exist there. Indeed, we do, like ants, need to decentralize from ourselves and recontextualize ourselves. Storytelling is one way to do this. We can reinvent ourselves as individuals by moving beyond individualism. Simultaneously, we can move beyond our human-centered world. By recreating our conception of society and creating new stories in which we define the common good as the thriving of all its members, we can once again start to become humble, compassionate, and empathic members of a community that will not just benefit the wealthy. A society that moves beyond the status quo will benefit all members, human and non-human, by creating a context in which all species and all members of the human species stand a chance to thrive.

Chapter One

Salmon Politics and Latour's Gaia

Halfway up the Indian River, the biologist who leads our group stops us, pointing to fresh bear scat, a dark brown heap of feces, along with footprints in the wet soil of the trail. The prints are bigger than a human hand.[1] When the biologist tells us that we must have chased a bear away, our excitement and anxiety grows. Unsuspiciously I check with my hand the bear spray in my jacket's pocket. These are not small Californian bears; these are brown bears, also known as grizzlies. The students and I, their professor, have all been hoping and fearing to run into a grizzly. Even while the California flag still displays the grizzly, they are long extinct in our home state. They thrive here in the forests of Baranof Island, Southeast Alaska. Grizzlies can and have killed humans in this area. They do not like surprises, but as a thirteen-person group, we have made enough noise to give them plenty of warning, making it unlikely to startle a bear. After we have all studied the prints and scat, we continue the walk, and a minute later, on the bank of the river we see a salmon still partially alive, while being held and poked by a bald eagle. The tail is still moving, while the rest of its pinkish body, a color indicating that it is ready to spawn, is clumsily lying on the gravel of the bank. Our guide's verdict is again clear: we must have interrupted the bear's meal, which was left for the eagle. The eagle would have received a nice meal regardless since the bear is only interested in the fat parts (the brain and eggs mostly) of the fish. It is clear: we are in the midst of a natural society, and for better or worse, we are part of it. We consume salmon or the berries that thrive on the nutrients brought here by the salmon. Alternatively, we can become food. We might be tempted to call it an "economy" in which animals and plants give and take. As discussed in the introduction of this book, Kimmerer calls this a gift economy in which different parties are engaged in a long-term reciprocal relationship. In this particular society of the Indian River, salmon play a central role. Bears and eagles are part of their beneficiaries who pass on the gift to the forest. The plants and trees are fed and fertilized by bears who feed on salmon. We can speak of a community here, as the local native Tlingit do. For them, all forms of life are in their essence the same, emphasizing kinship between different species. Community, politics, and cooperation are not special human characteristics. Humans find themselves in a world that is predominantly determined through the non-human.

In this chapter, my first approach to politics in the other-than-human realm discusses salmon, specifically by analyzing how they live with one another, with other species, and how we politically have failed the salmon (and the species of animals and plants that need them). We learn through the salmon how the whole natural world is interconnected and how we humans are affecting and are affected by salmon. We also learn how the disappearance of a species can have widespread effects. The state of salmon can be seen as an indicator of the Sixth Great Extinction: when salmon disappear, their loss is felt among many species of animals, trees, and plants.

What can we learn from the collaboration of salmon? One of the key questions in this regard is how they are able to work so well with one another and with other species. I will assume that salmon do not make conscious decisions, yet that does not mean that they cannot thrive and collaborate as a group. If we use human criteria, we would probably not call their collaboration a form of politics: they do not vote, nor do they have meetings; they do not try to sway others with arguments, nor do they put pressure on politicians, and so forth. As argued in the introduction of this book, I suggest that those characteristics, while often directly associated with politics, do not constitute the essence of politics, and that we in fact should consider the so-called political affairs in places like Washington, DC, the destruction of politics. Instead, I argue that the essence of politics consists of collaboration. The urge to work together in the world of the salmon is possibly similar to the human urge that leads us to collaboration and, thus, to politics. As Indigenous philosophies such as that of the Tlingit argue, deep down we are all the same. For that reason, they do not hesitate to immediately recognize the similarities between communities of salmon (or other animals) and our own. "Our" theory of evolution does not suggest otherwise, but our perception of the human-animal distinction is tainted with narratives that suggest a radical difference between humans and other animals.

One way to think about salmon is that they live in unity with one another, with other animals, with natural features (such as the gravel in the river under which they lay their eggs), and with the eagles, ravens, bears, and trees fed by the nutrients the salmon bring from the sea. If we can call this unity a society, as I argue, salmon are good citizens within this unity: they live in and off their place by being a healthy component, whose absence, rather than their presence, has severe negative consequences. It is in this regard that we can learn from salmon: how to become better participants of a greater unity in the different ecosystems we encounter on the earth.

To be clear, I want to steer clear of an ignorant claim that we should become salmon, but rather that we recognize the interconnectedness of ourselves with other beings and with the environments or ecosystems that sustain us. We do not become salmon. We become keystone species, like salmon. Yet, even while we do not become salmon or salmon-like, I will identify throughout this book certain similarities between all life-forms. Within that context, I will suggest ways to reevaluate human politics. First of all, we share with all other animals the need to cooperate, required for any living being to survive. While in some of the following chapters I will approach this through certain neo-Darwinist theories that emphasize cooperation over the struggle for survival, my approach to understanding the salmon is through Native American philosophies and Bruno Latour's *Facing Gaia*, which both emphasize, albeit in different ways, the communal interconnected existence of everything that is.

More particularly, in this chapter, I will answer some initial questions that we can ask about the very possibility of animal politics through Latour's Actor Network Theory (ANT). I use the salmon as a case study in order to analyze how we as actants are influencing and are influenced by salmon. When we listen to salmon, for example by noticing their decline, we can learn from them. More specifically, I analyze how salmon are (1) as actants part of our political system (partly construed through the natural sciences, restoration, and the Anthropocene), (2) interconnected with the rest of the world (which I will discuss through the worldview of the Tlingit), and (3) as themselves political through their relationships to one another, other species, and their environment.

Salmon Being, Being Salmon

For Martin Heidegger, dwelling has been designated as a particularly human activity. "Building thinking and dwelling humans" are opposed to animals who lack an approach to the things around them "as such." Yet, language points us in a different direction, as ecologists refer to creeks and rivers as salmon "habitat," derived from the Latin *habitare*, to dwell. We can wonder if they indeed dwell in these habitats since they only spend parts of their lives here, albeit two essential parts: birth and reproduction occur in the creeks and rivers. Both events typically occur at the same place. Since they return to spawn in the place where they were born, ecologists call this return "homing." Yet their home or habitat also includes the ocean, where the majority of their lifespan is spent. I am not sure if it is appropriate to call the place of birth and death—as opposed to the ocean—their home, but at least we can say that salmon are ambiguous creatures, seemingly homeless and yet returning home. Their bodies undergo radical changes in order to transition between salt and freshwater. Only a few species of fish can facilitate a transition that requires such radical adjustment to their bodies. Interestingly, biologists have given different names to the various stages of the salmon. When they hatch from their eggs at the bottom of the creek, they are not called salmon yet. They are first "alevin," "fry," "parr," and "smolt," before finally becoming "salmon." The latter occurs in the ocean, so the names suggest that the creature that starts its life in freshwater is not (yet) a salmon. The name changes of the numerous different stages indicate not only the radical developments these animals undergo, but also the "homelessness" at the beginning stages of their lifespan. During their time in the ocean, which can be up to seven years, salmon swim thousands of miles. When they return to the river, some species such as the Chinook, or king salmon, swim thousands of miles upstream without ever eating. Salmon return to their place of birth when they are ready to spawn. With the term "homing," language again indicates a sense of dwelling and home even while it remains a question of whether there even is such a thing as a home for salmon. As they move between different ecosystems, what they are capable of, how their bodies function, and what their appearance looks like radically changes. Besides the different stages named above, when salmon return to freshwater, they stop eating and again change color. Male humpback (or "pink") salmon grow a big hump. After they spawn, their body quickly deteriorates—a process visible by the white spots that grow on their bodies.

The relationship to their environment is thus a complex one, since they navigate between different ecosystems. Navigating creeks or rivers and the ocean requires cooperation. Salmon are born en masse and they migrate together. If the term *dwelling* is appropriate for salmon, we can say they dwell in a group or a "school." Salmon seem to have little to no trouble being part of a group. I will assume that salmons' experience of others is very different from what we experience, and it might be something very different from what we are even able to comprehend. Nevertheless, based on the fact that they always work together, I will compare their drive or tendency to group beings to our own drive towards the group.[2]

Group Being

While the term *herd culture* often has negative connotations when we speak about humans, being part of a group is a prerequisite for the very possibility of any political community. Even more, a tendency towards group being could be a first indication that salmon are social or even political beings. Besides the networks of connections with other species, salmon form groups among themselves, as seen through their behavior in schools. Generally speaking, animals that stay together in large numbers (such as schools) do so because, in a group, they are better protected against predators. If a school is attacked, only a few individuals will die. Studies of the hydrodynamics at work in a school have shown that fish move more efficiently when riding the wake of other fish upstream. Likewise, arriving with the collective at the spawning grounds is required to find a mate. The Darwinian story tells us that drives towards groups are part of a survival technique: fish that swim in groups are better suited to survive than fish that are solitary creatures. Be that as it may, the more interesting aspect is that in order for these schools to form in the first place, salmon have a continuous tendency to be part of a group, a trait we find in many life-forms.

Along these lines, it can be suggested that a school of salmon is a moving community, and individual salmon move between these communities. The schools of salmon are considered to be "loose." This means that individual salmon do not remain in the same school through the process of migration. Schools of fish are also not hierarchical. Instead, they are considered to be "self-organizing," that is, by the group as a whole, decentralized. Even while all fish move in the same direction at the same speed, there is no leader. Somehow the group as a whole organizes, moves, and orients itself.

One question biologists ask in the context of loosely organized schools of fish is how individual fish can recognize members of their own species. Scientific answers to such questions use "mechanical views" in which fish with similar bodies naturally group together. While I have no reason to doubt the answer, I have hesitations about the language used to express the answer. In a study from 1948, James Morrow discusses (and accepts) the idea that schooling of fish is what he calls a "mechanical" process: "Fish group together because other fish provide a reference point on which to 'take bearings' rather than because of any desire or urge for companionship, etc."[3] This mechanical view—and the very fact that it is called mechanical—is significant in this regard. It reiterates the Cartesian view that animals are basically machines. Any "social behavior" is to be considered "merely as an incidental result of the mechanically integrated reactions of individuals."[4] As Morrow describes the vision as the most important mechanism through which fish relate to other fish, we find an interesting example of such "incidental social behavior." As he describes the behavior of "normal" and blind mackerel, he makes an astonishing judgment for a biologist with a mechanical view of the animal world when he writes: "The eyed animals were unable to keep up with the steady, aimless movements of the blind, leading to 'resentment' on the part of the seeing individual and often resulting in its attacking and killing its blind companion."[5] While the word *resentment* appears in scare quotes, it seems that the researcher found that the mechanical terms failed to explain the behavior in this specific example and that words which express emotion and sentiment were needed.

More recent studies (focused on individual species and typically done in controlled environments) speak of "social behavior" and "social transmission," but whatever a natural scientist means with social behavior and transmission, such mechanisms are ideally expressed in numbers. There are some speculations about communication, yet it is again framed within a mechanical view as we find in the following example: "Social transmission of information about a predator could decrease mortality by allowing school members to initiate antipredator behavior earlier than solitary individuals."[6] In this explanation, social transmission is part of a survival strategy with the survival of the group as its goal. While the school of fish is explained in terms of "social behavior," it is ultimately staying away from any kind of feelings and framed as a mechanical strategy for survival. Instead of suggesting that these animals are social and therefore have a better chance at survival, the approach is result-driven and teleological: they are social in order to survive.

As we become more aware of the rich lives of non-human animals and their similarities to humans, we have to either step away from using the mechanical language to describe non-human animals, or we should also apply it to our own being and ways in which we respond to one another and our environment. In both cases, the point is that when it come to the most basic urges and drives, we are not essentially different from non-human animals: we also act by reacting, involving different stimuli. Thus, we can find similar mechanisms (if we want to use that language) or strategies that lead to group being in human societies. As I will discuss in much more detail in chapter 4 when discussing Steinbeck and Ricketts, we rely on one another to survive and protect ourselves by being part of a group. While we have less certainty about other species, we know that for us, beyond the pure mechanistic principles at work, we find a deeper level of social behavior functioning on the basis of feelings and emotions. We have instilled in us a deep need to be social. Similar to all other organisms, humans cannot survive and raise offspring without some form of cooperation. Social abilities have evolved over time, starting with the ancient forces that attract us to group being. Different social capacities make us and many other species successful at cooperation. I assume that salmon are moved by a basic drive (often referred to as an instinct) to collaborate as a group. Such a drive is innate to salmon (as it is to us, as well as chimps, mice, bees, trees, and bacteria, for example). Besides the primal drive to belong to a group, in some other animals we also find feelings, such as empathy, that make the dynamics of the group arguably more complex. Similar to chimpanzees (discussed in chapter 3), we recognize that we should help those in need and that we share the need for a leader.[7] Similar to rats and mice (the animals of chapter 2), we feel pain when we see another human being suffer. Underlying these different feelings, the basic drive to be part of a group is also found in these more complex species of animals and is the underlying foundation to be a social animal in the first place. Humans, I suggest, are no exception to this.

Because salmon (presumably) do not experience feelings such as empathy, they are an interesting species to better understand the primal urge to be part of a group. In the case of salmon and other fish that swim in schools, we find the continuous formations of loose communities. The basic drive that pulls them towards the group assists them in facing obstacles and challenges that otherwise could not be overcome individually. Human groups typically have leaders, whereas salmon lead "as a group." Yet, in both cases of salmon and humans, members are drawn to the group and participate. As we will see in the following section, Latour describes such participation in terms of "acting" and "reacting."

Latour's Gaia

Salmon collaboration in the form of schools can be seen as loosely organized societies. They might come and go or move from one school to the next, yet they are driven by a tendency to be part of a group in which they cooperate with others to (1) get to their destination and (2) optimize their chances of survival as (a) individuals and (b) as a species. The joining of a group for a salmon is, I assume, not a conscious decision, yet we find that a tendency towards the group, which increases the odds of survival of both the individual and the species, is at work in all animals, including the human animal. Some species of animals are more social than others, yet all need to collaborate at some point in their lives. While collaboration in human societies today often translates into monetary exchanges, it is obvious that without others who supply food, clean water, shelter, and so forth, the human population would collapse quickly. It is also clear that we cannot survive without other species, a natural environment that provides resources, clean water, technologies ranging from transportation to computer networks, medicine, and education to keep these technologies and health care running.

How then do we exist as individuals in human groups as well as in relation to both natural and technological environments that largely determine us? How do animals such as salmon relate to their environment as well as members of their own species? I set up the groundwork for this discussion by bringing in Latour's Actor Network Theory, which provides an initial approach in which the relationship between an animal (including the human) and its surroundings can be made more explicit. Although referencing some of his earlier research, the focus is on his recent work, *Facing Gaia,* in which Latour speaks of "animated agents" that interact as "waves of actions."[8] In some of his earlier publications, he has expressed a similar idea in terms of a "parliament of things,"[9] a "political ecology" or "politics of things" in which rights are swapped or crossed over between humans and non-humans,[10] and a "democracy of nature."[11] The Actor Network Theory proposed by Latour is a challenge to rethink who we are, and it provides a radically different way of seeing ourselves in the world of "things." Whether those "things" are technological or natural does not make an essential difference within this network. All things are actants: a tree, a rock, or a smartphone is not a passive thing, but rather an acting being that makes other things within its network react.

Thus, we find ourselves in a network in which acting and reacting or agent and patient often intertwine in their activities: the human actant is one among many other active beings, including things. Along these lines, in *Facing Gaia*, Latour uses the Gaia theory as a secularized model of a network of nature that is self-regulating and has a history but is not driven by either a *telos* or an *arche*. For Latour, science consists of ever-changing narratives and works with social (and scientific) constructs. As the narratives and constructs that are used to tell these stories change, our understanding of ourselves and how we act also changes. The network blurs the lines between subject and object, which means that we are not in control of the world (of objects). Moreover, we find ourselves in a network of relationships. In "nonhuman beings . . . , we find agencies that are *no longer without connection* to what we are and what we do."[12] Instead of finding only agency on the side of the human realm, we now locate ourselves in a network of agencies.

Within this network, Latour criticizes how our Western concept of "the environment" is viewed as separate from us, or at least not an essential part of us. His proposed idea of a collective in which "everything that was a simple *intermediary* serving to transport a slim concatenation of causes and consequences becomes a *mediator* adding its own grain of salt to the story."[13] Nothing is passive or merely an object to be manipulated. Instead, everything is an actant that acts and reacts to its surroundings. In addition, he adds that an organism not only adapts to its environment but "*bends* the environment around itself, as it were, the better to develop. In this sense every organism *intentionally* manipulates what surrounds it 'in its own interest.' "[14] The result of all individual organisms intentionally manipulating their surroundings is the disappearance of intentionality of the whole: it is not an organized system or oneness. On the contrary, it is "the chaotic history we know very well since we are living in it."[15] This interaction between an organism and its surroundings replaces the idea of "the environment." Thus, it follows that "there is *no longer any environment* to which one might adapt. Since all living agents follow their own intentions all along, modifying their neighbors as much as possible, there is no way to distinguish between the environment to which the organism is adapting and the point at which its own action begins."[16] Rather than speaking of an environment, we speak of interactions as "*waves of actions,* which respect no borders and, even more importantly, never respect any fixed scale."[17] Furthermore "the inside and outside of all borders are subverted."[18] Thus, we get to a messy picture in which there is not a single providence. We are asked to believe in "as many Providences as there are organisms on Earth. . . . The very idea of Providence is blurred, pixelated, and finally fades away."[19] Latour, then, moves away from any kind of *telos* or *arche,* and instead, we find a messy interaction of actants constituting a whole.

This "messy" interaction can be regarded as a reinterpretation of the political replacing the Aristotelean framework and teleological language. Instead of seeing the political as an arena where certain goals are set (such as increasing the number of jobs, the GNP, or financial indexes), we would redetermine our political community as a wave of interactions in which different people seek different outcomes. Instead of seeing this as a conflict between different self-interested people, the very recognition of this messy whole can help us to understand that like the salmon, we ultimately are group beings. Humans and salmon are similar insofar as they are involved in interactions through all kinds of processes within which they are both acting and reacting. We collectively adjust to the weather as salmon adjust to salt or freshwater habitats by altering their bodies, one of the many examples that indicate how the environment and actant(s) are one. Likewise, the salmon changes (or in Latour's terminology "bends") its "environment" around it. Swimming in schools creates an efficient hydrodynamic movement of the water and protects the group as a whole against predators. Salmon manipulate the bed of the river to lay their eggs. After spawning, one can clearly see the lighter colored spots (called "redds") in the river as a result of the salmon digging and flapping their fins to create a hole (or depression) and eventually cover the eggs. Salmon in all these actions are valuable members of a larger community. Besides being food for animals in the sea (and for those that bring their food to land), when returning to the creeks and rivers salmon bring valuable nutrients from the sea. These nutrients feed bears and bald eagles, as well as the forest. Bears are picky eaters, eating only the fat parts, such as the brain and the eggs, leaving the rest of the fish for others. Bears and other animals fertilize the forest after eating the nutrient-rich salmon. Trees, shrubs, and berries grow well on the nutrients the salmon bring. Although it might seem that in my description ecosystems are following some kind of telos, it is rather the result of each member—in Latour's terminology—bending their environment around them. An ecosystem is not designed; there is no plan. The members of an ecosystem live in overall mutually beneficial relationships. The forest with (among other things) trees, berries, bears, eagles, and salmon is maintaining itself in an interchange between these members, each fulfilling a role in the gift economy that is the ecosystem.

Thus, we see that the distinction between environment and actant is blurred. The same is true for the distinction between nature and culture. As Latour argues,

> The idea of a Nature/Culture distinction, like that of human/nonhuman is nothing like a great philosophical concept, a profound ontology; it is a secondary stylistic effect, posterior,

derived, through which we purport to *simplify* the distribution of actors by proceeding to designate some as animate and others as inanimate. This second operation succeeds only in deanimating certain protagonists, called "material," by depriving them of their activity, and in *overanimating* certain others, called "human," by crediting them with admirable capacities for action—freedom, consciousness, reflexivity, a moral sense, and so on.[20]

Here Latour criticizes the familiar philosophical story—a story that informs all of our thinking, including that of the natural sciences. We find agency only in the activity of the human, yet any "animation" of the natural world is met with great suspicion. By "overanimating" our side, we can quickly accuse anyone who animates the non-human side of anthropomorphizing—through "anthropofabulation" we separate ourselves from other animals by creating standards we ourselves cannot really meet. As a result, we see ourselves as radically separated from the animal world, as well as the inanimate world. Those other worlds we regard as lacking freedom, consciousness, reflection, morality, or politics. We have to wonder, first of all, if we possess these qualities ourselves.

What is so interesting about the salmon is that they negotiate with (and bend around) so many different environments. One example already mentioned is their return back "home," the place where they were born and where they will spawn. How they are able to make this return is still largely a mystery since salmon often swim vast distances over their lifetime. One hypothesis is that they use magnetic fields in order to orient themselves and find their way back. However, even with magnetic fields, studies suggest that this only puts them about 50 to 100 kilometers near the mouth of the river. It is therefore assumed that other mechanisms are also in place. It is suggested by some that they "smell" the water of the stream that is their home. David Montgomery writes: "Once they near the coast, smells imprinted on the journey downstream help guide the salmon back up their home river; they follow the scent of their river carried in surface waters to guide them on the final leg of their journey back from the ocean."[21] Perhaps salmon are operating on a similar memory as ours when we are reminded of home because of certain scents. Be that as it may, in terms of Latour's *Facing Gaia*, we can regard salmon as creatures taking part in a complex network of processes that involves actions and reactions of different animals and organisms, including the microorganisms that emit scents and are smelled and the magnetic fields that emit and are sensed.

In the water, salmon are fast and incredibly strong, as anyone who has caught one or tried to catch one can testify. Yet, they are also extremely vulnerable, and as a species they are struggling. Reproduction is fairly inefficient since very few fertilized eggs will become salmon. Many eggs will be eaten, become infected by a fungus, or end up in a section of the creek that is too shallow. Similar challenges exist for the early stages of the salmon—the alevin, fry, parr, and smolt—when we do not even fully call them salmon yet. Few salmon actually make it to the ocean. The United States Fish and Wildlife Service states that of the 1,000 to 17,000 eggs a female can lay, a return of three fish per parent fish is considered "good production." Of those salmon that make it to the ocean in the first place, many die before they return to the river or creek. They are on the menu of sea lions, whales, and other predators. Facing multiple obstacles, it is clear that the strength of the salmon lies in numbers. Yet, even strong numbers can be decimated, and it is no surprise that the biggest threat to the species is the *Homo sapiens*.

Other Than Human Politics

In the introduction of this book, I argued how politics is no longer to be seen as a human characteristic alone. We humans did not invent politics but inherited political tendencies from other species, made it our own, and morphed it into the dysfunctional mess that we today call politics. Throughout this book, I show different forms of animal collaboration involving different models of governance, most of them decentralized. While I have indicated some traces of a shared political community between the salmon and the human as a collective which includes both the human and the non-human, we are still far from actually facing Gaia. I will now take on a second approach which is to consider the salmon as being political in their own right, thus outside of human politics.

In Latour's work on non-human actants, he speaks of "a democracy of nature" or a "politics of nature." In *Politics of Nature*, he has suggested, among others, that ecologists can speak for other species. In *Facing Gaia*, he takes a slightly different approach in arguing that the very way in which we understand our relationship to the earth and how we understand the earth itself has serious consequences as to how we treat it. The whole that is called Gaia, for Latour, is not so much a thing or an entity, but rather a process. It is a "geohistory" in which all parts are active without being driven by some overseeing entity. Latour—playing on the word *anthropomorphism*—suggests that Gaia will "*morph* humans into a more realistic image."[22] Different stories, different narrations of this history of the world, and different geohistories will morph us differently. This context of a secularized narrative that will change us is one of the important insights that Gaia has to offer.

As mentioned, Latour regards the complexity of the interactions of different organisms as "messy" and adds: "Gaia is not a kindly figure of unification."[23] It is rather "the name proposed for all the intermingled and unpredictable consequences of the agents, each of which is pursuing its own interest by manipulating its own environment."[24] Within this context of the self-interest of all actants, Latour is rather pessimistic in his assessment of the ability of humans to become better political animals. The Anthropocene is for him a "postnatural period." Yet, the book as a whole argues for a new climate regime by "making the distribution of agency the political question par excellence."[25] This distribution of agency involves, "all the animated agents," which Latour considers political: "Can we become capable of limiting ourselves to the animation proper to the Earth, which would make it possible to redefine politics as well as nature? Yes, in fact, it is. Isn't it strange that we could once have thought that only humans were 'political animals'? What about the animals, then, and all the animated agents?"[26] The traditional realms of nature and politics (and society, culture, etc.) are challenged here. Logos, freedom, consciousness, reflexivity, and moral sense could possibly be found in the non-human realm, yet Latour does not seek such a redetermination of the animal. Rather, he proposes to rethink the world in terms of agency, in which we find an interconnected world of actions and reactions. Instead of a material world of objects that can be acted upon by human subjects, subject and object are now reevaluated in terms of agency, in which non-human entities are also determined as agents. Moreover, the concept of nature disappears and politics is the all-encompassing field that connects all agents. Interestingly, all beings are now becoming political agents (or political animals) in their interaction (or "bending") of their environment around them. Thus, following Latour, we find that, indeed, salmon can be called political in their own right, as they engage (or interact) with numerous different environments.

Salmon in Indigenous Cultures

Latour speculates that in the future, people might find it strange that there was ever a time when animals were not considered political. However, he does not mention any cultures that have always considered animals as political creatures.²⁷ Cultures much older than our own perceive the world as animated in which everything is interconnected, cooperation is necessary, and domination is dangerous. The introduction to this book already mentioned Kimmerer's "grammar of animacy." One example of an Indigenous culture that is directly connected to the salmon is that of the Tlingit in the Pacific Northwest Coast of North America. The salmon is a particularly important animal for their culture (besides other local animals such as the raven, eagle, bear, and killer whale). Not only do the salmon provide food, but their runs also mark the seasons, and they are seen as an integral part of the natural world.²⁸

One way to engage with Tlingit culture is through their stories. I will focus on the Tlingit story commonly known as "Salmon Boy," which tells us about a boy who was taken by the salmon.²⁹ When the boy throws away a piece of smoked salmon because it has a moldy corner, the salmon take him to the sea. There he learns about the salmon's life and how to properly live with them as a member of their community as well as those who subsist on them. When he eventually returns to his village he becomes a shaman and a spokesperson for salmon and herring.³⁰ The story warns us about disrespecting salmon or rather implores us to respect them.

Many Tlingit (and other aboriginal) stories describe a transformation between the human and the non-human. These transformations should not be taken literally but do contain a message about how close we are to non-human animals. The message of the Salmon Boy story is, first of all, to respect animals because they symbolize life. In this case, salmon nurture the people, whose lives depend on the fish. We quickly learn that salmon are more than their bodies and more than just food. The Salmon Boy can and does eat the salmon even while he lives with them, but their spirit remains. He learns how to treat them in the correct way. In fact, he creates suffering for the salmon chief when he neglects to return the eyes of the salmon to the sea. The eye of the chief turns sore, and he is only healed when the boy returns them properly.

It is certainly difficult for a Western mind to grasp the idea that salmon are just like us or that they live like us. This story suggests that the boy's transformation made it possible for him to recognize that all life is essentially the same. A common idea found among the Tlingit is that once we strip the bodily appearance away, all life is very similar. In the case of the salmon this means that just like human animals, salmon communicate, teach, and are capable of suffering.

When interpreting the story, we should be aware that this story comes from an aboriginal community, the Tlingit, that has subsisted on (or dwelled with) salmon for thousands of years. Stories such as this one contain ecological knowledge that is the result of thousands of years of living with and living off salmon. While it is hard to take the story literally—when kids ask whether a story really happened, Tlingit will typically answer with an "I don't know"—that part is not really important. As with the fables of Aesop, the question of whether or not they really happened misses the point of the fables. Likewise, most people do not take the stories of the Bible as literal true stories, but the significance lies rather in the allegorical values that they hold. Gary Snyder provides a valuable insight regarding myths: "I suspect that primary peoples all know that their myths are somehow 'made up.' They do not take them literally and at the same time they hold the stories very dear. Only upon being invaded by history and whipsawed by alien values do a people begin to believe that their myths are 'literally true.' "[31] These stories serve as lessons on what to do, how to live with one another, and in the case of Salmon Boy, how to live with salmon. Such narratives can be much more powerful than any policies. As David Montgomery points out, the problem is not that we do not care about salmon, but lies rather "in the way we make decisions and in the mismatched times scales over which societal and evolutionary processes operate, as well as the slow accumulation of little changes into large impacts that can radically alter natural systems."[32] Stories such as Salmon Boy warn us exactly against the impact we currently have on natural systems. The story suggests that salmon form a community that is very similar to a human community. The community can thrive, suffer, or even die.

Salmon in the Anthropocene

In our own politics, we have overall miserably failed the salmon. Humans have impacted all parts of the lifespan of the salmon, from creek to ocean, from water quality and creek destruction, to overfishing. While overfishing is arguably the biggest problem, it is really the combination of overfishing, the pollution of waterways, "spills" in the ocean, building of dams in creeks and rivers, and the destruction of creek and river habitats that has led to a serious decline in the salmon population. Each salmon run we can witness the consequences of our activity when we see how many (or how few) salmon return to spawn. Our politics has led us to an extreme "bending of the environment." Contemporary *Homo sapiens* are far from learning how to interact with other members without destroying a habitat for those creatures, which eventually also destroys human habitat(s).

In our collective Western mind, we are becoming increasingly aware of the precious state of species like salmon. Maybe we worry about salmon because of their culinary value, but it seems more likely that we are slowly beginning to recognize that the collapse of the salmon population is a sign of how poor of a state our ecosystems are in and how poor members we are to the larger community of the earth. In general, rivers and creeks often provide us with clear feedback on how poorly *we* are doing. The Cuyahoga River in Cleveland spurred the environmental movement when it caught fire in 1969. Many German rivers were polluted to the point that they were considered dead yet have been restored to some degree. Fish have returned to those rivers even while they are not recommended for human consumption. In the United States, creek and river restoration projects are occurring all over. Some rivers (for example, in New Zealand and India) have rights. Rivers and creeks should not just be considered things. They are the arteries of the earth, bringing life to the places where they flow. Salmon and other fish are an important part of this flow; they are—to use the metaphor of the artery—the oxygen that is carried by the river, not only going with the flow of the river, but also against it. In fact, upstream swimming against the flow is part of the important relationship between river and fish. It is a flow of life and death: at the start of this migration upstream, the salmon stop eating and they will completely exhaust themselves.[33] It will, thus, kill them, yet the process which involves their inevitable death, preserves their species.

We sometimes try to become better members of a community, for example through restoration. Rivers and creeks are important parts of ecosystems, and most need restoration. Habitat restoration projects are underway, yet these projects face all kinds of challenges, including a lack of funding and relatively little knowledge about salmon, which sometimes result in costly mistakes. One example of this was the removal of redwood tree stumps from places such as the Lagunitas Creek in Marin County, California. Mistakenly it was thought that the trees were obstructions for the salmon and that removal of the trees would produce better runs. However, it turned out that the water just downstream from the fallen tree stumps created great spawning grounds, as well as resting places for the salmon on their journey upstream. After the mistake was discovered, the stumps had to be brought back in with military helicopters, an expensive operation that further cut into the already limited amount of funding. Ecologists learn from these mistakes, but the trial and error process is costly, both in monetary terms and moreover in terms of the salmon population and the communities that depends on their continued existence.

While our attempts to restore habitats sometimes result in even bigger disasters and salmon would have been better off without our efforts, we slowly learn from the salmon. They provide us feedback and mostly tell us to back off or reverse our actions. Thus, in some cases we are listening to the signs salmon provide us. From these signs we can determine how to better bend our environments around us: reduce fishing, restore habitats in a meaningful way, stop the pollution of waterways, and so forth. In that sense, salmon have become part of our political unity in which they have a voice. We want them to thrive, yet we still need to learn how to make that happen. Such wishes and such listening did not occur when we destroyed the creek in the first place. Here we notice a human political community that is arguably improving in terms of including the voices of non-human actants: salmon now have a voice. Yet, we are far from the situation in which the human actant recognizes the full complexity of what Latour calls Gaia, or how the Tlingit claim that the lives of salmon are not essentially different and certainly not separated from our own. We still have to fully grasp the facts laid out by Latour's Actor Network Theory, that we are not in control and that we are part of the messy whole, a network of processes that shape us as much as we try to shape it collectively.

Politics then becomes a collective that is shaping and is being shaped. It is, arguably, one of the biggest failures of our contemporary Western societies to not recognize this dual relationship between our world and ourselves. We tend to think we can shape ad infinitum and even recreate the earth on distant planets that are quite hostile to any living thing. Instead of turning our collective energies towards saving our current world and learning how to live here sustainably, we think our genius is to create living conditions somewhere else. Against such massive failures of humanity, Gaia brings awareness to the reality that we are inhabiting the only living planet and that there is no escape because we "find ourselves at the center of its little universe, and because we are imprisoned in its minuscule local atmosphere."[34] As opposed to Galileo's discovery that the earth is similar to other planets, James Lovelock's Gaia story is one we find more difficult to accept: Latour points out that it is more comforting to hear a story that the earth is nothing special, just one of the heavenly bodies, part of an immense universe, while Gaia tells us that there is no escape. It is exactly the message the explorers of Mars fail to hear. It is a message that tells us we are living on a planet that is, first of all, unique and that, secondly, reacts as an agent or actant. Through these insights, we can recognize our dependence on it. In addition, we can then ask if we would change our actions in relation to the earth once we accept it as a living thing and thus as a thing that can die. Latour suggests that we are poor members of the collective because science and philosophy repeatedly have told us stories that disconnect us from nature. Gaia, instead, ties us back to nature. We need more and new stories that are successfully tying us back to nature.

Indigenous Knowledge and Practice

Returning to the Tlingit, stories such as "Salmon Boy" can be interpreted in a variety of ways. Disrespecting animals by stepping on them or by wasting parts of their bodies can be partly explained in a spiritual manner. To offend a salmon means offending the salmon spirit, and so all salmon will turn against you, your family, or even your community. You will not catch any salmon, they might disappear for a while, or you yourself might turn into a salmon. The idea that salmon have souls or spirits have an important metaphorical meaning that provides a clear ecological message: wasting food, or not taking proper care of the waste, can destroy the system that provides us with food. We have to recall here the idea of the gift economy, as described by Kimmerer: every gift puts us in a relationship of reciprocity. The gift of salmon should not be taken for granted. We have to give back by taking care of the shared ecosystems that both humans and salmon can thrive in. This, again, is ecopolitics as described in the introduction to this book.

It might be suggested that I am reading too much into the Salmon Boy story and that I am suggesting that the Tlingit were environmentalists long before that word was even invented. We should not forget that sustainable practices were at the center of Indigenous cultures. They learned to live in a particular place without destroying that place by actually contributing to it in positive ways. Tlingit stories consistently tell us not to waste food, overfish, or overharvest trees. Their knowledge of the land developed over generations, influenced by famines and disasters that they learned to avoid. The Tlingit knowledge found in these stories is a land- or place-based knowledge that shows the deep connection of all things. If we overfish one year or take things for granted, we will face the consequences in the following years. When "scientific" knowledge and Tlingit knowledge are in agreement we still find an essential difference: we Westerners fail to act on our knowledge, whereas the Tlingit are typically fairly consistent between knowledge and acting. Western scientific knowledge alone lacks the strength to convince us to change our behavior. Whereas an aboriginal community (such as the Tlingit) translated their knowledge through stories and rituals into practices, Western society fails to ground its practices in knowledge. This brings us to reflection on our own stories: what is lacking today in our stories? How do we fail to act upon the knowledge that, not only salmon, but the whole earth is destroyed and we stand by and participate in that destruction in more or less active ways?

The story of the salmon boy provides an idea of the interconnection of all life: the salmon people *are* people, not just in a symbolic or mythological fashion, but also scientifically. Darwin discovered evolution in the Western tradition, but Native Americans have called animals brothers and sisters for millennia. Some might call this an anachronistic reading of Native American narratives, but many Native Americans insist that their ancient knowledge is not that different from what Darwin discovered in the nineteenth century.[35] We tend to separate "Western science" from "aboriginal myths," yet if we think about the way in which Darwin made his discoveries, we immediately observe some significant connections. Darwin did not dream up his theory in labs and by simulating models. He made his discoveries by closely observing an environment, famously, the Galápagos Islands. His knowledge originated from a place-based knowledge, even though he ended up applying it to all places. Native American knowledge is a much deeper place-based knowledge as they were not spending, like Darwin, a limited amount of time in one place (three years and three months). The Tlingit spent generation after generation in the same places, living very closely with the animals on which they depended. I suggest that to think that they would have been unable to come to conclusions comparable to those of Darwin should be considered an insult. Returning to the earlier point about whether these stories really happened, we see that we can take these stories as metaphors full of important lessons and, thus, as scientific.

One story that is used in Tlingit science lesson plans regarding the moon, the sun, and the tides, involves Raven. It is the most important and sacred animal for the Tlingit. Like other animals, it is indicated in the singular and capitalized (although the stories were originally transmitted orally) to indicate that all ravens share one spirit. The raven is, actually, a sacred animal across Alaska and the Pacific Northwest, as well as in Japan, and is also important in Celtic and Nordic stories. For the Tlingit, Raven created not only the earth but also people. He is a creator who works through trial and error. He made rivers that flow in two directions simultaneously, similar to a two-way street, which he ultimately corrected. He also created immortal human beings, or beings that walked better than he did, mistakes he also had to correct. Raven is a trickster and not necessarily a benevolent being; he acts mostly out of self-interest. The trial-and-error approach also indicates that creation is messy.

What implications do the Raven stories have? In particular, the idea that an animal created humans, as well as the earth, is in great contrast to the Western Christian tradition in which God created the earth and then us "after his own image." While science tells a different story than the biblical story, Nietzsche already predicted that God is going to cast his shadow over us for centuries. Indeed, we still hold on to the idea that the earth was created with some *telos* and that we are somehow the fulfillment of that *telos*. Often Darwinism is misinterpreted along such lines in which the human is regarded as the highest or ultimate step in evolution. Whether taken as a myth or in a more literal way, the story is sometimes interpreted as suggesting that the earth was given to us, the Godlike creatures. Lynn White and others have discussed the problems of Christianity in relation to environmental destruction. Of course, Christian thinking has many other trends, including that of Pope Francis. Nevertheless, it tends towards hierarchy, one that suggests we as humans are the chosen ones to lead and that we are close to the creator. The stories we hear, even if we doubt that they are true and even if we simply take them as metaphors, have a tremendous effect on who we are, what we do, and what we do not do.

One of the important implications of this is that, as already suggested, science is not without religion. Our thought patterns and ways of theorizing and investigating have been directed by biblical stories and by some ideas that are in fact older than Christianity but have been solidified by it. As I have argued elsewhere, ideas regarding *arche* and *telos* still persistently play a role in the natural sciences.[36] Ultimately, fields such as ecology and ecological restoration seem to indicate that nature is ordered, not necessarily implying that a god ordered things, but at the very least indicating that we find balance in nature *as if* a higher being ordered it.

The Tlingit story of how Raven steals the moon and the sun from a chief can also be taken as an "as if." Raven disguises himself as a spruce needle that is swallowed by the daughter of the chief. She becomes pregnant and gives birth to Raven, who now lives in the house of the chief. The chief keeps many goods in a box, including the sun and the moon. Baby Raven cries for these goods, which are eventually given to him, and with that, he steals the moon and the sun. It is indeed a fictional story, but indicates why Raven stole the sun and the moon: after he crafted the world, there was no light. He wanted to see his own beauty and the beauty of the world. While it is not an act of benevolence on the part of Raven, the story recognizes that the moon and the sun are important for all. All are more important than the single chief who wants to keep the moon and sun in a box, which creates his power. Even the chief, after he loses possession of the sun and the moon, recognizes this when he feels the warmth and can see the beauty of the world as the sun is shining.

The moon and the sun are extremely important for the Tlingit people not only for the most obvious reasons but also in order to predict tides. This knowledge was and still is incredibly important for both food (certain foods can only be collected at low tides), as well as transportation. The tides are so important to the Tlingit that their name originates from the word tide: *Tlin* means "tides" and *git* means "human being." *Tlingit,* thus, means the "tides people." Since the regularity of the tides is referred to in another story involving Raven we see then that the stories show the sun and the moon for what they are in terms of their actual meaning and value for humans: besides warmth, light, and beauty, the stories provide the science that tells us how the tides behave.

Likewise, returning to the salmon, they are also regarded as indicators of change. As mentioned above, the changes that the salmon body undergoes and where salmon move correlate with the seasons. Many Native American people in salmon territory have named months after the salmon that run during that time of the year.[37] Salmon are in this regard fairly predictable, and their arrival marks the occurrence of certain events. Reflecting on this example of the relationship between an animal and its "environment," we step beyond the immediate insight that salmon are a source of food and income (even while that relationship is meaningful and often drives policies).

Stories (and names) thus provide ways to relate to important aspects of the world, such as geography, tides, or the seasons. The creation of the world by Raven puts us in a much humbler position than our Christian stories. It does not mean that we are subordinated entirely, but Tlingit stories imply that other animals, such as ravens and salmon are very similar to people. That does not mean we should become like them. In fact, we should not be like Raven, the trickster. Many Indigenous stories warn us against the selfish, narcissistic tendencies we have, and Raven is one of those.[38] Likewise, Yunkaporta describes the figure of Emu and our Emu narcissist tendencies. We are all a bit like Raven, or Emu, or as Yunkaporta states it bluntly, "Some people are just idiots—and everybody has a bit of idiot in them from time to time, coming from some deep place inside that whispers, 'You are greater than other people and things. You are more important than everything and everyone. All things and all people exist to serve you.' This behavior needs massive checks and balances to contain the damage it can do."[39] Indigenous stories about animals, thus, often tell us that we are like them, for better or worse. Moreover we are told we are connected with the natural world, not as leaders but as a part of a larger community in which we have certain powers or knowledge, yet lack knowledge and powers that other animals might have. Spending time in Tlingit territory can make one realize the reason for this humble position, as nature takes us out of the position of leader or master. One does not need to read Nietzsche to be told one is a mote of dust.[40] The landscape itself seems to tell one again and again that one's very existence is a matter of indifference.

It would be a mistake to reduce the story and the taboos we find in many Native American cultures to mere spirituality. Most of these traditions find ecological aspects just as important as spiritual aspects, or they cannot be separated from one another. The Tlingit also recognize the message of the Salmon Boy story as what we could call a scientific, ecological instruction, that is, we should not waste animals or parts of animals, since disrespecting animals will not be without consequences. The fact that the boy turns into a salmon symbolizes the close relationship between salmon and humans. The ecology of this story tells us that the material and spiritual aspects tie us to the salmon. The latter can be found in the ambivalent relationship between life and death that is expressed in the Salmon Boy story: only bodies die, while spirit continues. In terms of evolution, we can understand this as the survival of the species, and even across species we find the survival of certain characteristics in most forms of life, such as the tendency to collaborate. The boy in the story discovers that different life-forms share these same features.

When we connect salmon and human realms, we learn more than just the politics of the individual species, but ultimately, we start to recognize an interrelated or interconnected view of ecosystems as gift economies. From the perspective of the whole, these ecosystems regard all members as equals. Such a perspective is provided by the Salmon Boy story, in which we come to the understanding that the different parts of the collective depend on one another. Individual relationships within this politics are not equal. For Latour, the interconnections make up a messy whole of actions and reactions. The Tlingit provide a more organized view (even while recognizing the messiness of creation) but do—like Latour—recognize the human as an actant among many others. We live because of the salmon, raven, bears, or (in another well-known creation story) the turtle. We live with these other beings in relation to the sun and the moon. The tides change with the closeness of the moon, and we follow its movements, the ebbs, and floods as well as the monthly cycle. I will return to the sea and the biological significance of the moon in chapter 4, while discussing the community of the tidepool.

The Salmon Boy narrative tells us to respect other animals, the river, the sea, and the earth. Modern physics often seems to tell us a different story: things can and should be manipulated (which Heidegger explained in terms of *Gestell*). Within this narrative things are objects moved by subjects, a deceptive view of the world in which we think of ourselves as the only free agents and by that same token as the only political beings. The Salmon Boy story tells us how other creatures are like us, beings that can suffer and that interact with their environment through "bending it" (action) and morphing (reaction). The Gaia hypothesis, in many ways, supports the narrative of an animated world. Latour's Gaia "anthropomorphizes" all non-human actants. Both the Salmon Boy and Gaia do change (morph) the human and make us rethink all non-human beings as actants. They make us wonder if we have perhaps overemphasized our own superiority over other beings, and they provide ways to rethink the very idea of a society, not consisting merely of human agents, but of non-human animals, as well as the processes that constitute Gaia.

Conclusion

In this chapter, I have used salmon as an example of Latourian political animals. If we can accept that salmon group participation is political in nature and follow Latour's gesture to extend the political to all animals, we can now start to wonder if we humans can learn something from salmon politics. Salmon are necessarily involved with other salmon. Without them, they would not survive. The same is true for all humans, yet our political, social, technological, and economic structures seem to focus mostly on isolating us from others. For example, I can make purchases that sustain me without interacting with or even encountering another human being. When I do encounter others, I am protected by a physical barrier consisting of steel when I am driving in a car, or otherwise some form of technology directs my attention and that of others towards our own self-enclosed world. What we call politics today (the messes in Washington, DC, London, Brussels, or any other governmental place) is arguably an extension of this individualized anti-community. We have resorted to representation through voting. We rarely vote on decisions, and if we even bother to vote, we elect others to represent us, which allows us to withdraw from all political life, including the local. We only show up (if ever) to a local town or city meeting if an issue is discussed that has an immediate effect on us. Even while everything in life is political, most of us do not participate in political decision-making. I suggest that this is a problem in a global society in which humans collectively are destroying the very conditions of life. When politicians can do and say whatever they want because most citizens have tuned-out of so-called politics, we are in a self-destructive mode that is already presenting long and lasting consequences. Citizens are not encouraged to engage in politics. Instead they are encouraged to consume more because we have equated success and happiness with consumption. Even more, the benchmark of the successes of government itself is the growth of the economy, which is directly tied to the level of consumption. We can only be successful by living unsustainably—a self-destructive predicament indeed.

Salmon, like most other species, on the other hand, cannot live without participating in processes that I consider to be political in nature, since their survival depends on it. They are actants in different "environments," acting and reacting to all kinds of changes they encounter. If we can accept that deep down all life is similar in nature, we open up the possibility for entirely different discourses, including Latour's Gaia and Tlingit narratives. Both stories provide a much-needed alternative to our Western narratives. Yet, Tlingit stories are exactly that: *Tlingit* stories. They are rooted in a particular place and encompass a particular history, a science, an ecology, a value system, and an identity. All those are only of real use in the part of the world in which they originated. It is not my intention to suggest that we should take up these stories, nor is it my intention to compare and contrast Latour's account of Gaia with aboriginal stories, which would be a futile attempt. What I want to suggest is that the stories we tell about the history of the earth and the places in which we live, whether rooted in religion or science, are impactful. Thus, we have to tell and create different stories that influence the way we understand the places around us and how we act in those places. It is in this regard that we can translate one important lesson from the Salmon Boy story to our own narratives: we are deeply and fundamentally connected to non-humans, sharing all kinds of drives and abilities.

Where do we start in creating stories? Perhaps we can, first of all, listen to the salmon. Most people will find salmon to be amazing creatures. Many will also agree that they constitute a community. Yet, the majority of people will also seriously doubt that salmon somehow engage in politics, as I argue here with Latour and the Tlingit. As far as we know, salmon do not vote, deliberate, collect in caucuses, protest, or engage in civil disobedience. While Latour argues that politics does not have to be limited to human agents, it is clear that salmon politics does not fit our categories. I suggest that this is precisely the point of researching salmon—or any being that lives in a group: we have to challenge and change our own categories. The ultimate goal is to better understand our relationship with a world that is much larger than ourselves. By recognizing the large whole of which we are a part, we can ultimately become better members of the group ourselves. What does that mean in terms of salmon? We have seen that other species rely on salmon. When salmon suffer, the sea and the forest are suffering. Salmon being is the kind of existence we should aim for: as a keystone species others can rely on. This is in many ways the opposite of our current state of affairs, even while we know that our actions have great effects on salmon and other species. Even as a dynamic species that adjust their bodies, and with survival techniques such as the self-organizing school, salmon cannot evade the human predator. Perhaps their politics is lacking, but considering the fact that the decimation of the salmon population greatly affects us, it seems that it is our politics that is failing.

We have seen that we can learn from salmon and many other non-human animals that we are in essence very similar and that our lives are intertwined with theirs. This insight can change our discourse and rethink what politics is and can be. This does not mean that we adopt "salmon politics," which would result in an obvious rejection: we are not salmon. Nonetheless, even while the issues of our polis are not identical to those of salmon, we quickly learn that ignoring "their issues" leads to a catastrophe for us as well, an insight presented in the Tlingit Salmon Boy. One of the important conclusions regarding the redefinition of politics is that it is now determined as a collective that is shaping and being shaped. The collective thus is fluid and not limited to one species or group. The interaction between individuals and between a group of individuals and their surrounding environment, the others that are shaped and shaping, is a tremendously complex ecosystem.

It is an *oikos* in which different agents are involved in relationships that I call political, or ecopolitical.

It is likely the case that salmon do not have an understanding of the significance they constitute as members of a larger community that bridges several ecosystems and involves other fish, mammals, birds, trees, fresh and saltwater, soil, and so forth. Yet, the lack of understanding does not undermine the fact that the species fulfills an important role for all these other beings. The irony, then, seems to be that while we humans do (or at least can) understand the impact we have on other beings, we fail so miserably to act on that understanding. To truly understand would mean that we act in a more salmon-like way: as a member of a larger community on which other members rely. Salmon make several ecosystems thrive. The challenge of our time is to take up this feature of the salmon and to learn how to be a member of Gaia, bringing as many benefits to other species as the salmon do.

Chapter Two

Crossing Borders

On Rats, Mice, and Other Decolonizing Packs

Harry liked to bring in a little surprise once in a while: a mouse or a small rat, still alive (of course). Typically, he dropped it on the floor and after the mouse pretended to be dead for about twenty seconds, it would attempt to make its escape, only to encounter Harry's large feline paws to redirect it. I did not appreciate the torture of the rodent, especially since most of the time Harry lost interest before the game was truly over. Thus, we were often stuck with a rat or mouse slowly dying, bleeding, but still able to move and hide too quickly for our clumsy human bodies. One time I locked the cat and a rat in the bathroom ("you brought her in, so you take care of things!") and to my astonishment, I found them sitting next to one another. Our, at the time, seven-year old son concluded that they had become friends. Whatever the cause of this unlikely friendship (for one, Harry was well-fed by us and did not need the rat for nourishment), we did not want a pet rat, and moreover, the rat was now terrified of me rather than of the feline that had brought him in. I had to hesitantly accept the obvious: it was my turn to take action. With some luck, I was able to catch the rat under a bucket. While aware that the rat might not survive, I did not want to kill it prematurely, and instead, I released her a few miles from our house.

Human encounters with mice and rats are obviously common, and none of my experiences as described in this domestic scene are unique, nor is my reaction. I have to overcome my resistance to mice and rats. Questions such as *"Is it still alive?"*—and if it is—*"What will it do next?"* *"Where will it run?*" are really hopes such as "*I hope it is dead! I hope it will not bite me! I hope it will not run up my arm!*" I know my worries and anxieties are not very rational. It is a *tiny* animal. Yet, the long tail and the fast, skittish, unpredictable movements seem to create the image of an apocalyptic horror film creature to be avoided at all costs. Obviously, our cat knew better.

Why is it that rats and mice—while in many ways, quite fascinating animals—are often seen as disgusting pests? Their tail is perhaps a telltale characteristic that shows this contrast well: the tail is used for balance, coordination, and controlling their body temperature, but it is also often judged to be appalling because it is much longer than the rest of the body. We also know that rats are very sociable, experience empathy, and even seem to care for sick members of their own species. They have good memories, have different moods, and have individual as well as collective identities which determine their behavior as a group. We know they can be good, clean, and smart pets. Rats are worshipped in the Karni Devi temple in India, and the rat is the very first of the twelve animals of the Chinese zodiac. We find a stark contrast between the worshipping and the warfare often waged against rats and mice. The animals themselves also seem to behave in radically different ways: as good pets and sacred animals deserving worship, or as pests carrying plagues and other diseases. While some of this might be "in the eye of the beholder" this chapter dives into deterritorial and territorial tendencies displayed by mice and rats and seemingly dictated by different circumstances.

In literature and films, this vast difference in terms of rat behavior is reflected: Kafka's last story explores a singing mouse. Numerous films that explore rats fall in the category of dark, postapocalyptic, science fiction, or horror genres. As discussed in this chapter, John Steinbeck explores human and animal relationships through the imagery or metaphors of mice.

When we want to imagine rats in a philosophical way, as a political animal even, some work has already been done, most famously by Deleuze and Guattari. Len Lawlor explores the zigzagging of the rat through Deleuze and Guattari. We should, he argues, follow the rats in our writing. I will argue that we, indeed, should explore the movements and motives of rats and mice in order to envision new ways of moving, thinking, and relating. In order to think about this systematically, I will discuss our relationship to rats and mice as the colonizing animal species found in ecology, as a metaphor for fleeing opportunity seekers in Steinbeck, as subjects of laboratory research, and as a sacred animal. Through this strange smorgasbord, I will attempt to argue that while mice and rats are often colonizers and invaders, they do present political strategies that are deterritorializing and decolonizing.

This insight partially explains the choice of rats and mice in this chapter. Whereas salmon are loved by many, rats and mice typically have a bad reputation. They come into our houses, multiply "like rabbits," spread diseases, eat our food, make a mess, or even worse, destroy our house. They are extremely hard to get rid of and they always seem to come back. In pretty much all of these characteristics, rats and mice are characterized very similarly to many people's perception of immigrants who cross borders and flee away from war, political unrest, hunger, and poverty. We think about rats and mice in the same way we think about unwanted human others. These others are regarded as the carriers of diseases and the instigators of violence. They eat our food, multiply by the day, infringe on "our" space, and make a mess.

Lastly, I discuss how rats and mice act differently depending on their environment. They can cross and break down borders, and we share the same part of the brain that is responsible for empathy, but they can also be greedy and protective in certain situations when empathy is overruled in order to protect privilege. I want to think through what kind of political community we can have with rats and mice, not merely as an exercise, but as a way to think about our political community grounded in a colonial past. Packs, in the form of rodents or those who cross borders, disrupt boundaries, and I argue that we can understand both as decolonizing. Rats and mice confront us with conflicts, deep tensions, and the territorial nature of contemporary politics. In a time of tremendous tension around issues of refugees and migration, by following the politics of deterritorializing mice and rats, I will suggest to not merely rethink immigration and refugee policies, but instead to think beyond borders. This implies a rethinking of what it means to be an insider or outsider, and with that, a challenge to politics based on identity, so that we can move towards a politics of inclusion.

Warfare I

We find rats and mice in all kinds of places, and we mostly seem to think that wherever they are, it is not their place. I already provided the example of our cat bringing mice and rats into our home. They are also often unwanted in the wild. For example, we find mice thirty miles off the coast of San Francisco on the Farallon Islands in the Farallon National Wildlife

Refuge. On these islands, uninhabited by humans, mice have joined the thousands of birds and marine mammals, presumably unknowingly transported there by seal hunters in the 1800s. As a *San Francisco Chronicle* article states bluntly: "The mice do not belong on the Farallons."[1] The argument is that since humans introduced the mice, they should not be part of the island ecosystem, even while they have lived there for at least more than a century. The population of mice fluctuates dramatically: in the summer, so many mice live on the island that, according to the same article, the ground appears as "a gently rolling tide of rodents."[2] Most of the mice die in the winter when food supplies are very low. The presence of mice has changed the behavior of other animals. One example is the behavior of owls, which used to migrate to the mainland during the winter but now can stay on the islands year-round because there is enough food. Ecologists certainly do not like this: their idea of the Farallon Islands does not include mice, and owls are supposed to migrate. The fact that living creatures adapt to changing environments and ecosystems themselves adapt to changes is, for most ecologists, not a valid reason to allow mice to exist on the island. Mice have been introduced in an unnatural way, by humans (using the assumption that humans and their activities are not natural).

Although the standpoint of these ecologists can be problematized, we should be suspicious about human (voluntary or involuntary) activities. As exemplified in the failed salmon habitat restoration projects in chapter 1, it is not easy to reverse even some of the destruction. Restoration or taking out nonnative species is at least a start in rectifying some of the problems we have caused on a massive scale. Nevertheless, we should be careful about the methods we use in our attempts to "rescue nature" since we often produce or introduce bigger problems. I discussed how in the restoration of creeks to recreate salmon habitat, big mistakes have been made that actually created more problems.[3] Unintended consequences are exactly the worry in the situation of the mice on the Farallones, especially since the proposed method to kill the mice is the use of poison (nicely called "rodenticide"). A poisoned rodent continues to live for a while, and as it weakens, it becomes particularly easy prey for predators, who then eat the poisoned animal. In a 2008 effort to eradicate rats from the Aleutian island of Hawadax, an estimated 46 bald eagles and 320 glaucous-winged gulls were killed after eating poisoned prey. Poison can also spill into the ocean, getting into the food chain. When a similar war against mice was waged on the Catalina Islands, permits were issued to use poison. The problem for the ecologists working at the Farallon Islands is that the islands are part of a national marine sanctuary, and special permission needs to be granted. The Department of "Fish and Wildlife admitted [that] some seabirds would likely die as part of the initiative."[4] Last but not least, the method of using rodenticide also involves severe cruelty. The poison blocks the production of vitamin K, which results in the failure of blood clotting. After one or two weeks, the animal will die of massive internal hemorrhaging. Interestingly, the ecologists working on the mice problem on the Farallones present their solution—poisoning the mice—as one that avoids rather than creates suffering. Their argument is that killing them prevents further suffering: each year thousands of mice die because of hunger, a cruel and unnecessary event that will end after the poison has done its job. The argument seems to apply some utilitarian principle of avoiding as much suffering as possible but lacks any other principles. If the subjects were humans, the problematic nature of such an argument would be immediately obvious. Should we euthanize any human who is about to face great suffering? Should we kill populations that suffer from food scarcity? Decisions around euthanasia for pets and certainly humans are very difficult and can only be made on an individual basis. When thinking about the suffering of mice, I suggest we should apply at least the same criteria used when ending the life of a pet, making the argument proposed by ecologists highly problematic.[5] If we are really that concerned about suffering mice, we should bring them food as opposed to poison that will lead to internal hemorrhaging.

    The other proposed methods to eradicate the mice included introducing predators (such as cats), infecting the mice with a lethal pathogen, or the use of traps, but for a variety of reasons, none of these are seen as better alternatives. In 2021, the plan received initial approval by the California Coastal Commission. According to *The Guardian*, the plan now includes capturing owls and other raptors and using "hazing" techniques such as lasers, pyrotechnics, and effigies.[6] The organization Wildcare, which has opposed the use of poison, mentions that legal hearings have led to additional conditions, including the addition of a stormwater runoff plan and a call for the plans to return to the commission for "informational review" prior to the execution of the plan.[7] Besides these small victories for Wildcare and wildlife, the last hurdle for the ecologists working for the US Fish and Wildlife Service is likely to be met.

    We have to wonder if the mice are indeed such a tremendous problem, that this allows for these radical measures, such as dumping 1.5 tons of rodenticide in a marine sanctuary. Since the measures are resisted by others, we find an interesting political debate about the future of the mice:

Do we allow them to remain there? If we want to get rid of them, what methods will be used? Can we justify the killing of animals for the sake of preserving an image of nature that excludes human influence? The wildlife refuge provides a special political status to the islands and their inhabitants (which does not include humans), creating a sanctuary in which mice, or any creature that makes it to the island, enjoy some form of immunity. Even while they are unwanted, the prohibition on poison saved them at least for some time.

Becoming Rats

If there is such a thing as a rat, mouse, or rodent philosophy, we might be able to find it in Deleuze and Guattari. As Len Lawlor writes:

> If we want to understand becoming in Deleuze and Guattari, then we must understand becoming rat. As we shall see, when I become rat, the rat becomes a "feverish thought" in me, forcing me to think. And, in response to the gnashing rat thought, I do not start to look like a rat. No, instead, I start to write like a rat. To write like a rat is to write in the style of the rat's agony, to tabulate a tale of rats—so that the work produced will call forth a new people. Writing like a rat, we might be able to call forth a people who themselves have the feverish thought of the rat in them, forcing them to think differently. Perhaps this thoughtful people would say, "This right that I seem to have is not justified." Then perhaps we would see coming a people who would no longer enclose the world in a globe.[8]

This seemingly strange project of Lawlor, inspired by Derrida, Deleuze, and Guattari, discusses "becoming" and criticizes "globalization" and its attempts "to enclose the world in a globe," which is, for Lawlor, the dominion of man of the world. It is a dominion based on an unquestioned right that is "not justified" and assumes a territory. The focus of Lawlor is that territory excludes the non-human. Likewise, we can speak of the exclusion of other humans, who are considered "aliens," "refugees," "illegal immigrants," or "undocumented workers." Such acts of exclusion are, moreover, acts of affirming inclusion: by determining who is "out," one also states who is "in" without the need to explicitly state the latter. Today, we are all too familiar with this dynamic when, for example, the citizenship of American people of color is questioned. The implicit message (although little effort is made to hide this) is that to be American is to be white (or that "make America great again" means "make America white again").

Lawlor's idea to write like a rat is an attempt to become something else, to become-animal, as Deleuze and Guattari propose. To become-something in the sense of Deleuze and Guattari is, as Lawlor discusses, not a simple act of the imagination or the understanding. Neither is it an experience of memory or perception, "It is not a process governed by an eminent form or endpoint; it is not a relation of recognition in which the subject and the object would be outside of one another, and it is not a representative relation of one thing standing in for another."[9] Becoming involves both subject and object, challenging the strict dualism that we often assume in such relationships. Thus, becoming-animal does not only change oneself; it also changes that which one becomes. As Lawlor quotes from Deleuze and Guattari's *What Is Philosophy?:* "We become animal so that [pour que] the animals become something else."[10] What the animal becomes is not clear, but we are not exchanging positions: the animal is not becoming me. To contextualize this becoming, he then takes a step back and discusses becoming in terms of gender. When man becomes woman, Lawlor explains, she does not become man, she becomes animal "so that she may be able to attack an enemy."[11] This is a helpful thought insofar as we are familiar with changes to gender identity and gender roles. If a male person becomes more feminine or takes over tasks that are traditionally assigned to women, this can open the opportunity for a woman to become something else. One option is for woman to become man or more masculine, yet a reversal of roles is not a true becoming for Deleuze and Guattari. Indeed, thinking about gender in terms of a reversal would simply maintain the binary opposition. A reversal is merely reactionary in which one's becoming is already determined by what one is not yet. Instead of this dichotomy, becoming has to be entirely open, in which one can become something entirely different. "He" and "she" can become something beyond gender dichotomies and beyond past models of gender, beyond concepts of gender. Deleuze and Guattari express this in terms of woman becoming animal, which should not be interpreted as a step back. It reunites us with our less rational, bodily existence, with our instinctual drives. Given the history of portraying woman as an emotional, irrational creature, the metaphor has possible negative ramifications. Yet, for Deleuze and Guattari—who write in a Nietzschean tradition in which reason is regarded with much suspicion—becoming-animal is a positive and forward movement, not only associated with woman, but with humanity: man first becomes woman, so that woman can become animal.

The next step is, admittedly, even harder to grasp: when woman becomes-animal, the animal becomes something else (the child and the molecular). This implies that when I become-rat, the rat becomes something else, something other than rat. Lawlor eventually identifies becoming-rat in terms of writing. Characteristics such as "feverish" and "zigzagging" are translated into writing as a rat. Writing is an act that should not be underestimated, certainly for Deleuze. Text and writing are predominant features in Lawlor's essay, in which writing is considered an ontological, ethical, and political activity.

Lawlor writes, "We have gone from Derrida's thought to that of Deleuze and Guattari."[12] He uses the notion of deterritorialization in order to explain becoming in Deleuze and Guattari. Deterritorialization—I suggest now—is not only a matter of writing differently, it is a radical rethinking of who we are, what we are (and who/what we are not), what we are entitled to, and what we allow others to be and do. When I become something else—let's say a rat—I give up my territorial notion of self and other and recognize that boundaries can become fluid, that *everything* is, in fact, fluid. Thus, my very being is determined not as an identity such as "I am human" but rather through the possibility to become. Not only can I explore "being human" in a variety of ways, wearing different masks; I can also become something else. Significantly, it is not a self-centered activity. It is not about the self, but rather the other that I become so that this other—woman, animal, child, the molecular—can become something else. Thus, we find the politics of becoming, in which nothing is fixed and all boundaries are challenged. For Lawlor, this implies in particular that we stop enclosing the world in a globe. This idea is mostly explained at the end of the essay, where he states:

> Is this collectivity a people (as in Deleuze) or a democracy (as in Derrida)? Again, it does not matter. All that matters is that, since the collectivity would be called forth by rat-writing, the collectivity would have a different relation to the animals than we do. Perhaps this collectivity to come would be themselves a people who thought feverishly. Haunted by the specter of the agony of animals that they find, within themselves, perhaps they would say, "This land that I seem to possess is not my own." They would say, "Let's open all the doors and destroy the walls."

Perhaps they would be a people who loved the world so much that they would want to let everyone, without exception, enter in, and to let everyone, without exception, exit out. Perhaps, we could call this people to come "the friends of passage."[13]

This is a powerful idea, especially in today's political climate. And yet: as enticing as a world without borders might sound, can we even seriously engage with this thought, especially in today's political climate? My answer to that objection is that we have to rethink property and borders in the most radical way possible. I might not want to share our home with rats, mice, or ants, yet the fact that we pay the mortgage every month does not entitle us to eradicate rats and mice with poison. Of course, sometimes circumstances leave one with very few options (for example, when dealing with termites that might destroy a home), yet in becoming-animal, one recognizes that one is to never take decisions to eradicate any creature lightly. Thinking, then, about human others, we come to recognize that this land is not mine, yours, or ours. Even if we ignore the acts of violence against Native Americans and the slavery that largely built this country, we can still not claim a right to exclude others from what is known as North America. The "right of exclusion" that we speak of is exactly established under a system of law that specifically excluded Native Americans, African slaves, and their descendants. Perhaps we should rid ourselves entirely of the language of rights, which assumes inclusion and exclusion.

We are in a situation in which we can praise ourselves for letting in some refugees, while others are literally drowning. Capitalism itself has embraced a similar ethical strategy. It has become standard practice for businesses to include some sort of community plan. These plans typically satisfy the consumers enough to avoid feeling any form of guilt about the products or services they purchase. We can purchase a gas-guzzling monstrosity without guilt since it is a hybrid car and the dealer "gives back to the community." If we are worried about people displaced by the politics that ensure gas flows cheaply, we can always volunteer, or donate to a refugee center to feel assured that our own lifestyle and the borders that protect it are justified. We rely on legal documents written by the ancestors of those who benefit from them (just as their ancestors did). We can raise practical objections: if we open borders, the Western world will be flooded by refugees. This will indeed happen, but let's not forget that this is already occurring—under the most inhumane circumstances. Yes, there will be more, and we can learn from pack animals such as rats and mice—a system that moves en masse without leadership yet collectively knows what to do. What we are witnessing is the chaos that occurs in moments of transition.

Unfortunately, this will occur and is already occurring all across the globe after natural environments have been destroyed and political systems have been destabilized. People will have to move in packs like rats if they want to survive. Of course, there will be walls and guns, and political candidates will do their best to keep "the others" out under the pretext that opening borders will be a threat to national security. Unless extreme and unacceptable violence will be used, we have to accept the only other possible answer: to overcome our sense of the insider and outsider, of who belongs and does not belong. In a shared world, security will be shared as well. In a world beyond borders, a terrorist attack will attack the terrorist as much as anyone else. Terrorism is a symptom of the disease that is the world of borders. Anger at the Western world is not without reason, and we can start to understand and overcome our fear through the strategy of Deleuze and Guattari: becoming and deterritorialization. Thus, the fearful Westerner becomes the oppressed so that the oppressed can become something else.

David Graeber put the dilemma of borders well in a proposal to create "an immediate amnesty on international debt . . . an immediate cancellation of all patents and other intellectual property rights related to technology more than one year old [and] the elimination of all restrictions on global freedom of travel or residence."[14] For those who object that this is dangerous and will create chaos, he adds: "The moment the average resident of Tanzania, or Laos, was no longer forbidden to relocate to Minneapolis or Rotterdam, the government of every rich and powerful country in the world would certainly decide nothing was more important than finding a way to make sure people in Tanzania and Laos preferred to stay there. Do you really think they couldn't come up with something?"[15] Graeber's provocation is indeed challenging us (the industrial Western world) to make sure to stop the decline of the living conditions in the developing world. For instance, even while we often buy away our guilt through some fundraising action for a "poor country," the depletion of their natural resources and the political instability is often directly linked to our consumption. The typical refugee is not defined by seeking opportunity but by fleeing a disaster. It is the opportunity-seeking mindset of the first world that creates these disasters in the first place.

The similarities between unwelcomed non-humans and humans are plentiful. We do not want mice or rats where they do not belong as we do not want refugees. Our solutions are shortsighted, to say the least: poison or patrolling walled borders, as opposed to addressing the true causes. Deleuze and Guattari, in relating to the animal, woman, child, the earth, or molecular, place us in ecologies where we become aware of the natural beings we are but often attempt not to be. We can then argue that for them, this oppression of our inner natural being translates into the oppression of women, people of color, animals, as well as the earth. It is that which we oppress that we need to become.

Of Mice and Men: Becoming Mice

Rodent politics might sound interesting, yet rats and mice are infamous for being horrible members of the earthly community, especially when they collect as a pack. Mice plagues can cause extensive damage to food crops and farmlands. While we target these populations, we have to, first of all, recognize that mice or rats are not to blame. While they naturally have peak years in reproduction, plagues are the result of numerous factors, including an open landscape, a lack of predators, and abundant food sources. In Friesland, the Netherlands, the plagues are associated with relatively dry years resulting in lower water levels. While winters will usually partially flood the land, in recent drought years without floodings, the population of mice can rapidly increase. In Australia, plagues occur around the enormous scale of human food production. Storage of grains can provide excessive conditions for a plague. BBC video footage shot in Australia shows enormous numbers of mice running through the grounds and buildings around farms. The video shows the floors, ceilings, and walls swarming with mice. Opening a door produces a flow of mice at least a foot deep. The whole world seems to be taken over by mice, covering every visible square inch, often piling on top of one another. There simply doesn't seem to be a place that is not covered with mice. What a human being can do against such a force is far from obvious.

When discussing today's immigration issues, we likewise seem to think that we are facing a force that is beyond our control, unwilling to admit that it is we, the industrial world, who caused the problem in the first place. When discussing immigration, we can first of all say that while the issue is pressing, it is far from new. History is full of stories of those who do not belong, or those who were forced to move elsewhere only to meet exploitation and oppression. In the United States, one infamous event revolved around an environmental crisis, known as the Dust Bowl.

Famously, Steinbeck chronicles the hardship, prejudice, and injustice that farm workers from Oklahoma, among others, faced during their journey to and after their arrival in California. *The Grapes of Wrath* follows the escape from a land without hope to a land full of (false) promises. Another famous work by Steinbeck, *Of Mice and Men,* chases a false dream, as two men look for work and eventually a place of their own in that same land of false promises. The dream consists of the idea that things will get better, eventually. To discuss our mice-like existence, I will focus on *Of Mice and Men* and pay particular attention to the correlations between the characters in the story and mice.

Lennie and George, the two main characters in *Of Mice and Men,* who make a living by working on farms in California, are like many other farmworkers who dream of owning their own place someday. They are unlike other farmworkers in always traveling together—the others all are by themselves. The story is partially about friendship in a world full of loneliness where "ever'body in the whole damned world is scared of each other."[16] Lennie is the strong giant who likes to touch soft things: mice, bunnies, puppies, a dress, or the hair of a woman. His strength combined with his love of soft things keeps getting him into trouble. While never meaning harm, he kills mice, a puppy, and eventually a woman. George, the smarter of the two, reminisces on his own situation on several occasions and expresses that his life would be easier without Lennie: "I could get along so easy and so nice if I didn't have you on my tail."[17] A long rant about their previous trouble with a girl in a red dress ends with the following words: "All the time somethin' like that—all the time. I wisht I could put you in a cage with about a million mice an' let you have fun."[18] What makes it all bearable for George, it seems, is their romantic dream of owning their own place someday. They know it is a dream, yet the real trouble starts when they think they can make it come true when Candy, an older farm worker who has enough money saved, wants to join them.

Thus, their dream laid out in a scheme with Candy is closer to realization than ever before. Yet, there are abundant signs that the farm they are at is going to bring trouble, bigger trouble than ever before. The title *Of Mice and Men* is important in this regard. It is taken from the poem "To a Mouse" by Robert Burns. The most relevant lines, although the whole poem is very relevant, run like this:

> But Mousie, thou art no thy-lane,
> In proving foresight may be vain:

> The best laid schemes o' Mice an' Men
> > Gang aft agley,
> An' lea'e us nought but grief an' pain,
> > For promis'd joy![19]

They are left with grief and pain when Lennie accidentally kills the wife of the farm owner's son. She had been flirting with him (and the other farmworkers), tells Lennie of her own failures—her schemes that have gone askew—and eventually asks him to touch her hair. Here, her scheme to seduce one of the workers comes closer to fulfillment than ever before, yet goes awfully wrong. When he touches her, Lennie's strength scares her. The screams and resistance cause Lennie to freak out and he accidentally breaks her neck.

Of Mice and Men is in many ways rather hopeless, especially since collaboration between the moving farmworkers has greatly diminished (especially in comparison to *The Grapes of Wrath,* which is arguably a much more hopeful book). The killing of the woman reflects the kind of world they live in: a world in which no one trusts one another. In a world full of distrust, people behave accordingly. The son of the farm owner is hyperaggressive, his wife flirts with everyone, and the owner and other farmworkers distrust Lennie and George because they travel together. Farmworkers are typically isolated, and in this situation, isolation might be the best survival strategy. Yet, even in that isolation, the men are drawn to one another, indicating an important instinct (further explored in chapter 4).

As already indicated *The Grapes of Wrath* is more hopeful, even while it is a devastating story as it follows the struggles during the journey of the Joad family from Oklahoma to California, where they face nothing but more hardship, disaster, and exploitation. The book ends with the powerful image of the Joad's daughter breastfeeding a starving man. Even while their family went through so much hardship, the story ends with an act of love for a stranger, a fellow Okie, who is fed the milk that was meant for the stillborn baby. Maybe their schemes have gone askew, but they have not given up.

Likewise, in *Of Mice and Men* the powerful image of George killing his best friend provides hope as it is an act of love. In both cases, the hope is rather twisted. *The Grapes of Wrath* provides an ironic kind of hope (a man is saved from starvation because an unborn infant died), and *Of Mice and Men* provides a troubling and dark hope with George shooting Lennie out of love. At least we know that Lennie is not lynched and tortured to death. We can even admire George for his heroic act. Yet, we find ourselves wondering how horrible the circumstances must be that we find hope in death and killing.[20]

In a world where everyone turns against one another, it is perhaps the gentle giant Lennie who softens people, at least some. George recognizes that Lennie does not mean harm. Other characters in the novella recognize that being alone makes one mean, and the stable buck Crooks, who as the only person of color is forced to live all by himself, offers the following: "A guy goes nuts if he ain't got nobody. Don't make no difference who the guy is, long's he's with you, I tell ya."[21] The "who the guy is" comment presumably reflects on race. Within the context of the novella, it also reflects on the relationship between George and Lennie. It doesn't matter that Lennie is who he is. Nevertheless, their friendship raises suspicions among the lonely guys who have become mean, suggesting that the social environment of farmworkers that isolates people generates meanness.

We can return here to Burns's poem: "man's dominion / Has broken Nature's social union." The dominion of the landowners in California has broken the social union. They exploit and crush those who need to make a living. With that, they break nature's social union, and mutual aid is made impossible. Lennie and George's scheme goes against the interests of the landowners. It crushes them because it cannot be realized; the closer they get to realization, the deeper their trouble grows.

This is explicitly tied to an environmental theme when loneliness is discussed as a "loneliness for land."[22] This expression comes from Crooks, who a few pages earlier makes a comparison between land and heaven: "Nobody never gets to heaven, and nobody gets no land."[23] Here, the problem of exploitation of cheap hands by the farm owners comes full circle: in a world without any kind of social network, everyone has to fight for themselves and loneliness turns into meanness. In a world in which the law is always on the side of the farm owners, their frustration can only be expressed towards one another. Love seems impossible as is expressed through the strange marriage of the farm owner's son. His wife flirts with all the farmworkers, and after she gets killed, he is only concerned about taking revenge for a fight with Lennie he lost earlier. Representing the mean world of the landowner, (as the owner's son) he only cares about regaining some of his lost reputation, not about losing his wife.

We typically react with violence in order to eradicate mice. The influx of people in places like California leads to abuses, another form of violence. A plague in nature indicates an imbalance, often caused by our domination. It is disturbing since a plague shows us that we are not in control, rather, we are controlled by the forces of nature that overwhelm us. Lennie and the other farmworkers are in their behavior reacting to the circumstances they find themselves in. The way they live together (or apart), the violence, and the distrust is a result of the social environment in which they are treated as mice, as a plague. In the case of refugees (such as the Okies, today's political refugees, or tomorrow's "climate refugees"), we also find an imbalance at the root of the problem. Both mass migrations of humans and of rodents are an indication of our political failures. In the case of mice invasions, the storage of grain and other foods on a massive scale provides the possibility to sustain massive amounts of mice. When we store food that can feed thousands of people, it can feed millions of rodents. Large-scale production causes large-scale problems. Mice become part of this system and interrupt it so we are forced to engage with them. Mixed with climate change that provides dry conditions and pollution that leads to extinction of predators, mice and rats can be virtually boundless in numbers.

The mice in places such as Australia find a true heaven in a world of virtually unlimited food supplies. Rats and mice then form a political community, yet we fail to recognize this political gesture. Our response to their gestures is limited to warfare, and we fail to grasp their motives and, as I will discuss in the next section, we fail to think like a rat. While I sympathize with farmers who have to deal with plagues that threaten their farms and source of income, I suggest we have to take a step back as a political global community and economy. Mice and other unwanted others are a creation of the industrialized world of globalization with the availability of massive amounts of food. Human "plagues" are caused by similar circumstances. The violent, dangerous, or poor conditions in one place force people to places that seem to promise a much better future. Refugee problems are caused by a global world in which natural resources are taken from third-world countries, often destabilizing them. Here is then the truth of our "rat politics:" the rat or mouse is not to blame, as the refugee is not to blame. It is we who have created the conditions for the pack that is now considered to be our enemy.

Humans, like most social animals, often show a tendency to move towards groups. Yet, we also see that humans often isolate and stab (or shoot) one another in the back. Mice seem to be better at sticking together than humans. Their strength in numbers can have positive and negative consequences. Whether one is a mouse, a rat, or a human being, traveling as a pack provides power. The famous Critical Mass movement is based on the idea that bicyclists acquire power over cars when enough bicyclists gather. The phenomenon occurs, for example, in Asian cities where bicyclists stop for cars at intersections, and once enough bicyclists have accumulated, mostly within a minute, they obtain the right of way over cars purely based on their mass. Arguably, migrants have also acquired some power by traveling together. Nevertheless, such packs also become easy targets for people who take advantage of them and for political movements that oppose the invasion or even hype it up for their own benefit.

To think about how to encourage positive movements that attack oppression, racism, injustices, and so forth, I propose here a decolonizing politics: packs of people (and animals) that carry messages we cannot ignore. In Levinas's terms, it is the face of the other that shows itself to us, in this case en masse, and makes a deep, massive, ethical appeal.[24] It tells us how we as a human political community have failed: colonization, which includes war, environmental destruction, and exploitation, has brought us to a point at which the other responds as a pack. This decolonizing politics is a politics of mice and rats. We can take the politics around the Thirty Meter Telescope (TMT) as an example. This telescope was proposed to be built on the sacred land at the top of Mauna Kea on the island of Hawai'i. Mass protests involving thousands of people blocked the access road to the site of the planned construction, drawing enough attention to the situation to block it in court. While lady justice is depicted as blind, we know too well that she is not and that she will give in to political pressure—in this case to decolonizing tactics. In many cases, organizations, developers, and builders regard such protesters as rats disrupting their agenda. The strategy of "the rats," though, is to become a pest in order to resist and disrupt. When that strategy is successful, they become a political player. The typical Western mind cannot understand the Native Hawaiian mind. To most Western scientists, the summit of Mauna Kea is a place far away from any community (the site is over 13,000 feet above sea level) and without vegetation, making it unworthy of protection. To them it is simply an ideal place for observing the sky. Yet, they now have to reckon with a conflicting story in which the mountain is a sacred dwelling place of deities and ancestors, as well as the meeting place of sky father and earth mother. It is the most sacred location, the center or beginning and ending (*piko* which means "navel") of the island of Hawai'i. It is, thus, not surprising that a strong opposition developed against the construction of an enormous telescope. This opposing force is constituted by a group of humans who want to protect the site, who want to mark the place as something off-limits.

Thinking Like a Rat

Perhaps Steinbeck suggests that we are too much like mice. We assume we can escape or have already escaped our animal tendencies. We think we plan ahead in order to move out of our current misery. The plans of George and Lennie in *Of Mice and Men* are similar to the hordes of young people who currently are attempting to start their own business with some brilliant scheme. A few will indeed become wealthy, but the vast majority will fail.[25] The failure, for most, will not be as dramatic as the one of George and Lennie, but the results are still painful. The cause of the failure of today's entrepreneurs is similar to that of George and Lennie: somehow, they are not going to be like everyone else. It is in this denial of being like everyone else that they are exactly homogenous. Thus, we find the denial of our animal being, the scheming mice whose plans often go askew.

Steinbeck, mostly, shows us our own animal characteristics. Are we simply stuck in rat-like or mice-like schemes? I suggest we should not give up our attempts to overcome those rat and mice tendencies that lead to pain and sorrow, yet we can only do so by first acknowledging that we have such tendencies. By first of all recognizing how our societies are not very different from those of rats, mice, or ants, we can better understand who we are. This understanding can ultimately lead to new ways of fighting the oppressive and other negative aspects of our own societies. We can also start to think about new ways of being and living together that emphasize cooperation and mutual aid, as opposed to competition and oppression, such as we find in the world of farm owners and farmworkers in Steinbeck's California.

Maybe we do need to overcome our rat- or mouse-like being, but we can only do so by first of all fully grasping who we are. Following Deleuze and Guattari, we can only do so by "becoming-rat." In this endeavor we have to acknowledge the difference between human and rat being, between different ways of being in the world and in thinking. Yet, such differences can ultimately tell us more about ourselves, such as how we fail in our relationships to the world around us.

The work of Vinciane Despret, and in particular, her essay "Thinking Like a Rat," is helpful here. The article, and many of her other publications, discuss the issue of how animal researchers typically fail to ask animals about their interests and to acknowledge their specific way of being. In some of her works, she has discussed the disappearance of *mētis*, the knowledge that we shared with animals. Instead, in researching animals, we have to find a way to "get to know" the animal that we seem to share nothing with. The way animals think is foreign to us (if we even acknowledge that they think), and thus, we must "ask them to teach us the good explanation, the right motive" for the behavior we try to understand.[26] We then have to "become with" the animal we are studying, not by merely investigating from our own (mistaken) questions, but by becoming their biographer, so we can ask the right questions. This means that the researcher is not the only one who is recruiting (for example, by setting up experiments in the hopes that they will display the behavior we seek to understand and provide clues to understand it); the researcher should also be recruited by the animals so that they can teach the researcher. Despret discusses, among others, the efforts of Bernd Heinrich to explain the seemingly unpredictable behavior of ravens around carcasses. Answers are only found when Heinrich starts to think like a raven, which is made possible by becoming their biographer, through which the ravens teach him to ask the right questions.

While her question is very different from mine, in "Thinking Like a Rat," Despret provides quite helpful phenomenological accounts of rat thinking, rat being, or being "ratish." Her analysis is grounded in the work of Jakob von Uexkull and his criticism of animal researchers. Von Uexkull argues that for an animal, meaning is acquired through action. With this in mind, Despret asks the question, "When observing rats, what can produce the activity of translating their behaviors in terms of meanings?"[27] She approaches this through research that focuses on forcing animals, in particular, rats, through a maze. For her, researchers fall in the typical trap that many psychological experiments encounter: the subject—human or non-human—answers a different question than the one posed by the researcher. When a rat is researched in order to discover its "abstract relation . . . to a neutral object," researchers fail to take into account von Uexkull's idea that meaning is acquired through action.[28] Even for human beings, known for their ability to think abstractly, there is not such a thing as a purely abstract relationship to a purely neutral object. Even while I can think of "route" in its neutral, abstract form, it is only through former specific actions (such as planning, taking, or describing a route) that the idea "route" has a meaning for me. Likewise, a rat does not learn a particular route through the maze in an abstract way but learns it through action. The more interesting question then is: how does the rat learn a route through a maze and how does it memorize it? Despret brings in a seemingly simple observation: "Rats always touch the walls as they go along them."[29] She then invites us to think like a rat:

> It [the rat] inscribes the course of its route in its body in the form of lines, curves, and turns, or even roughnesses, textures, sensations of cold or humidity . . . The rat draws, marks, soaks up, in its muscles and on its skin, the map of a lateral landscape . . . It is not only a matter of "marking" the places one passes . . . it is also a matter of letting itself be marked by the space, itself organized by the trajectory, and of incorporating the organization.[30]

While we think of memorizing as abstract mapping, the rat thinks differently. It does not remember to go fifteen steps, then turn left at the green wall, and take another left at the second opening. The rat does not "mark" the places in such memorization but is rather "marked by" the place. The memory consists of the physical experience through which the place is "soaked up" by the body.

It could be suggested that the rat is involved in something we have lost as human beings. In a world determined through technology, we "know" exactly where we are without interaction with that location. The rat does so well what we fail to do: (1) today, without a smartphone, we are quickly lost. We fail to find our place and we fail to recognize the interaction between self and environment. (2) We are poor political animals and fail to incorporate the organization of whatever environment we find ourselves in, besides of course the ones that we have learned so well (such as the school and the workplace, which for some of us are one and the same). While the latter is an important issue in itself, my focus here is really the lack of the ability to learn from the organization of the world in which we find ourselves. We refuse to let ourselves be marked by the places we pass daily. Instead, we have marked them. This in itself is an animal activity, yet in a technological world, we refuse the interactive bodily experience of the world, as the phenomenological rat does so well.

So, to think like a rat is then more than zigzagging and being feverish. A rat is touching by being touched and marking by letting itself be marked. It can then be a respectful member of its community, and perhaps, we find here the first outline of what rat politics would look like: a recognition of self and others not as absolute boundaries, but rather as co-constituted in action. I am the wall in my openness of letting myself be touched by it, as I am the air that I breathe in letting it in through visible and invisible holes in my body.

Decolonization

We have seen how Deleuze and Guattari suggest a decolonizing movement. They suggest becoming a child, woman, or animal that crosses, and moreover, questions boundaries. An echo of this can be found in the work of Despret. She suggests the rat thinks differently and crosses boundaries between self and other by both marking and letting itself be marked. The rat and mouse play a significant role in crossing boundaries and can be regarded as decolonizing creatures.

So far, my argument to become rats is to suggest that we take steps towards decolonizing and crossing boundaries. However, such crossing of boundaries is not without complications. Rats themselves sometimes depart from their own decolonizing strategies. An example of a different rat strategy can be found in the behavior of the rats at the Karni Devi temple in India. The temple is a place to worship about 20,000 black rats, who are well-fed and considered to be sacred. It is quite a fascinating place, but what is truly amazing is that the rats seem to be extremely healthy, and no infectious diseases have ever been found, even during times when the whole country was experiencing the bubonic plague, or when rats in the country were infected with other communicable diseases. The reason why these rats have remained healthy is somewhat mysterious, and the most logical explanation suggests that the rats are highly territorial and, thus, do not allow other rats in their community. Rats are either in or out! By keeping others out the plague has been left out.

With that, the idea that rats and mice can be symbols of deterritorialization is brought into question. It seems that the strength of these particular rats is their territorial behavior, as opposed to many other rats that seemingly take over without limitations. Through the latter, I have tried to challenge our ideas of borders and boundaries, and I have argued to let in the stranger and challenge the boundaries between self and other, native and nonnative, familiar and strange.

Again, we have to ask the right questions here. Instead of suggesting that rats have to be either territorial or deterritorializing, we should, first of all, consider the environment (the place that marks them) in which they exhibit this behavior. The temple rats are "wealthy" and privileged. Perhaps, we can say that rats and mice are not very different from humans in the sense that their respective circumstances generate different ways of relating to their fellow earthlings. In human societies, social and organizational context, class, race, and gender, as well as infrastructure related to those characteristics, set up patterns of behavior. The temple rats of Karni Devi have embraced the social contract in which, according to Rousseau, the wealthy become powerful by successfully protecting their property. While the rats do not use written laws or contracts, other strategies are similar to those of humans. In both cases, privilege leads to borders; wealth leads to securing and strengthening them.

The Karni Devi rats are not so different from this class of humans who want to protect their territory. While some rats explore and seem to know no borders, others build borders. The reasons why rats are either territorial or deterritorial depends on their circumstances, and I suggest that the reasons are more or less similar to why humans are territorial or deterritorial. Typically, territorial groups of humans have something to protect, something to lose, whereas those who are on the move, like Steinbeck's farmworkers, are looking for better opportunities or fleeing disaster. Today, undocumented workers find themselves in a similar position. They are here, but those who are "in" fail to recognize them as fellow human beings who deserve our empathy. Likewise, a rat pack such as the temple rats can set their feelings of empathy aside when they decide to keep strangers out. They, like human territorial beings, have something to lose. Perhaps human territorial behavior is then just like temple rat behavior in terms of the refusal to share. Empathy or sympathy is put aside for selfish reasons. It is the situation in which exclusion of others is very beneficial to those who are included.[31]

Interestingly, our relationship with refugees mirrors the relationship the Karni Devi rats have to outsiders. Likewise, we have similar relationships with most animals. We welcome some in our homes, if they benefit our well-being, while rodents such as rats and mice are either kept out or exterminated. When we consider the rat as a sacred animal or as a pet, we open up the possibility of a different kind of political relationship, one not characterized by destruction and warfare, but by mutual aid. Likewise, we welcome some humans, while we attempt to keep other humans out. Similar to rats and mice, we can be welcoming or hostile, depending on the circumstances.

Rats and mice can tell us a few things: when they are invading packs, just like human packs, it is not the pack that is the problem. We are the problem. When rats take over our food storage facilities, we can and should recognize the political ecological message contained there: our systems might be way too large, creating problems that outpace our practical and ethical capacities to deal with them. Yet, instead of solving the issue at hand, for example by reimagining our economy, we become even more territorial. The mice overrunning food storage facilities should not be regarded as a pest, but as ecopolitical messengers. We need to learn to hear their message. This means we need to interpret the issue and address it.

One thing we can learn from Despret is to think like a rat. When we build walls, such as the walls of a maze or walls around our country, we fail to think like a rat or to think like the pack of others that is, in fact, treated like rats. The rat is part of a collective, the pack, and acts as a collective within an environment. The individual rat runs along the wall and touches it, without us noticing. Yet the rat is ultimately the pack. Likewise, the refugee that has been othered, colonized, and is now decolonizing by perhaps behaving as a rat, is trying to jump or climb over the wall not as an individual, but as a pack. Perhaps the pack brings a hacksaw to cut a hole in the fence, or digs a tunnel (like a rat or a mouse) and goes under it. The fence or wall mostly has a symbolic meaning: if the border was not porous we would be in trouble because we actually need the others we do not want. While we fail to think like a rat, we can understand and think like the refugee, not in order to block their next move, but rather to deterritorialize. If we allow and nourish our empathic capacities instead of blocking them with territorial instincts, we can move towards a more just and shared world. Instead of walls that attempt to block the other, not only from entering our country but moreover from entering our thoughts and feelings, we need to tear down any thought of a wall. The real wall is not the physical barrier but the barrier in our feelings. Empathy (further explored in the next chapter) seems to be lacking.

Of Mice and Men (and *The Grapes of Wrath*) provides a testimony of our dominion, yet of course, we do not have to resort to works of fiction to find examples of people who are portrayed and treated as invading rats. The current refugee crisis, undocumented workers, and police brutality against black people are just a few examples of such treatments. I, now, suggest that in becoming-animal, we should not just become a rat, but also become the human other who has been portrayed as a rat. We fail to think like a rat as it touches and is touched by the wall. Likewise we fail to understand how the refugee is touched by the wall, and, most importantly, we fail to be touched ourselves.

Conclusion

What is interesting is that as we have moved from salmon to rats and mice, the picture of the political community we find is becoming messier. Salmon are fairly predictable even to such a degree that many Native tribes name months after the species of salmon that spawn in that period. We have just seen that mice and rats are a lot less predictable, even while we might think that feelings such as empathy would make them more predictable. It seems that "more complex" beings can "turn" their feelings on and off, depending on the circumstances they are raised in and the conditions in which they live. We can, thus, compare this to our own rat behavior in that we do not seem to care about certain others. Like the temple rats, humans often put certain others, somehow identified as more similar to themselves, before those who less resemble us. In the human realm, this dynamic can lead to racism, sexism, classism, nationalism, and speciesism.

Besides this interesting (yet highly problematic) dynamic at work in both (some) rats and humans, negative antagonistic feelings can be at work in all animals. Kropotkin and the neo-Darwinist biologist discussed in chapter 4 on Steinbeck and Ricketts make very clear that besides mutual aid or cooperation, animals can and will fight. Yet their point is that rather than struggle, cooperation is the predominant instinct and behavior among animals.

As (social) animals can behave in either cooperative or selfish ways (and sometimes these two might merge), is this "more basic" drive possibly overruling more complex feelings such as empathy or altruism? So far, it has been argued that the dynamic is more complicated since other circumstances play a role in determining the outcomes of behavior. The oppressor, as we have seen with Lawlor, needs to become something else in order to face a new reality and to rethink notions of inclusion in a language and landscape without borders.

To call certain politicians rats is then mostly an insult to rats. What we need today is not a wall, but we need rat politics, that is, a politics that recognizes that our schemes often go askew and that pests and plagues are the results of our dominion of the world and of human and non-human others. We need to deterritorialize every aspect of our being, starting with our empathy. In other words, we need to feel for, and be touched by those others who are the victims of our actions.

Chapter Three

Chimpanzee Politics

Towards Empathy

> If biology is to inform government and society, the least we should do is get the full picture, drop the cardboard version that is Social Darwinism, and look at what evolution has actually put into place.
>
> —De Waal, *The Age of Empathy*

"These boxes all go to the first truck. The smaller boxes first, the bigger ones last!" It was another day of intense physical labor for an Amsterdam moving company. As an undergraduate student I worked through a temp agency, sometimes once a week, mostly every other week. Temp workers like myself did not have the experience of the full-time employees, but we worked hard. The experienced crew did most of the stacking and more delicate work; the heavy lifting was typically done by us. This seemed not unfair (we were not experienced after all) and we did not complain, especially because the tips were often pretty substantial.

Everything changed this very day when it was announced (at the end of the day) that a new company policy had been introduced, which determined that tips were no longer shared with the temp workers. Many of us, if not all of us, including myself, never returned. Looking back on that experience, I recognize how the full-time employees were given a position of privilege that they wholeheartedly and seemingly without empathy exploited. The employer wanted to keep their full-timers happy, and the class system in which the full-timers could let us do most of the hard labor, while they reaped most of the benefits, was a small-scale model of how much of the capitalist world functions.[1]

It might be tempting to describe such injustices as "monkey business." Likewise, the political scenes in state capitals and board rooms seem to be led by some "alphas" who are running the show, until they are ridiculed, or hooted down, by another alpha. In fact, in 1994 Newt Gingrich, then Speaker of the House, or "alpha male," assigned De Waal's *Chimpanzee Politics* to all incoming congressmen. De Waal later stated in an interview that Gingrich should have read his book on peacemaking among chimpanzees instead. Indeed, monkeys, such as chimps, are often much better politicians than we humans are.

In comparison to other non-human animals discussed in this book, it is arguably easier to recognize chimpanzee animal communities as political. As in the other comparisons with animal politics, it is certainly not my aim to argue that chimps are just like us or that we should become chimps. Instead, I want to understand the political constitution we inherited from chimpanzees.[2] Moreover, I argue that "monkey business" in Washington and other places of power is exactly what not to aim for. I believe a comparison of our governance to that of chimpanzees is rather an insult to chimpanzees. As suggested in the introduction to this book, politics does not necessarily equal government, and perhaps government is not worthy of the name "politics." In order to rethink our political future, I seek to grasp our past by establishing a better understanding of our own biological being. This will help us to understand the political and social difficulties as well as their possibilities. As suggested in earlier chapters, cooperation is as much part of animal nature (including humans) as competition.

We find the dual nature of cooperation and competition in primates such as chimpanzees. Primatologist Frans De Waal, particularly in his later work, argues that empathy is the foundation for cooperation. His earlier work *Chimpanzee Politics* largely focuses on power, and as the title suggests, he recognizes the chimpanzee colony as a political unit. He argues for this on the basis of the complex social organization he finds in chimps. As can be read in his study, not only is their social life "highly subtle and complex" but it also undergoes changes.[3] The relationships and order of a colony are not set in stone by any means. The central part of his analysis focuses on a couple of changes in leadership, in which an alpha male establishes alliances while strategically and slowly grabbing power. Through such strategic mechanisms, as well as senses of reciprocity and triadic awareness, coalitions are formed.[4] De Waal shows the colony as a political unity, a dynamism of "everchanging systems of relationships within the group."[5] Chimpanzee politics is not centered in a leader; instead, it involves the whole group. The leader has to follow their will, without which he cannot even become a leader. As De Waal states: "Each individual has his or her role to play in this web of intrigues. The future new leader shows the way, but he can never act entirely alone; he cannot impose his leadership upon the group single-handedly. His position is granted to him, in part, by the other chimpanzees. The leader, or alpha male, is just as ensnared in the web as the rest."[6]

Although he acknowledges the importance of the group, he defines politics through leadership as Machiavellian manipulation, arguably missing out on some other aspects of the successful social organization, a caveat he acknowledges and discusses in later works. We see here that politics for De Waal is about leadership and how different individual members of the group are involved in the processes that undermine and establish leadership. He describes a web of intrigues and collaboration, as well as the idea of "granting" leadership.

As previously mentioned, chimpanzees resemble us very closely, possibly more than any other animal. And yet, chimpanzee politics seems very different from our politics, and when it resembles ours, it seems undesirable "monkey business." Although actual fights are rare, the constant threat of physical aggression, male domination, and the extremely protective behavior of the female apes towards their own children, are some examples of what I deem to be undesirable traits of their societies. Needless to say, we do find such traits in human societies. Verbal aggression along with displays of power through gestures such as the handshake and body language are sometimes displayed subtly, other times shamelessly. Either way, aggression is a major part of politics. Insights into these dynamics are the first step towards fighting them, because, arguably, this is an area in which we can improve our current selves.

In his work De Waal has discovered all kinds of political and social behavior in primates and—as he himself stated—made a risky move when he published a book on chimpanzee politics as a primatologist at the beginning of his career. Cooperation, as well as solidarity and empathy (a focus of De Waal's later work), are natural characteristics that make a society with complex dynamics possible, such as we find in chimpanzees.

One of the main questions of ecopolitics is what we can learn about our current political situation by studying other non-human political societies and how we can think about redesigning our own society. When specifically studying chimpanzees we can think about setting up structures that are more natural and do not promote violence but empathy and cooperation. I use De Waal's studies of primates as a way to think about power, the appearance of power, and what kinds of background structures make leadership possible. His work also reflects on the different kinds of artificial and removable structures or barriers that cause frictions in a chimpanzee society. I relate this to human societies as we find comparable structures in our society that create violence.

Although the other chapters in this book discusses more distant non-human entities (such as salmon, rats and mice, and ants), this chapter on chimpanzees will be an important transitional chapter precisely because they are evolutionarily much closer to us. Analyzing what happens to chimpanzees when natural circumstances are disturbed, thus, might indicate ways to think about our own circumstances and the way they influence our behaviors and feelings. In the previous chapter I made some suggestions regarding our correspondence to mice and rats. How they behave (and what they feel) depends on their circumstances. Chimpanzees display similar traits. For example, fights over food rarely occur in the wild, yet can be extremely violent and lead to a lot of tensions in zoos. The abundance of food in one location seems to generate greed in some of the apes. As primates' behavior is determined through the situation in which they find themselves, so is human behavior transformed through the kind of social organization they live and work in. We can start to answer then what the causes of greed and selfishness are. Wealth and power are often associated with one another in our world. Selfishness and greed seem to be both the cause and the effect of wealth. Analyzing chimpanzee politics will be helpful in trying to formulate a different kind of politics, one that minimizes the inclination to selfishness and maximizes collaboration. Learning from chimpanzees we can think about creating political situations that cultivate solidarity and avoid hatred. Empathy is a significant component in this regard. We have seen in the rat and mice chapter that while they are able to feel empathy, it is not guaranteed. The temple rats are highly territorial and lack empathy for those who are not part of the temple community. The circumstances dictate feelings and behavior of rats, chimps, and human beings. When rethinking our own society these issues have to be taken into serious consideration. Before getting into a more in-depth discussion of empathy, I will start with a discussion of De Waal's analysis of politics in the world of chimpanzees, through which I challenge the basic premises of real politics.

Chimpanzee Politics

When thinking about politics in the chimpanzee colony, we might first of all think about the real politics of Hobbes and Machiavelli. I will argue, with the aid of the chimpanzee studies of De Waal, that such comparisons are mistaken. The leadership of chimpanzee alpha males extends far beyond creating fear and expanding territory; the same can be said for humans. Nevertheless, the point of departure in this chapter is real politics.

Hobbes's state of nature is determined as a war of all against all and can for him only be resolved by giving up our natural rights to a sovereign and seeking protection in the state. Even if the political society we live in is not perfect, it is always better than the war of all against all, he argues. Machiavelli similarly (unless his work was a parody of the leaders of his time) proposes a real politics consisting of controlling the population in which moral considerations are set aside and only practical or pragmatic considerations are valued. The people that constitute the state consist of individuals who all want the same: the best for themselves. Thus, the task of the sovereign (in Machiavelli's case "The Prince") is to direct those selfish forces in such a way that they work together in harmony.

Both Machiavelli and Hobbes regard leadership as a straightforward and easy task, exactly because they consider human nature as straightforward. Their view of human psychology revolves around fear and greed, leading to insights such as it is better to be feared than loved (but avoid hatred). For Hobbes and Machiavelli, their political thinking was highly influenced by the times during which they lived. Hobbes witnessed the devastating effects of the Civil War (which for him should be avoided at all costs), and Machiavelli lived in a turbulent political climate in which small republics were either in war or threatened by war. A leader could not afford to simply hold on to power. A republic had to expand and conquer new territories in order to become more powerful and to avoid being conquered itself. Instead of wondering whether the behavior of people was influenced by the political and social contexts of war, they seem to have taken this behavior at face value as human nature. While it would be impossible and foolish to argue that selfish tendencies are not a part of who we are, throughout this book, I argue that cooperation is another part of our (and other animals') being.

Prejudices that suggest we are only acting based on selfish grounds seem to be made in the context of corporations. Machiavellian or Hobbesian politics are often seen at work in the decision-making processes of CEOs. Their situation is not unlike that of the Machiavellian prince: in the competitive capitalist environment, a corporation loses if it does not expand. Even growth is often not enough: growth of growth is what one pursues. Moral issues are not part of this climate as the economic goal dominates, and as a result, feelings such as empathy are suppressed.

Thus, a Hobbesian or Machiavellian society or organization will, indeed, consist of selfish people because selfishness is the only possible strategy to survive in such a society. De Waal argues in his work that we (and primates) are not only selfish beings but also possess feelings such as empathy that form for us the condition for the possibility of cooperation. Nevertheless, *Chimpanzee Politics* focuses less on empathy and regards the primate colony as one ruled through Machiavellian leadership. It is in particular a study of a colony of chimpanzees in the Burgers' Zoo in Arnhem where the animals have two acres of outdoor space, including trees. The zoo setting is not without issues but provided De Waal with a rather unique opportunity to study the animals. While, obviously, a zoo is not a natural environment, it provides accessibility for researchers that cannot be matched in the wild. Moreover, because of their access to the outdoor space, their behavior is more natural than that of chimps in zoos with cramped cages. The large group (about twenty-five chimps) live mostly harmoniously, for example, evidenced by the fact that adult males are "solicitous toward the children and tolerant of their behavior."[7] He is particularly interested in the politics of these animals, an interest that developed by him witnessing leadership changes in the colony. He writes in the introduction about these changes that "took many months and, contrary to what people so often think, they were not decided by a few fights. My own research has been particularly concerned with the endless series of unobtrusive social maneuvers leading up to the dethronement of the leader. The stability of the group is slowly undermined."[8] The fact that the social order changes and the complexity involved in such changes indicate that a colony is not purely based on "instincts" nor is leadership simply a "natural" given based on strength. We find a whole range of different types of social behavior in chimps, such as seeking refuge and reassurance, recruitment of support, instigation, reconciliation, and the formation of coalitions. With regard to reconciliation, it is particularly interesting that chimps (and De Waal also mentions bonobos) have a need to resolve conflict. Chimps do this with hugging and kissing (and bonobos with sex).[9] Letting conflicts linger can lead to tensions that can ultimately lead to extreme violence.

Some important aspects of the study involve the idea of unique personalities in individuals and the recognition that every single chimp has a distinctive "genetic make-up, life history, and social background."[10] The first chapter is dedicated to the topic of personalities, and by focusing on the characters of the different members of the colony De Waal shows that decisions are not made by pure instinct. All the chimps might be driven by similar urges, but how they act on those urges and how they go about their daily lives, set up alliances, and attempt to break down other alliances is largely driven by their personalities.

The focus on personalities already breaks with the idea that there is one "chimpanzee nature." Moreover throughout the chapter, it is evident that chimps' character traits are far from stable. The situation in which they find themselves or which they are able to establish for themselves shapes their personalities: "If, for instance, we have known a male only in the role of alpha male, we probably think he is very self-confident. That need not be the case at all. As soon as his position is seriously threatened, the self-confidence may vanish."[11] So, as the social organization changes, individuals change as well. This shows the complexity of these animals and, moreover, the relation between the social organization and the individual.

In his analysis of two power takeovers, De Waal finds that power is not merely based on physical strength, as we often seem to think. In fact, it is partially the other way around since bodily appearance changes when a chimp is in power:

> In the years of his supremacy Yeroen's hair was constantly slightly on end—even when he was not actively displaying—and he walked in an exaggerated slow and heavy manner. This habit of making the body look deceptively large and heavy is characteristic of the alpha male, as we saw again later when other individuals filled this role. The fact of being in a position of power makes a male physically impressive, hence the assumption that he occupies the position that fits his appearance.[12]

De Waal distinguishes formal and real dominance. The first category consists of, among other things, submissive greetings of the alpha male and involves the acceptance by the group of their leader. The real dominance does not always align with this. For example, in fights, alpha males do not always win. Even children (who have no formal dominance) "can put an adult male or female to flight or even coerce them into doing something."[13] Real and formal dominance largely overlap, and changes in leadership are instigated and developed through both forms of dominance. Yet, De Waal makes the interesting observation that the physical strength of the chimps is to a degree relative to their social status. In one of the power takeovers, his research group observed a series of fights, and within the span of a few weeks, the roles between the two alphas were reversed. Since their actual strength must be approximately the same, De Waal concludes: "The outcomes in fact reflect the change in the relative social status."[14] The social status of a leader provides a sense of confidence, and when the support of the group diminishes, confidence diminishes as well. I assume we have all experienced this ourselves. When I find people staring at me as if I just uttered a sentence in a language they don't understand, while I thought I made a succinct and clear statement, I start to doubt myself. If, on the other hand, people nod and start to share examples reflecting my point or idea, I feel more confidence. We also know it cuts both ways: when I express an idea with doubt in my (body) language, it is likely to be doubted or dismissed. We are constantly in these kinds of dynamics, and while some of us are better at displaying confidence, or hiding insecurities, we all feel it. Along these lines, De Waal describes how chimps try to hide their insecurities (such as trying to hide showing their teeth, a sign of insecurity).

Some of the chimps seem to quickly turn to the potential new leader, others keep supporting the old one (for example by bowing, greeting, or grooming the alpha male), and some try to stay out of it. An extremely important aspect is that leaders have to form a coalition, and as the study of the colony makes obvious, these coalitions are far from stable, need to be maintained, and will ultimately shift. Coalitions work partially as a strategy to isolate those individuals that might threaten one's position directly or indirectly. Besides alliances, coalitions, and isolations, there is also a lot of mediation, especially by the females. Males do eventually reconcile, and this can be initiated by hand gestures, and often involves the mediation of others. Reconciliations include expressions of power as well, partially determined through the chimpanzee who initiates the reconciliation. Yet, power is not all about force and overcoming threats. One also needs support from weaker members. An interesting mechanism, in this regard, is "loser control" in which a stronger male supports the weaker individual in a conflict.[15] The fact that when males come to power they show much more solidarity with the weaker than they did prior to their ascent to power shows how complex their social order is. Leaders who support the weakest typically receive their support in return.[16] I will return to this mechanism in the next section, discussing empathy.

In the political systems of chimps, maintaining power is an ongoing effort. A chimpanzee leader needs the constant support of the group, as well as a coalition with other strong males. While we might think of hierarchies as vertical, De Waal points out that chimps notably establish many horizontal relationships that form a hierarchy. Chimpanzee power is not to be understood in terms of a ladder, but rather as a network that involves other strong males, weaker males, females, and children.[17] What, then, does power mean for a chimpanzee? While showing the complexities and the horizontal aspects of power, De Waal cites Machiavelli and Hobbes, and references Freud, because male power is for chimpanzees closely related to sex. While the most powerful male in principle mates more than the others, male chimpanzees also bargain with one another (often involving grooming one another) after which the alpha male can allow the other to mate with a female. Yet, the females are not powerless in this process. In fact, mating only occurs if the female allows it to happen. They, first of all, need to recognize the leader as a leader, and they play a crucial role in establishing alliances. De Waal, at least in this book, stays away from speculations of this sort, but to a reader, it sometimes appears that the females just let the males exert and display their power by showing off, while the females secretly run the show. De Waal, as mentioned above, in some of his later works admits that he earlier underestimated the power females have in the colony. While females are physically weaker, they can be the center of power, and this is specifically exemplified by the controversial introduction of the males to the colony in the zoo, involving another power takeover with the assistance of human intervention. After the males were introduced they were harassed by the leading females who scared the male newcomers into "intense screaming, diarrhea, and vomiting."[18] Fearing severe injuries or even deaths, the ruling female and her companions were taken out of the colony for some time. The move has been criticized, and although De Waal was not part of the team when this occurred, he defended it as a necessary intervention that sped up the process of returning to a "natural state" that would eventually have happened anyway but was now (presumably) established with less violence. Although I have no grounds to make a fair judgment about the matter, I find it interesting that female apes can rule. In addition, I would like to bring into question the idea of a "natural state" for it seems there is a fluidity to the formation of the colony. To use the argument that the "natural state" of the female members of human society is to be subordinated to the powerful male is highly problematic. To assume that there is only one natural way for chimps to form a colony is likewise problematic and ignores the possibility that a colony might be able to develop its own culture. In other words, we find here the assumption of a nature (as opposed to a culture that might be different from the one thought to be found outside of the zoo environment), which chimpanzees have to submit to. In the case of this colony in the zoo, it is also quite clear that after the males have taken over, the former female leader, "Mama," still plays a very powerful role and is often the individual who assists in resolving conflicts between both females and males. She seems to be the quiet leader who stays away from the messy action.

Besides the fluidity of gender in terms of power, the colony studied by De Waal also displays some gender fluidity as well as a homosexual orientation in the female chimp "Puist" who looks like a male, refuses to mate, and is described to act in "a lesbian fashion" consisting of mounting other adult females and being around mating females.[19] "At times it seems as if, like the males, Puist also has a say in whether intercourse is tolerated."[20] What is interesting for the purpose of my project is that the variety of roles female chimps can take suggests again that these animals do not simply display a single nature, but are dynamic as both individuals and as a group in developing and changing their behavior dependent on the circumstances.

Empathy

We have seen, so far, how complex of a social organization the chimpanzee colony is. Power is not only established by physical strength, suppressing other males, and aggression. Instead, power involves alliances and establishing support by different members of the colony, including the weakest. Establishing and maintaining a peaceful society involves continuous work. While in his earlier work De Waal is very interested in the establishment and recognition of power as a key to the success of a chimp colony, in his later work the significance of empathy is emphasized. Using Peter Kropotkin's idea of mutual aid (discussed in more detail in chapter 5) he argues strongly that in many animals, including humans, empathy is a feeling that can determine actions. Interestingly, empathy can also be shut down and overtaken by aggression. This is true for chimps and other primates (as it is true for us humans, and rats—as we have seen). Primates are often regarded as aggressive animals, and they certainly can display such behavior. Yet it is not their determining character trait, and part of the value of De Waal's work is that it shows the complexity of their social relationships. Instances of extreme aggression are rare in primates but do occur. He describes a few instances caused by circumstances that go against their typical natural situations, such as how in the London Zoo a group of hamadryas baboons ended up killing one another. The problem, he points out, was not the nature of these baboons, but rather how their group had been formed: "The hamadryas baboon is a harem holder where one male mates with multiple females. Normally you would want to introduce just a few males and a much larger group of females if you were to set up a stable colony. They did exactly the opposite. They put a whole bunch of males together and then introduced just a few females. The males started fighting like crazy over those females in order to build their own harem."[21] Likewise, in the colony that he studied for *Chimpanzee Politics*, one of the males was attacked and castrated by two other males.

One might use these examples of extreme aggressions as an argument against the existence of politics in primates. For if their "natural environment" is a prerequisite for them to behave well, it seems that their behavior is entirely "instinctual." If it is otherwise, they would be able to adjust their behavior, the argument would suggest. Yet, De Waal suggests the opposite: this particular zoo setting triggered violent behavior, not unlike the occurrence of violence among humans in prisons. He describes the failure to keep peace as an eye-opening experience that (ironically) turned his career in the direction of empathy, or "what holds societies together."[22] The extreme violence (the attacked male eventually died) was caused by a failure to establish a society in which conflicts were resolved and empathy could be cultivated. Instead, tensions and aggressions developed to this extreme.

De Waal describes the significance of empathy for animal (including human) societies. One of the failures of empathy at the human level is, for him, exemplified in the American corporation Enron. American capitalism, he argues, is heavily influenced by Herbert Spencer's social Darwinism, which circles around the idea of survival of the fittest. For Spencer the idea of the fittest is itself becoming a prescription: the fittest *should* survive. De Waal, first of all, shows the problematic nature of this as evidenced by the adoption of social Darwinism through the American capitalist notion of competition, in which individualism is the reigning concept. As with the Machiavellian or Hobbesian state in which subjects are treated as fearful and greedy, his example of Enron analyzes the same culture at the corporate level and shows the consequences.[23] Jeff Skilling, the CEO of Enron, created a corporate culture based on a literal (and false) interpretation of Dawkins's "selfish gene." Skilling assumed that all humans have "only two fundamental drives: greed and fear. This obviously turned into a self-fulfilling prophecy. People were perfectly willing to slit one another's throats to survive within Enron's environment, resulting in a corporate atmosphere marked by appalling dishonesty within and ruthless exploitation outside the company."[24] The point here is that in a society (or corporation) that is built on the assumption that humans are selfish, they will indeed act in selfish ways. By creating structures built on the assumption that humans only want the best for themselves (the Hobbesian/Machiavellian notion of human nature), humans will indeed follow these expectations of selfish behavior.

De Waal's example of Enron's corporate climate that cultivated greed and fear is a good way to show how humans are determined by their environment. In both human and chimpanzee societies, behavior of its members is heavily influenced by environmental factors. Chimps can become violent and competitive, as all other animals can. Cooperation is also a possibility. The basis for these two possibilities, in both chimpanzees and humans, is biological, yet triggered (or blocked) by the circumstances in which they/we live together.

It could then be suggested that we can improve human behavior by improving their social environment, just like we can trigger their worst instincts in a poor social environment. While we should avoid behavioral approaches à la Skinner, we could aim for societies and/or communities that foster empathy and cooperation. Some might say that we cannot change human nature itself. De Waal, in this regard, stays away from behaviorist tendencies for the simple reason that human nature is for him permanent.[25] It consists of a mix of positive and negative tendencies. Aggression and empathy are significant parts of who we are, and while our environments can encourage one over the other and influence our actions, they will not fundamentally change who or what we naturally are.

This argument of De Waal assumes that we know what human nature is and what we are capable of (as well as what we are not capable of). This is not a problem for his argument: within those limitations, we can still find possibilities to change the circumstances that make us greedy. In the case of chimpanzees, De Waal discusses a zoo's practice to feed the animals at the same time, without proper facilities to separate them, which led to fights and tensions, even long before feeding time. A few of the individuals would attempt to dominate, and this led to "an extremely tense and aggressive atmosphere in the group."[26] In their natural environment food is scattered, and competition over food is very rare. Needless to say, basic requirements such as food are tremendously important, yet it is very interesting that this conflict is not about the need for food. In the case of an abundance of food, some chimps want more than they need. The situation of wealth or abundance seems to bring out greed. In the Indian temple rats we found a related dynamic, as they behave territorially by blocking other rats from accessing their palace, not very different from how wealthy countries block access to their riches.

De Waal thus argues that we (and chimpanzees) have particular capacities and urges. An ensemble of feelings such as empathy and greed constitute our nature. The circumstances dictate which feelings are triggered. Cooperation is a requirement for the success of any form of life, and empathy assists animals such as mice, rats, chimpanzees, and humans, to function together well. De Waal suggests that empathy is a true feeling, yet often can be considered a "self-protective altruism."[27] For example, the self-protective mechanism might be at work when one watches another animal in pain and feels pain oneself. Aiding the other animal to end the painful scene can then be considered selfish since one wants their own pain to end. Empathy is for De Waal then to be considered as a merging of selfish and unselfish behavior, as one truly feels with the other, as the pain of the other is felt.

In the human realm David Hume argues that we should aim for a political society in which feelings such as sympathy are encouraged. He argues, indeed, for the use of the word *sympathy* over *empathy*, because for Hume we feel along with a person who suffers, yet our feelings are not the same. We do not "feel into" the other person (as in the German word for empathy, *Einfühling*). As discussed by Jacqueline Taylor, for Hume sympathy is not a specific emotion, but "a principle that allows us to communicate our passions, sentiments, and opinions to others."[28] Thus, it is really a sympathizing with the passions or sentiments of others. Sympathy is not merely an act of or sympathizing, though, it also can strongly evoke feelings "and produce an equal emotion, as any original affection."[29] Thus, I feel sad about my friend losing his mom. My feeling is not necessarily exactly the same as that of my friend, but that does not mean it is insincere or less powerful. I feel with my friend. I do not feel the emotion of losing a parent, because at this instance I do not experience the loss of my own parent as he does, but I feel his loss. De Waal uses the word *empathy* in a very similar way Hume uses the word *sympathy*. Thus, while trying to avoid losing the significance of the difference between these two terms, I will use them somewhat interchangeable and in reference to De Wall will use *empathy*, while using *sympathy* in relation to Hume.

Framing sympathy within his overall philosophy, against the tendency of his time to see humans as predominantly rational, Hume argued that we are mostly determined through passions and habits. Deleuze explains Hume (one of his important "nomadic thinkers" of the history of philosophy) through Bergson's insight that "habits are not themselves natural, but what is natural is the habit to take up habits."[30] The clear implication is that we can create different habits, and for Hume the habits we take up are largely determined through the society in which we live. In fact, in Deleuze's reading of Hume, all our institutions are up for change: "Take, for example, *one* form of marriage, or *one* system of property. Why *this* system and *this* form? A thousand others, which we find in other times and places, are possible."[31] Deleuze then continues with drawing a distinction between drive (the habit to take up habits) and institutions (particular habits): "An institution exists when the means by which a drive is satisfied are not determined by the drive itself or by specific characteristics."[32] Quoting from Hume's *Enquiry*, he then ties specific habits to the influence of reason and custom.

Deleuze's reading of Hume can be used to answer the question: how can we live? It does not have to be like rats, chimpanzees, or human beings. We have an urge to generate institutions and habits, yet which institutions and habits we take up is not determined. The fact that we feel empathy or not is, as I have suggested, dependent on the circumstances, which includes particular institutions and habits.

Experiencing sympathy starts, for Hume, with an idea and is set within the context of particular customs. Cultures and customs can start from different practices regarding loss and mourning. In Hume's language this can be explained as the way in which a culture associates different ideas. One custom requires to not shave and/or wear black clothing while mourning. Another culture relies heavily on rituals such as a service and burial. In some cultures, family members wash the bodies of the deceased and have them in their house for days. Other cultures dispose of the body as quickly as possible. Some ceremonies center on the dead body, and in other cultures the body is entirely absent during the rituals. We then observe different feelings about who or what we lost, about souls and bodies, about life, and remembering or paying tribute. Some want to remember the person as they were alive, others want to honor and take leave of the body that once was alive. Our feelings are then given shape within the context of all these rituals.

Here we can return to Deleuze: our societal context has an influence on what we feel or fail to feel.[33] We can think of gendered feelings, as well as "class" feelings (such as pride). Different languages as well as cultures allow for different feelings, and as class and gender examples indicate, within the same society we can find a variety of degrees of those feelings. Following Hume's insight that a passion starts with an idea, certain situations will not call for sympathy or empathy if we suppress particular ideas or connect ideas in ways that obstruct feelings of sympathy for certain groups. Going back to the example of mourning, cultural differences could dictate a failure to feel sympathy ("You did *what* with the body?") or a merging of ideas could lead to even deeper feeling of sympathy ("*That* is such a beautiful practice!").

Within the work on chimpanzees by De Waal, the possibility of "feeling with" or "feeling into" is framed in terms of bodily synchronization, for example through infectious yawning or laughter, or how different animals (including humans) imitate walks or gestures. Emotions then not only move us, but they also arise from our bodies.[34] As we will see in the next chapter, the arising of emotions from our bodies has important consequences for the dynamics of a group. We are moved towards a group, and once part of a group we are affected through the body. Emotions arise out of bodily presence. Jean-François Lyotard writes about the way we are affected by the body of the other, something that lies beyond human language. Many of our interactions with others are indeed through bodily affections. Interestingly for Lyotard, this brings the possibility of an ethical moment. The other makes an appeal to me, through the body. As I have argued elsewhere, we can for example think about the body of a suffering animal in a cage. For Lyotard we have the responsibility to bear witness to the wrong that is left unspoken, generating a sensitivity towards the panther in the zoo, the cow on its way to the slaughterhouse, the chicken crammed into a cage, or the human other living on the street. Whether we call this sympathy (Hume), empathy (De Waal), or a general sensibility (Lyotard), in all cases this raises the possibility of a different kind of politics.

As we saw earlier in De Waal, empathy itself is sometimes regarded as a selfish trait. We can do something for another person with hopes and expectations that the favor will be returned. Especially in work settings, the quid quo pro attitude is omnipresent. Yet, even situations in which we expect a return do not imply that empathy is an insincere feeling, De Waal argues. Evolutionarily we can make sense of the feeling of empathy because it benefits the group. Citing examples of cross-species adoption he suggests that indeed such adoptions can be regarded as conflicting with "evolutionary aims" (adopting an infant of another species will not aid the species, eating the infant of the other species would), but they make sense psychologically, as the feeling of empathy takes over.[35]

Thus, here we encounter an example of what De Waal calls "the other Darwinism," the neo-Darwinist approach emphasizing cooperation over the survival of the fittest, discussed by, among others, Peter Kropotkin. De Waal describes Kropotkin's "struggle for existence" not in terms of "each against all, but of masses of organisms against a hostile environment. Cooperation is common."[36] From the field of primatology, he brings in examples such as colonies of baboons on the Kenyan plains, whose female members "with the best social ties were shown to have the most surviving infants."[37] It is from these examples that we humans should take lessons, in which social or communal ties are essentially different from our contractual understanding of society.

Discussing peacemaking De Waal discusses the importance of "value" in primate politics. He speaks about "relationship value" in terms of economic interest. If there is a shared economic interest between two parties, violent conflicts are less likely to occur. He states, "I can say that studies of reconciliation in primates have demonstrated that if the relationship value increases between two parties they are more willing to make peace."[38] While I think the dynamics are interesting, and similar to human ones, I want to raise some concerns about the use of the economic "value" language in De Waal's analysis. The alternative economy I have discussed, among others in the introduction of this book, is the gift economy. It would be very interesting to translate the chimpanzee colony into Kimmerer's language of the gift economy, in which all members give and take. Such a language might also point us to some problems in the human realm. Considering his critique of Friedman and others who prioritize profits over humans, it seems fair to assume De Waal does not want us to reduce chimpanzee relationships to economic insights, but his analysis does not account for those who lack economic value. Chimpanzees do not have to worry about a monetary system that ignores the circumstances of large parts of our human societies—such as groups of people that are not given a fair chance to cooperate, but find themselves in the position of the powerless in a society that is based on competition. One of the interesting outcomes of De Waal's study is that chimpanzee leaders can only obtain and maintain their leadership position if they protect the weakest members of their society. We, thus, see in the chimpanzee colony that the weakest members are protected, and the protection, one could say, has "value" within the colony, which could not occur within a system entirely based on economic value. The language of value tends to pull us into the economic, capitalist mindset, where indeed competition reigns.

Personalities and Self: Confucian Reflections

Besides my hesitations about the use of the economic language, when it comes to De Waal's discussion of selves and different chimpanzee personalities, a different language and way of thinking could be helpful. He shows us that their characters are not fixed. Their position in the colony changes their behavior and even their physical appearance. Likewise, the behavior of the chimps is influenced by the collective, the colony. While in his analysis De Waal holds on to the Western understanding of a self as an independent and absolute entity, one could suggest that a Confucian approach might actually further his analysis, which would also assist my attempt to differently approach human politics.

In the West, we find an emphasis on reason, freedom, and individualism. Agency, and in particular rational agency, is regarded as crucial. Kant famously sees the individual as a rational and universal lawmaker: I decide for everyone else. In addition, we find absolute respect for individuals as ends in themselves. A Confucian lens provides an alternative approach, which I discuss in the following through the multicultural pluralist ideas of Henry Rosemont: in his work *Against Individualism*, he provides an interesting reevaluation of Confucian ethics.[39] Rosemont discusses how in Confucian and Buddhist notions of identity a self or individual is always understood within a context: as acting within a family, a state, a culture, etc. This is then how Rosemont (as well as Ames) emphasizes that an individual is always in a role-bearing position.

Despite these differences, Confucianism, Buddhism, and Western approaches, for Rosemont, should not be regarded as at odds with one another. He argues that even while different ideologies provide a different emphasis, the basic values are almost identical. The values that we find in Confucianism, Buddhism, Christianity, or in the Western formulations of ethics (as we find them in deontology, utilitarianism, or virtue ethics) are quite close to one another. To describe this idea of human universality, he uses the term *homoversal*, which is a play on universality for all humans, mentally and physiologically as they are: a shared human attitude and behavior.[40]

Against the common belief today that cultures across the world are radically different and incompatible in terms of values, he argues that the difference in all these ideologies is how values are prioritized. With the idea of the homoversal, Rosemont indicates that we share certain attitudes and behaviors across cultures, while with the idea of prioritization we do sometimes make different choices. His soft or pluralistic relativism is thus not based on a difference in values, but rather on a difference in priorities.[41]

When Rosemont contrasts the ethical consequences in the Confucian and Western contexts, he argues that while ethical decisions within a Confucian context are made by individuals, these decisions are not regarded as absolutely free and independent from others. Rather, these decisions are made by role-bearing individuals, who find themselves in a network of relations. Confucianism often emphasizes family relationships, and so indeed we can say that I make decisions based on the fact that I am a father, a husband, a son, and so forth. Yet, I bear roles beyond the family, as a friend, a teacher, a philosopher, a colleague, a member of the community, a citizen of a country (or a "stranger" or "alien"), and so forth. Responsibility is then constituted differently, as a duty towards the community that constitutes me. If I withdraw myself from my family or take up some high-risk sport such as base jumping this does not only concern me but my family as well (beyond mere financial aspects). Admittedly, we can make similar claims with the ethical systems we find in the Western tradition, yet the emphasis is very different: the autonomy does not lie in the self that is then responsible (or not) to a community, but rather the community constitutes the self. In fact, it seems then that what it means to be a human being is formulated radically differently.

Can we look at non-human communities in a similar way? Chimpanzees have a lot in common with us, even in terms of our values. For example, we have seen that care for the most vulnerable is essential for an alpha male to maintain his role in the colony. Empathy plays a huge role in this both for the dominant males, as well as for the other members of the colony who either support or fight his leadership. Such shared values among human and non-human societies are only possible because of shared capacities. We also find differences: intelligence and reflections on our feelings might change our behaviors, as do the kinds of political societies, work environments, communities, and economic realities we live in play a tremendous role in how we act towards one another.

As mentioned above, De Waal could, from such a Confucian perspective, have paid more attention to the way in which personalities are created through the multitude of changing relationships within the colony. In contrast to the role-bearing model, even while it is clear that the roles of the individuals are changing, he makes use of the conception of the self as we find it in the Western traditions: an absolute unchanging self prevails, and with that notion, we find that the individual is prioritized as free and independent. From a Confucian standpoint, we could say that in studying primates and other animals we see that the context of family and community is not only constitutive for humans. We might come to a better understanding of the workings of the chimpanzee colony by using a Confucian role-bearing model as opposed to a Western understanding of the self. Likewise, the other animals discussed in this book are determined through a social context. Biologists today even consider life itself as a network. Individuals are constantly connected in networks that constitute them. I have discussed such networks at length in chapter 1, through Latour's theory. We can also propose a role-bearing Confucian model in order to think about life as a network. In the chimpanzee colony, the interaction between individuals shows a network of relations, which could be explained in terms of role-bearing individuals. Even while there is a hierarchy, the top would tumble down without the support of the bottom.

The consequences of these different ways of thinking about the self as context or network are rather significant. Individuals are always in a context, and that context largely determines what one does. This does not mean that there is no individual responsibility, but it means that bad circumstances can lead to bad actions. In De Waal's work, we have seen this with the baboons in the zoo, employees at Enron, or inmates in a prison. For a reevaluation of our own society, it is first and foremost essential to understand that individuals are not entirely autonomous and that their decisions are not made independently of their context. If we live in a context in which aggression and violence are encouraged, or cooperation is discouraged, we will act accordingly.

We can take up these insights regarding the context in which we live as selves and discuss in particular the ways in which our understanding of evolution shapes our current political system as well as our moral obligations towards one another. Ideas of social Darwinism translate into a situation in which competition is not only allowed but even encouraged to function in a ruthless way. De Waal suggests that it justifies an immoral society in which empathy is replaced by fierce competition. The fact that some do not receive healthcare, proper compensation, or other support that is required for a reasonable standard of living, is justified through the idea that these are weaker or "less valuable" specimens of our species. It is then argued that competition will and should take care of these weaknesses. Social circumstances and the lack of opportunities provided to these individuals are disregarded. This situation would be unacceptable in the chimpanzee society.

With the emphasis on the network as opposed to the independent self, we can also express the influence a poor social and communal network has on the individual. In the next section I will reflect on our human societies and the role identity politics plays in our current xenophobic world.

Identity Politics

Today we find identity politics in the oppression of those who have a different skin color, are from a non-Western country, non-Christians, women, homosexuals, or of a "non-conforming" gender identity or expression. We can blame reason, religion, capitalism, and overall our tendencies to oppress those who are not like us, or our egoism for all this. Yet, why do such tendencies emerge? If we follow De Waal's idea that we can be both egoistic and empathic, what triggers one or the other? When discussing selfish and aggressive behavior, as well as a lack of solidarity, social-political philosophers such as Rousseau, Marx, and Foucault (to name a few) have attributed these tendencies to our social systems, as opposed to regarding it as part of human nature (as for example Hobbes did). These three thinkers provide interesting and detailed analyses of the problems that underlie our behavior that acts against a just society. Private property, the social contract that legalizes class systems, capitalism, prisons, or panopticism are some of the well-known themes in their rich analyses. Rousseau, famously, criticized Hobbes's take on the state of nature, which according to Rousseau is a rather peaceful and innocent state. The reason lies in his assessment of human nature as overall neutral. It is society, not human nature, that is to blame for greed. The social contract is nothing but a ruse of the wealthy, who through the contract become powerful and protect their wealth. Of course, for both Hobbes and Rousseau, the social contract is a thought experiment, as are various later versions, such as Rawls's veil of ignorance. Charles Mills explicitly calls the "racial contract" real, and indeed the consequences of the idea or thought experiment that is called the social contract are very real. As argued in the introduction of this book, the idea of a state of nature creates the idea that we are the first and only political beings: we created it. I will return to this in the conclusion of this chapter.

Our view of human nature determines how we relate to others. If a leader assumes that all people are egoistic, this will determine not only their leadership style and organizational culture. That culture will determine the behavior of the people in it. As De Waal showed through the earlier discussed example of Enron, this becomes a self-fulfilling prophecy. We have all witnessed the effects of managers on employees. In workplaces that are run by Machiavellian or Hobbesian leaders, employees will react to their expectations. A micromanaging boss who is suspicious of their employees will create an environment in which morale is low and workers will feel alienated. In that environment, employees will indeed work as little as they can and be overall less productive. This is not to say that an extremely laid-back manager is the key to success. In one of my first full-time jobs after graduating from college, and before I started graduate school, our boss was very close to retirement, and in between her mandatory meetings she played games on her computer. I do not believe she had any idea of how most of us were spending our days and what we were actually working on. There were no deadlines, and projects that could have been completed in a few weeks lasted for months. It is fair to say that the work we completed could easily have been done by a third of us. To be clear, I do not blame our boss for the lack of productivity. In fact, when she retired and was replaced by a younger person, little changed, except that we had to put more effort into appearing to work. David Graeber has extensively written about this phenomenon of bullshit jobs, and my job at that time was certainly one of them. Interestingly, I did not mind the job. I liked most of my colleagues, some of them became friends, and I learned some skills that I still use. This is not unusual: according to Graeber's study, most people do not mind their bullshit jobs.

On the other side of the spectrum, we find jobs that are physically challenging and not fairly rewarded. I started this chapter with my example of working as a temp worker for a moving company, where I witnessed a quick development of a class system. I was, of course, in a much better position than, for example, undocumented workers. Yet, even for those who are legally working and who are protected by laws, exploitation occurs. As De Waal points out, capitalism is set up in such a way that it encourages egoism and competition and suppresses empathy and cooperation. While in my example of the moving company, no one seemed to care about the temp workers, the underlying problem in my office job example is that we, the employees, did not care much about the company. These labor situations have parallels with our relation to society and politics from which we are alienated in a similar fashion. In countries such as the US, a two-party system implies polarization. In other countries, more parties are added with each election in order to represent the multitude of perspectives and ideas. Regardless, we do not identify with politicians, or if we do it is for the wrong reasons. For example, many people indicated they voted for George W. Bush because he—more so than his opponent—seemed to be a guy they would want to drink a beer with. Leaving aside the fact that Bush hadn't touched a drink in years, it seems hardly a qualification for leading one of the most powerful countries in the world. Arguably this part of politics is not very different from that of the chimpanzees, in which appeal to all parts of a colony is important. Nevertheless, it remains a question if Bush after several rounds of corporate tax cuts (and thus not supporting the weakest) would have remained in a position of power in the chimpanzee colony.

What we call the political in our world is a show of display of power that is often hard to identify with. Patriotism is used as a way for people to identify with their country, but it is also explicitly exclusive and leads to hostility by other nations.[42] Identity politics can be regarded as a symptom of our alienation from our own societies. The problem is that ideologies, religion, race, gender, and other identities often constitute exclusion and hostility.

Amartya Sen describes these complexities in terms of identity and violence. Although not argued in a biological or evolutionary way, in Sen's analysis of our global world we find similar tendencies towards violence as opposed to cooperation. When we identify others, for example, as Muslim (the focus of Sen's book, published five years after 9/11) we assume ideologies and end up with a situation that encourages violence. As Sen argues, the politics of identity often leads to a single identity, neglecting the many different ways in which one can be (for example) a "Westerner": besides the fact that one lives in the West, many more important aspects make up one's identity. We can think of ideologies, education, jobs, hobbies, gender, or sexual orientation as some of the important aspects of our identity. Sen's point is that when we use identities such as "Muslim" we make the mistake of assuming a singular identity, lacking any other qualifiers.[43] Against the politics of identity in which we place "the Arab World" in juxtaposition to the Western world, Sen, on the one hand, argues for the recognition of the multiplicity of identities.[44]

Against the backdrop of non-human politics, it is perhaps all the more scandalous that we humans with our shared rationality, ethical codes, studies of morality, and instilling of justice in education, keep failing to live by our own standards. We encounter or exercise exclusion, suspicion, and violence. We often seem to think that human cultures consist of such extreme differences that we cannot translate one culture into another or that a Westerner cannot fully grasp the rationality of someone living in the "Arab World." Interestingly (yet, not surprisingly) we use similar arguments when it comes to non-human animals.

In the chapter on rats and mice, I discussed ways in which we create boundaries between human and non-human others, which creates a false identity of non-human animals and moreover of who we are. If we fail to recognize that politics is more than human endeavors, we isolate ourselves from our own evolutionary history and do not recognize what makes a functional community possible in the first place. Thus, both on the human–non-human divide and the divide between different human cultures, creating differences on the basis of false identities leads to exclusion. It is these false identities that feed current anti-immigrant movements. Xenophobia is largely based on a fear of some false identity and notions of belonging and not-belonging. It is essential to step beyond this politics and perhaps chimpanzees can help us along the way. We see that the circumstances that encourage empathy are essential to a well-functioning colony. Through Hume and Deleuze (as well as Rousseau, Marx, and Foucault) we can argue that our behavior and feelings depend on the kind of society we live in.

Conclusion: We Have Never Been Nonpolitical

As discussed in the introduction to this book, Aristotle defined us as the political animal, and throughout Western thinking, it is typically assumed that politics lies in the human realm alone. Politics is assumed to be something we invented or even gave birth to. This idea leads us to social contract theories. While these are thought experiments and explicitly speculative, they all suggest that there was a time when humans lived without a political form of organization. We lived independent of others, only had chance encounters, and depending on the author's view on human nature, we were either content and at peace, or under constant threat and thus scared to death. Considering the remarkable similarities we find between human and chimpanzee societies, I propose to reject (once again) the claim that we are the only political animals. The human species came into existence in a world that was already politically organized. We inherited structures and mechanisms of an organization from other primates. Even while we changed the structures and continue to change them, we did not give birth to politics/the political.

Humans, thus, have never lived by themselves. The earliest human societies were mixed hominid societies in which Homo sapiens and Neanderthals lived together.[45] As the Homo sapiens developed, their great ape predecessors already were living together in the form of societies. Early humans did not have to reinvent the wheel and were from the beginning already in society. Yet, as both feelings and the brain developed in different ways, skills, language, governance, rules and laws, and so forth changed these societies from the great ape or primate societies out of which they emerged. Thus, as opposed to Hobbes's and Rousseau's vision of a state of nature in which we lived all by ourselves, it is a lot more likely that humans have always lived in communities. Those first humans did not find themselves alone in the forest (like Adam and Eve). They found themselves in the company of others, and as evolution is gradual (even with some jumps) there were no first humans, distinct by a radical difference of kind from their hominoid predecessors, who lived along with them. The radical difference only occurs when humans introduce laws, contracts, and institutions of governance.

When discussing the social contract we find "natural orders" juxtaposed to human artificial orders. While Hobbes's "artificial body" or Aristotle's *zoon politikon* suggests that politics is constructed or born in the human realm, my argument suggests that politics already occurs outside, or before, the human. That the human species came into existence in a world that was already political can be made explicit by looking at other great apes, such as chimpanzees. In their colony, we find complex political structures that involve all members, including the weakest members. Their political structure is far from a mere instinctual drive as we see in the establishment of alliances and the development of personalities. The context in which the chimps find themselves (or work themselves into) has a large influence on their behavior and appearance. In this sense, as I have suggested, they are role-bearing individuals.

If we compare their colony with ours, we can first of all point to the enormous scale of our political systems. We could regard ourselves as successful at being a social species in the sense that through cooperation we have colonized all of the earth and changed the surface of the earth to such a degree that we can call a geological era after ourselves. Here we encounter the failure of our species as we find it in wars, racism, genocides, sexism, classism, speciesism, and so forth. The massive scale of our colonization of the earth also radically challenges our ability to be social, which might have been easier in "natural" circumstances in which we lived together in small groups. Even at the local level we typically do not know our representatives, not even all the people on our street, or all of our colleagues. While the chimp community is a tight one, we, on the other hand, are disconnected from one another.

Institutions change our behaviors and encourage or discourage certain feelings. The good news is that these institutions (and our habits) can change. Much older and deeper than our current habits and the institutions that support them is our forgotten shared history with primates (and other species). The ability to live together successfully is not lost. It is deep down in our DNA and is still part of our existence and nature. In the next chapter, I turn to group being and how we are instinctually attracted to groups. I turn here from chimpanzees to some much older life-forms, as we find them in the tidepool.

Chapter Four

From the Tidepool to Human Migration
The Biological Roots of Politics[1]

Up until now I had never understood the attraction of tidepools. Here, on the side of a beach in Monterey, where rocks and water meet, after stepping over some green rocks, carefully, the water opens up. A moment ago, I had just seen the sun and sky reflected on the still surface of the water of the tidepool. Under my new angle my eyes break through the surface, and the anemones, sea stars, sea cucumbers, and crabs become visible. The intense colors are marvelous against the background of black rock, barnacle, and limpets. The creatures open the crust that is me, showing their non-human community. It resembles a modern artwork, yet one that can survive the violent impact of waves and the incoming and outgoing tides. The community brings life and non-life together in the form of a beautiful and resilient society.

In chapter 1 I argued how salmon can be considered political beings in their own right and how we can see ourselves within the context of a larger political unity. The political character of salmon, I argued, lies in their ability to cooperate and work together. Even while the drive to be part of a group such as a school can be put in mechanical or instinctual terms, my main point regarding the group being of salmon is that we find a similar drive in us humans. In chapters 2 and 3, I have discussed animals with (presumably) more complex emotional lives. Both rats and chimpanzees are empathic beings. To now return to the drive towards the group, and ultimately consider how this drive can influence our emotional being, I turn to the work of John Steinbeck and Ed Ricketts. Both the writer and the marine biologist provide philosophical insights into the human condition by studying human group tendencies through the lens of biology.

Throughout his work written in the 1930s and 1940s, Steinbeck provides a fascinating analysis that brings nature and humans together. Specifically, through his friendship and collaboration with Ricketts, Steinbeck develops a theory about the group being of humans as deeply rooted in our evolutionary history. Influenced by neo-Darwinists, such as W. C. Allee, who emphasized cooperation over struggle, they regard cooperation as old as life itself. Even single-cell organisms, such as bacteria, need to cooperate in order to survive. For Allee, as well as the entomologist William Wheeler, societies already existed a long time before humans came into existence. In his work *Animal Aggregations* he writes: "From the lowest to the highest forms in the series, all animals are at some time in their lives immersed in some society; the social medium is the condition necessary to the conservation and renewal of life."[2] Wheeler describes the political society of insects such as termites, while Allee compares the effects of crowding in all kinds of species to human societies, even explaining international politics along these lines. The basic premise is that while we humans do often fight, deep down instilled in us is a feeling for the group, an instinct to cooperate with one another.

What exactly can we learn about ourselves and the human condition from group-centered societies we find in other life-forms? Within the context of the greater project of this book, a redefinition of politics as ecology is made possible by placing our social and political systems within the natural world. A redetermination of politics also means that we become something else. This chapter studies, in particular, tidepool communities and the "ecology of all" as proposed by Ricketts and Steinbeck. The latter ties these insights specifically to human notions of group being and its rootedness in our evolutionary history. I will turn to *The Log from the Sea of Cortez*, written in collaboration with Ricketts, as well as Steinbeck's unpublished essay on "The Theory of Phalanx." We will see how the influences of biologists W. C. Allee and W. E. Ritter had a significant influence on Steinbeck's novels, in particular for recognizing both positive and negative forms of group being and in the idea of *westering* as a movement to the unknown and as openness to otherness.

The Sea of Cortez: Deep Ecology in the Tidepools

The Log from the Sea of Cortez describes the preparation and journey of Ricketts and Steinbeck to study the ecology of tidal areas in the Gulf of

California. Contrary to the tendency to specialize, limit, and close oneself off as scientists or philosophers, Steinbeck and Ricketts in this project instead want to "go wide open. Let's see what we see, record what we find, and not fool ourselves with conventional scientific strictures."[3] This means that they break with the scientific objectivity in which subject and object are strictly separated. Ricketts and Steinbeck, instead, recognize that their research in the Sea of Cortez makes them a part of it, permanently: "That our rubber boots slogging through a flat of eelgrass, that the rocks we turn over in a tide pool, make us truly and permanently a factor in the ecology of the region."[4] This kind of engagement between researcher and that which is researched, we also find present in Latour's thinking, among other things in his Actor Network Theory. Despret, we have seen, discusses this in terms of asking the right questions and becoming a biographer of the animal. Along similar lines, Ricketts and Steinbeck note that in asking questions and in our attempts to answer them, we are already becoming part of an ecosystem.

While Steinbeck needs no introduction, Ricketts is the lesser-known of the two. Ricketts, a very close friend of Steinbeck, worked as an independent marine biologist out of his "Lab" (the Pacific Biological Laboratories) in Monterey, which was a small company (as well as a place to gather for writers, philosophers, and bums). He made a small profit by collecting and shipping specimens of different marine species to schools and labs. This profit funded some of his research (Steinbeck funded the trip to the Sea of Cortez), and he did extensive research, focusing on tidepools on the West Coast from Mexico to Alaska. His *Between Pacific Tides* is regarded as a groundbreaking work and still, today, considered an important reference work.

As an independent marine biologist, Ricketts was able to chart his own course and did not have to follow the trend of specialization in his field. In his study of Ricketts and Steinbeck, Richard Astro describes how Ricketts "believed that so-called experts who carefully localize their interests so that they can boast that they know *one* thing really well really have no organon at all. . . . Ricketts believed that any kind of intensive specialization, vegetable or intellectual, is self-defeating in that it destroys the dynamic unity in nature."[5] This is a powerful claim which suggests that the detachment from the whole, in our biological and intellectual living, leads to the very destruction of unity. If we live and think separated from the other parts, we, indeed, create a separation. Ecopolitics is emphasizing exactly the unity and holistic view we find here in Ricketts and Steinbeck. Different from the specialized approach, the *Sea of Cortez* approaches nature in terms of the ecology of all, as the unity of humanity and nature. Ecology itself is described as synonymous with "ALL."⁶ Deeply rooted in evolutionary theory, they emphasize the connection of all life forms. Along these lines, Astro writes that for the two men the tidepools represent "an unmasked replica of man's social structure," and in Rickett's own words: "Here the struggle is unmasked and the beauty is unmasked."⁷

The idea that the tidepool contains a social structure is an idea that is heavily influenced by biologist W. C. Allee, with whom Ricketts studied at the University of Chicago. Allee's work is holistic and is sometimes referred to as behavioral ecology. He is influenced by entomologist William Wheeler, who in the early twentieth century described political structures in colonies of termites and ants as communitarian and democratic (as discussed in chapter 5). Both social and asocial characteristics of these insect colonies can, according to Wheeler, also be found in our societies. Allee, along similar lines, argues that communal activities can be found in all forms of life. While a group can become so large that it creates negative effects for the individual members of the group, all organisms need others to thrive as individuals. His research includes, among other things, the communal activity of bacteria, goldfish growing faster in water "contaminated" by other goldfish, and the growth rate of mice (they grow faster in smaller groups, but slowest in isolation).⁸ Cooperation, he argues, does not only translate into successful reproduction and the maintenance of the species, but also creates an environment in which individuals are healthier, as evidenced in growth, or phenomena such as the curing of lesions in mice.

Allee relates the idea of cooperation and group being to human beings. While we are conscious creatures, aware of what we do, we do not fully grasp the nature of our actions, especially within the context of cooperation. As Allee writes, "Conscious cooperation at the level of psychosocial facilitation is so comparatively new in the animal world many millions of years old that we may underrate its strength and importance if we are not reminded of its foundations in simple physiology and primitive instinct."⁹ The two fundamental principles "which consciously or unconsciously, penetrate all of nature" are "the struggle for existence and the necessity for cooperation."¹⁰ The basic premises in this regard are that no organism could have been successful without cooperation and that all lifeforms (including human) are driven by an instinct to cooperate.

Besides Allee, the work of the biologist Ritter is also seen as an important influence, in particular on Steinbeck. One important idea coming from Ritter is discussed in the *Sea of Cortez*: "each member of the colony is an individual animal, but the colony is another individual animal, not at all like the sum of its individuals."[11] This theory of organicism suggests that the group itself, such as a colony, forms an organism. Life is here regarded as a system of interrelationships. We could call such a system "intelligence," which is not conscious awareness. It is within this insight that we can understand the passage that discusses the behavior of a school of fish which "seems to be directed by a school intelligence."[12] This school "intelligence" (or what seems to be an intelligence) is the idea I discussed in chapter 1 on salmon, who loosely organize themselves and move collectively without any kind of leadership except for the leadership of the group as a whole. Steinbeck and Ricketts explain the self-organization of the group, not as driven by an external goal or intelligence, but through its internal drive to be alive: "Life has one final end; to be alive; and all the tricks and mechanisms, all the successes and failures, are aimed at that end."[13] The school intelligence is in Steinbeck's and Ricketts's wording nothing but a collection of tricks and mechanisms that enhance chances of survival. Even while we should be somewhat suspicious about the mechanical language that tends to deny the possibility of any feelings (as discussed in chapter 1), the point here is that the group intelligence is not a designed intelligence, but the result of long evolutionary processes. From the very beginning, in its most simple forms, life is characterized through a drive to be.

While there is some debate about how Ricketts and Steinbeck either took Allee's ideas in slightly different directions or interpreted the ideas differently, both were very familiar with the theory, and Allee's book *Animal Aggregations* was part of their library during their trip. For his part, Ricketts emphasizes the interrelatedness of "the animal or the community *in* its environment."[14] Ecology itself is understood here as the study of relationships, particularly "living relationships."[15] With that, he does not imply that ecology only involves living beings (the tide pool, obviously, is only possible because of rock formations and water), but rather that these relationships themselves are alive. The emphasis, following Allee, is on the community as opposed to the individual, and there are strong connections between all forms of life, as well as nonlife.

Evolutionary theory, especially the social Darwinist version discussed in the previous chapter, emphasizes survival of the fittest. The theory of "animal aggregation" suggests that the fittest is often not the individual that is most apt to survive, but instead is part of a group of individuals that can cooperate. "Fitness" is often found in species that collectively deal with challenges. Following Allee, for both Steinbeck and Ricketts, cooperation is a principle much older than humans, and we follow the same principles that are followed by other animals. Since all life, as well as nonlife, is relational: "Not only the meaning but the feeling about species grows misty. One merges into another, groups melt into ecological groups until the time what we know as life meets and enters what we think of as non-life: barnacle and rock, rock and earth, earth and tree, tree and rain and air. And the units nestle into the whole and are inseparable from it."[16] The "fullness of nature," or what they refer to as "the deep thing," however mystical it might sound at times, is, by the end, the evolutionary unity of all life, the relationships between living and nonliving beings. As they write, "Most of the feeling we call religious, most of the mystical outcrying which is one of the most prized and used and desired reactions of our species, is really the understanding and the attempt to say that man is related to the whole thing, related inextricably to all reality known and unknowable."[17] Species merge into one another and science merges with religion in the sense that science itself ties the known and the unknowable together and reaches "the knowledge that all things are one thing and that one thing is all things."[18]

Human Struggles and Cooperation: The Phalanx

Throughout his work, Steinbeck reflects on the human individual as part of a group. Ultimately, our group being is rooted in our biology. Our tendency to cooperate is an ancient memory we share with bees, ants, and probably even older organisms. Within this context, he writes that "man is a unit of the greater beast, the phalanx."[19] The phalanx is the Greek and Roman battle formation of a group of soldiers that forms, when well executed, a destructive tactic. Steinbeck wrote about the phalanx in 1933 (in an unpublished essay called "Argument of Phalanx"), six years before the publication of *The Grapes of Wrath*, describing a movement of people we could call a phalanx. Although he rarely uses the term explicitly, the theory is arguably at work in most of his writings.

When we are part of a group, our behavior is largely determined by the group. As Astro states, "Individuals often behave not as they would like to behave, but rather as the group to which they belong demands."[20] This is, in a way, Nietzsche's problem of the herd mentality (or Heidegger's *das Man*, or Foucault's power-knowledge relationships). Nietzsche was very well aware of our biological tendencies to act like pack animals. The problem is that we think we are free, while we are merely doing what our instincts tell us we are supposed to do. Spinoza points us to the same issue when we think that following our will is an act of freedom, even while what we want, and even more *that* we want, is not chosen freely. Steinbeck analyzes our natural tendencies specifically within the context of the group. He writes, "Man is a unit of the greater beast, the phalanx. The phalanx has pains, desires, hungers, and strivings as different from those of the unit man's as man's are different from the unit cells."[21] The individual person, the unit, is made out of cells that collectively create a whole that is more than its parts. Those cells strive for different things, yet collectively they create a larger unit. Likewise, the larger group of which we are a part wants and feels differently than the individual. It is foreign to us, to some degree. Yet, we can key into it: "Within each unit-man, deep in him, in his subconscious, there is a keying device with which he may become part of the phalanx."[22] Deep down we know (or feel) that we cannot survive without the group. This "keying device" is as old as life itself, and the tendency to be part of a group is found in all forms of life.

The ideas of keying in and the subconscious are taken from Jung, who writes, famously, about the collective unconscious consisting of inherited archetypes. Steinbeck and Ricketts interpret this concept as the imprints that have developed over the history of life. In the *Sea of Cortez,* they describe (and rewrite an insight of George Darwin, son of Charles Darwin) how the tides and the corresponding weight differential in pre-Cambrian times were "tremendous." All life was influenced by these cycles and is imprinted in us as what they call "a rhythm sense or 'memory' which affects everything and which in the past was probably more potent than now."[23] It has, indeed, been proven that during the earliest period of life on earth the moon was much closer to the earth, its gravitational pull much more forceful, resulting, among other things in larger tidal differences. As they write: "displacement and body weight then must certainly have decreased and increased tremendously with the rotation and phases of the moon . . . Consider, then, the effect of a decrease in pressure on gonads turgid with eggs or sperm, already bursting and awaiting the slight extra pull to discharge."[24] This then would result in an "instinctual awareness" or "memory of a cycle," which is imprinted in all forms of life. In the context of humans, they mention the menstrual cycle (which has the same length as the lunar cycle) as a manifestation of this memory. The main point here is that the cyclical and rhythmic existence of the human is inherited from some of the earliest life forms and now is a part of our collective unconscious. Likewise, our ability and need to cooperate can be traced back to the earliest forms of life (or to the tidepool).

The interconnectedness of all is sometimes described as a mood or feeling. For example, after describing their collective bad feelings as a crew about the Estero de la Luna, Steinbeck and Ricketts describe an attunement between the mind and the nerves with reality "neither segregated nor understood on an intellectual level."[25] This is followed by a quotation from the philosopher John Elof Boodin: "Thought and things are part of one evolving matrix, and cannot ultimately conflict."[26] Thus, they assume some primary unity between thought and thing, which cannot be explained but only felt.[27]

Boodin influenced Steinbeck in particular, but it is questionable whether Steinbeck took to Boodin's underlying religious ideas. Boodin believed that in the larger unit a higher intelligence is at work, and it is very unlikely that Steinbeck and (in particular) Ricketts agreed with that idea. The section in which the Boodin quote appears ends with the non-teleological idea of Lucretius who "was not so far from us" and who argues against the guidance of "steerman nature."[28] Moreover, the passage from Boodin is immediately followed by the idea that "everything is an index of everything else,"[29] indicating that ideas are an index of non-ideas, of things. Of course, we could also reverse that claim (things are an index of ideas), yet considering the emphasis on non-teleology, it seems that Ricketts and Steinbeck here are thinking about the biological evolutionary imprint or memory. While the Boodin reference creates some confusion because of his religious motivations, in a way Boodin is here read against Boodin. It seems that Ricketts and Steinbeck appreciate the relationship between things and thinking but reject the teleological metaphysics proposed by Boodin. They agree with Boodin that the larger unit takes a life of its own, but this is not run by a divine intelligence. For them, the relationship between thought and thing is not driven by a greater or original mind, but rather by the interconnectedness of all. The moods that places can create, negative or positive, are described as an awareness that is at the prediscursive level and cannot be understood. They make clear that it is not segregated from an intellectual level, although they do not explain that relationship.

In the human realm, the phalanx can be both negative and positive. On the negative side some human groups take away individuality, as well as creative expression. It can also take more dangerous shapes. Steinbeck wrote the phalanx essay in 1933, the year Hitler came to power and a time of fascism in Italy and militarism in Japan. It is not a surprise that during this time when the world faced the threat of totalitarian regimes, Steinbeck provides clear warnings about the danger of group thinking and feeling.[30] In our time of social media and conspiracies that quickly attract followers, evidence of the dangers of group thinking is abundant. Yet, Steinbeck also makes clear that we cannot do without groups. All forms of life need cooperation in order to survive, and in this regard, *The Grapes of Wrath* can be analyzed in terms of the phalanx theory: a large group of people that need one another in order to move towards a promised land. A group of people fleeing away from the Great Dust Bowl is not necessarily negative (even while the causes are). They collectively manage to move to a new future, even while that future is full of false hopes. We could suggest that the novel describes a disaster (leaving one tragedy just to find another tragedy at the other end of the journey), yet the Okies collaborate and mostly get to their destination. In this regard, the novel describes the positive aspects of the group. Steinbeck suggests this by providing all kinds of tokens of hope, many of which can be found at the end of the novel. The oppression of the California farmers is symbolized by sending the body of the stillborn baby downstream to the landowners, telling them how rotten their system is. Meanwhile, as mentioned in chapter 2, the Joad daughter's breastfeeding of a starving man symbolizes a sense of dignity and solidarity among the Okies. These dramatic events hint at the potential to collectively resist and organize against the farmers, as well as to help one another. The journey itself is a tragedy with families piled in overloaded makeshift vehicles that constantly break down, no means to feed themselves properly or to make repairs, constantly being ripped off along their journey, as well as the death of older family members. Yet, Steinbeck is in the end, a romantic, finding something beautiful in this journey. That any of these families or vehicles makes it might be regarded as a miracle in itself. For Steinbeck, this is the phalanx in the positive sense at work: the group that supports its members, not ensuring that all will make it but that most will make it. We have seen this same mechanism at work with salmon discussed in chapter 1. Their strength consists in numbers, in which salmon support one another by being part of the school, even if the school is loosely formed. In the case of the migrating Okies, the individuals can share and trade directions, parts, skills, and food in their collective attempt to move out West. Despite the hope and the sense of adventure in moving to a better place, the group moves while receiving fairly clear signs that the promised land will disappoint.[31] The feeling of the group simply takes over.

The move from Oklahoma is the result of an environmental disaster, to which humans naturally respond with migration and exploitation of the situation through a (natural) influx of mass amounts of cheap labor. This is, on the one hand, an example of an event in which it became very evident that the destruction of the land—in that case, because of agricultural methods—has tremendous effects on the lives of humans. In addition, it is a perfect example of the natural workings of Adam Smith's invisible hand and how laissez-faire is only benefiting the wealthy powerful class. Although the government, after the disaster, made attempts to avoid similar issues in the future, during the Great Dust Bowl governments mostly stood by. In the Great Plains, banks and large agricultural conglomerates took over, leaving the former small farmers powerless and without land. On the West Coast, governments and laws mostly protected the farmers, leaving farmworkers on their own and vulnerable. In works such as *Of Mice and Men* (discussed in chapter 2) we find the result of isolation, such as extreme distrust of others, even between those who are oppressed. Steinbeck writes to protest all these developments, from the perspective of communist ideals, without necessarily being a communist. Steinbeck offers a blatant assessment of the capitalistic machine that turns us all into mean, selfish, lonely creatures that fight one another, and who destroy the land and the sea, not because we want to but because we are told to do so.

The most dangerous situation occurs when members blindly follow a group, which can happen when individuals are grabbed by the emotions of a group, that makes one act in a way one normally would not. It is, arguably, the nature and the goal of the group that determines the nature of the participation. We have a natural tendency to collaborate, and the group thinks for us and generates emotions we would otherwise not experience. Individual reason can disappear as it is taken over by the collective rationality or emotion of the group. In our time we can consider the January 6, 2021, storming of the Capitol as an event driven by group emotions. Astro argues that "Steinbeck voices his preference for groups which heighten consciousness and increase the freedom of the individual."[32] That preference is one easy to agree with, yet it is not so clear how (and even if) we have a choice.

In his 1933 letter to Albee discussing the phalanx, Steinbeck explains the phalanx in terms of the biology of Allee: "The phalanx has its own memory—memory of the great tides when the moon was close, memory of starvation when the food of the world was exhausted. Memory of methods when numbers of his units had to be destroyed for the good of the whole, memory of the history of itself. And the phalanx has emotions of which the unit man is incapable. Emotions of destruction, of war, of migration, of hatred, of fear."[33] The phalanx is more than the unit of man and organizes humans in a way a cell arranges atoms, and how the human body arranges cells. In each case, it is the larger unit that is in control, yet not in a conscious way. Because of the ancient memories of cycles, hunger, destruction, and one's own history, "new phalanxes are born under proper physical and spiritual conditions," Steinbeck writes, in the same letter.[34] Referring to Jung, he writes about the unconscious and a keying mechanism. "It [Jung's unconscious third person] is the plug which when inserted into the cap of the phalanx, makes man lose his unit identity in the phalanx."[35] Even art is then described as an expression of the phalanx, but more dangerous is the situation of vice and war. "When your phalanx needs you it will use you, if you are the material to be used. You will know when the time comes, and when it does come, nothing you can do will let you escape."[36] This idea is at work in *The Grapes of Wrath*. The Joad family is part of "the material to be used" in the great migration to the West. The call to participate in this movement comes from the phalanx which creates a feeling of oneness, a group mentality.

The same happens in much more negative groups: fascism and militarism in Germany, Italy, and Japan, or racism in the United States. In relation to the latter, Astro ties the negative effect of the phalanx to one of Steinbeck's short stories, "The Vigilante." In that story, he describes the behavior of Mike, a man who takes part in a lynching of an African American man. Half an hour after the brutal act in which he participated with enthusiasm, he realizes he does not recognize himself any longer. He has lost his identity, his self to the group. What just happened has become unreal, and with that, he himself has become unreal.[37]

The character of Mike exemplifies our animal being in which we do not rationally make decisions but are driven by our feelings. We are not unlike the amoeba discussed by Ricketts in his essay "The Philosophy of Breaking Through." An amoeba is moving in the direction of the greatest weight. About the pseudopodia, the temporary parts of the amoeba that expand and contract, he suggests that if pseudopodia had a consciousness, they would think they were leading, whereas it is really the organism as a whole that leads.

At the human level, we have already seen that "when your phalanx needs you it will use you."[38] Along these lines, Steinbeck adds that even Hitler is not the creator of "the present phalanx in Germany . . . he merely interprets it."[39] As Williams points out, the leaders are "ultimately its [the phalanx's] products rather than its creators."[40] In "The Leader of the People" (the last section in Steinbeck's *The Red Pony*), we find a similar stance on leadership when he describes the settlement movement out west, as "westering," discussed in more detail in the next section. This collective movement, the phalanx of westering, is a more positive one: "Every man wanted something for himself, but the big beast that was all of them wanted only westering. I was the leader, but if I hadn't been there, someone else would have been the head. The thing had to have a head."[41] With a similar creation of leadership and the image of the big crawling beast, it is unclear how to stay away from the phalanx of fascism, militarism, or xenophobia and how to move ourselves and others to a more positive phalanx. It is clear that Steinbeck has a preference for groups that are inclusive, that do not oppress, that are not driven by greed, and that are not manipulated by demagogues who play with our feelings. Yet, how to avoid exclusion, oppression, greed, and manipulations is far from clear. The phalanx will use you if you are the material to be used. Unless we can shape our material, little agency and freedom seem to be left for us.

We saw earlier how all lives, for Steinbeck and Ricketts, are morphed into a group being through the basic urge, or drive, to be. We just read how Ricketts suggests that if the pseudopodia of an amoeba had consciousness they would think they are leading. While the inspiration for Steinbeck and Ricketts was mostly Jung's "collective unconscious," we find here also some interesting echoes of Spinoza, who discusses a stone that would think itself to be freely flying through the air if it had consciousness. We can also compare the "drive to be" to Spinoza's *conatus*, which emphasizes that in our basic being we are ultimately lacking freedom. We are *natura naturata*, nature natured, the result of a causal chain, and we are tied to our emotions, as he speaks of a "human bondage, or the strength of the emotions."[42] We often mistake the following of our will for freedom; yet for Spinoza, it is only in understanding our will as unfree that we can find some sense of freedom. Just like the stone flying through the air because someone threw it, or the pseudopodia moving because of the bigger organism they are a part of, my will is not causing itself but is moved by other causes. For Spinoza, by grasping how I am moved by other causes I can then understand myself as a being that is related to others, which then can lead to a "freedom-within-relation."[43] The problem for Spinoza is very similar to the problem Steinbeck has to address: How can we find freedom in a world in which our will is determined by forces outside of our control, or how can we become the material to be used by a positive phalanx? Can there be autonomy while being part of the phalanx?

On the Move

In one of his last works, *Travels with Charley*, which documents his journey across the United States, Steinbeck mentions people living in mobile homes and discusses mobility and roots.[44] At first, he seems to be surprised that people do not care much about roots, yet then quickly, without mentioning the word, turns back to the phalanx. He argues that land ties us down, and roots us, but land is scarce—only a few have it. Thus, the majority of people have to move when famine comes or we lose our job. We have always done so. It is again the ancient instinct of adaption imprinted on us ever since we were simple organisms. This has always (at least since we were insects) translated into mobility. Steinbeck reflects:

> Land is a tangible, and tangibles have a tendency of getting into few hands. Thus, it was that one man wanted ownership of land and at the same time wanted servitude because someone had to work it. Roots were in ownership of land, in tangible and immovable possessions. In this view we are a restless species with a very short history of roots, and those not widely distributed. Perhaps we have overrated roots as a psychic need. Maybe the greater the urge, the deeper and more ancient is the need, the will, the hunger to be somewhere else.[45]

Over thirty years earlier Steinbeck described this hunger to be somewhere else in the already mentioned loss of westering. Westering is the spirit of moving, the great migration out west. Echoing the phalanx essay, he describes the migration as "a whole bunch of people made into one big crawling beast."[46] Once the group reached the Pacific Ocean the migration was completed, and he describes that this has killed the spirit of westering. Why is the end of this spirit a bad thing, we can wonder. Westering as the frontier movement, as well as colonization more generally, have resulted in genocide, continuing racism, and oppression. Wallace Stegner's *Beyond the Hundredth Meridian* discusses the mistaken ideas about the west. Promises that included miraculous rainfall once the land was plowed did, of course, not materialize. Steinbeck himself writes about and worked with the migrants of the 1930s, who were driven by misconceptions of the west as plentiful. They thought their hunger, poverty, and exploitation would end, yet faced all of it along the way and at their destination. Needless to say, Steinbeck does not want us to western for such mistaken purposes.

What then does he want? He, first of all, wants us to understand that we are driven towards groups. Groups can move, settle, dig in, ignore, and even kill. During the history of humanity, people have been nomadic, either fleeing away from something or moving towards opportunity. When we think about the frontier movement we even find a perceived need to settle the west, almost as some sort of ethical duty. When Steinbeck discusses westering in "The Leader of the People" he provides a different take: "It wasn't getting here that mattered, it was movement and westering."[47] Interpreters have emphasized that Steinbeck here appeals to the beauty and power of being part of a group. The group is significant, indeed. Other works, such as the phalanx essay, as well as the *Sea of Cortez,* emphasize our biological rootedness as a tendency to be part of a group. Yet, besides the group, movement is also a focus. Westering is, in its very core, biological, both in terms of being a group and in what it does: move. The biological rootedness is made evident through a comparison to ants: "We carried life out here and set it down the way those ants carry eggs."[48] Life is movement forward, the striving to survive as a group.

In the case of westering as told by Steinbeck the biological principle to move seems to have been curbed. Steinbeck, through the character of the grandfather, explains:

> "Then we came down to the sea, and it was done." He stopped and wiped his eyes until the rims were red. "That's what I should be telling instead of stories." When Jody spoke, Grandfather started and looked down at him. "Maybe I could lead the people some day," Jody said. The old man smiled. "There's no place to go. There's the ocean to stop you. There's a line of old men along the shore hating the ocean because it stopped them." "In boats I might, sir." 'No place to go, Jody. Every place is taken. But that's not the worst—no, not the worst. Westering has died out of the people. Westering isn't a hunger any more. It's all done. Your father is right. It is finished." He laced his finger on his knee and looked at them.[49]

His son-in-law and the other adults in the story disregard the story of the grandfather. Maybe we should do the same. After all, movement leads to displacements of others, violence, oppression, and so forth. Why then does Steinbeck give the grandfather and the death of westering such great authority by building the story up to this climactic moment? The question remains, what have we, according to Steinbeck, lost after settling the whole continent?

One way to approach this is to think about the death of westering in terms of traveling without really opening our senses and mind to the places we visit. *Travels with Charley* describes the highway as a way to travel from coast to coast without seeing anything. Moreover, today's global world (as Marx already indicated) creates new places as a copy of the old. Perhaps westering has to be taken in a more metaphorical way, somewhat influenced by Thoreau who writes we should always walk "West." For Thoreau, too, there is an emphasis on being homeless, yet the activity of walking and being homeless for Thoreau means one is at home everywhere. In the following section I will make some further suggestions on how to interpret the move to unknown places and explain westering by tying it back to the societies of the tidepool.

The Tidepool Society

If the phalanx is an animal instinct that can take over and/or shape our feelings, and can destroy our individuality as well as our creativity, should we not celebrate the fact that we are overcoming this force of nature of westering—so that we can instead become who we are? The problem is that we are not becoming who we are. Instead of westering, we will be the material of a new phalanx. Perhaps one of war, technology, industrialization, consumerism, capitalism, (sub)urbanization, patriotism, racism, sexism, and/or xenophobia. What we lose with the death of westering is then a loss of a cooperative and creative model that turns into a combative and destructive model. Even while neo-Darwinists such as Allee emphasize that all living beings are driven towards cooperation, the opposite—fights—can be the result of the drive to survive. The two principles of the struggle for existence and the need for cooperation can be opposed to one another, yet, Allee claims that "there is evidence that these basic forces have acted together to shape the course of evolution, even the evolution of social relations among men and nations of men."[50] He then even speaks about "the biology of war."[51] While war or fighting could be understood as a natural mechanism that takes care of overpopulation and makes the strongest survive, later parts in Allee's chapter seriously doubt those effects of war. Fighting is an inherited trait of much earlier life forms, a trait we find—in one way or another—in all life. Nevertheless, the other natural traits at work here are the need for cooperation as well as adaption to change.[52] Despite his long reflections on international relations determined through war, Allee remains optimistic that ultimately the need to cooperate is stronger.

Arguably, Steinbeck is less optimistic. It seems that he, in the death of westering, sees a dangerous move towards destructive tendencies that are deeply rooted in us. In many of his works, as well as his Nobel Prize acceptance speech, we find warnings about our advancing technological knowledge, resulting, for example, in the creation of nuclear weapons. Technological developments, he argues, often outrun the development of our ethical capacities. In fact, Steinbeck was often criticized for being too political and too concerned about what should be. In his Nobel Prize acceptance speech, he responds to such criticism by stating that it is the responsibility of the writer to serve the human race's needs for hope, improvement, and survival, which is especially needed in a time of advanced technological knowledge, which has developed faster than our ethical dimensions.[53]

Likewise, when our technology makes it possible to gut the bottom of the ocean (which Ricketts and Steinbeck witnessed in the Sea of Cortez), (threaten to) drop atomic bombs, pollute the air, destroy the mountains and rivers, or extinguish other species, the living relationships that constitute our society as an ecology are destroyed. Every living being changes its environment in collaboration with members of its own species and those of other species. The possibility of the long-term thriving of a species depends on this. Yet, when we act as destructive members in an ecology, the living relationships themselves are killed. The phalanx of consumerism feeds our destructive instincts and suppresses our collaborative instincts, and our politics as ecology.

Does this mean that when we reach the Pacific Ocean and run out of land, we ultimately turn against one another and against non-human beings? Other outcomes are possible. Lisca has suggested that, for Steinbeck, "we are all pioneers" and that westering is possibly an openness to the unknown.[54] This Nietzschean reading of westering could explain the difference between the big crawling beast that moves to the unknown through which the individual can become something new, as opposed to the beast that fears and destroys the unknown.

Going back to the tidepool, we find that without teleology the world is described in terms of how things are, without a principle that guides as a first ground or a goal. Even without such ground or goal, the creatures in the tidepool collaborate with the other living and nonliving beings, creating living relationships—an ecology that is not very different from ours.

Non-teleological thinking does, however, not lead to a world without any direction. The unconscious intelligence of the group provides guidance.

Tying this to the ecology of politics, we can open ourselves up to the insight that we are beings in relation, not only collaborating with our kin and own species, but with other beings, living and nonliving. Partitioning in terms of species, gender, race, ethnicity, etc., is in the end detrimental to collaboration and to survival. Crossing the borders and boundaries is what constitutes the living relationships of the ecology of politics. We can thrive only if those living relationships are kept healthy.

Conclusion

Through a reading of Steinbeck and Ricketts and their studies of human groups and tidepools, I have argued that the instinctual memory that either drives us against one another or makes us cooperate is deep inside us. Recognizing these animal tendencies is a first step to the freedom to sculpt ourselves as the material for the positive phalanx, the one that westerns, that is, moves towards and is open to the unknown.

Steinbeck describes and argues vehemently against militarism, fascism, exploitation, racism, and classism in his time and shows how easily we can be pulled into a group that actively supports such structures of oppression. Needless to say, our own time is a dangerous time as well: from police brutality to separation of families at the border, deporting parents after they have dropped their kids off at school, not providing legal status to those who are the backbone to our food systems, or not providing health care to those who clean our homes and care for our children. Undocumented workers are today's Okies of *The Grapes of Wrath*. They are exploitable, as they have no rights. In the 1930s the government stood on the side of the farmers, acting against any humane standards, and against decency. Today the government has taken side with corporations and can get away with violations of human rights and indecency. These government stances are a representation of the feelings of the phalanx, sentiments that are further fueled by demagogues and their social media messaging. The task of ecopolitics is to emphasize and encourage the more supportive and collaborative sentiments.

Both in Steinbeck's time and today we can recognize the relationship between the treatment of others and the treatment of the natural world. As the Okies left land that was depleted, today's stream of migrants move away from environmental destruction and political instability. Considering the fact that environmental destruction is not slowing down and climate change is upon us, it is not a farfetched suggestion that this stream of migrants will exponentially grow, that this is just the beginning. Instead of the phalanx that rejects these migrants on the basis of selfishness (expressed as nationalism), we should support the phalanx that generates cooperative tendencies that we can also find in our natural constitution.

It is these issues I will discuss in the last two chapters and the conclusion, in order to provide a possible way to redirect the forces that constitute these movements and to convince others to become part of a more positive phalanx. Steinbeck inspires us to create ethical capabilities for the twenty-first century, driven by hope and the need to survive, along with the other creatures and beings that make our lives possible. In short, instead of building walls, ecopolitics (guided by Steinbeck) seeks to knock down both the walls and the builders of walls. It does so by forming a new phalanx that forms a strategic formation based on mutual aid.

Chapter Five

Human and Other Ants

Decentralized Ecopolitics

> I am against all forms of government, including good government.
>
> —Edward Abbey, *The Monkey Wrench Gang*

Standing on a stepladder on our deck, blasted by the hot sun, covered with protective glasses and a mask, holding a spray can, I coat our power line in ant poison. The absurdity of the situation is a confrontation of our limited abilities to keep the group intelligence of the ants out of our home. They, indeed, did it again: finding yet another way into our home. This time we have carpenter ants—who really should be given a different name, because they destroy the work of carpenters. As our home is under attack, quite literally, we have to take measures that are a bit more drastic than creating barriers of pepper or baby powder (which they typically do not like to cross). The tiny creatures that presumably do not have much intelligence on an individual basis are incredibly smart as a collective, and they are with many. A recent "conservative" count concluded that for every human on the planet 25 million ants exist.[1] Because collaboration is their strength, the collective intelligence and power of ants should not be underestimated.

In the study of salmon, chimpanzees, mice, rats, and tidepools, the non-human world reveals itself as one full of different models of collaboration. Some animal communities seem hierarchical, yet none seem to have incorporated centralized decision-making. Sometimes our descriptions indicate hierarchies. For example, we find "queens" in "colonies" of ants and bees. The word *colony* might be appropriate to some degree, yet bees and ants do not conquer new territories or make new settlements, unless the old one collapses. Moreover, the title of queen is misleading because she does not lead by giving orders or by making decisions. Instead, ants and bees make decisions collectively. Finding food or nesting sites are collaborative efforts that require the consensus of the whole group. Well-known studies of bees have shown that they are able to communicate about potential nesting and food sites through dances and have some math skills to calculate directions. The queen does not give orders, and in that sense, the monarchist title is problematic to say the least.[2] Yet in the case of the death of a queen, chaos emerges. She seems to rule by mere presence. In that regard, an important detail is that she is (mostly) the mother of all bees or ants in the colony. In the case of both ants and bees, queens do not rule by making decisions, yet the insects as a group know what to do, function efficiently, and survive different challenging situations. These colonies seem to be run anarchically, in which I use the term *anarchism*—going back to the Greek meaning of *anarchos*—as "without a leader." To most of us, anarchism seems unrealistic and radical. We are convinced that we need bosses, job descriptions, and contracts to tell us exactly what to do and what not to do. Likewise we believe we need laws to protect our rights, etc. Yet, if social insects are our evolutionary predecessors, or if we had a common ancestor, might we still possess this ability to function without a leader? We have seen in the previous chapter through Steinbeck's phalanx that power often resides in groups, suggesting that leaders in the human world might be much less powerful than we generally assume. They simply follow the phalanx of the people— what the group wants. The "instinct" to be part of a group suggests that humans often act politically in decentralized ways. Quite differently, many aboriginal communities suggest that anarchism is possible as they functioned for thousands of years without a top-down government and without a social contract. While the modern mindset deemed such cultures as "uncivilized" we might finally start to appreciate the wisdom of these cultures.

Some of the key questions in this chapter are: What did we inherit (directly or indirectly) from old predecessors such as ants? How did those inherited qualities change and function differently within the human context when other factors, such as feelings, rationality, and spoken and written language play a role? I want to suggest that even while we seem to have little in common with ants, we act and function "ant-like" much more frequently than we generally assume.

In the human realm, it is certainly not democracy itself that drives collective decisions, even though we find a certain collective mind at work in elections (as discussed earlier) in terms of the phalanx. In the act of electing new leaders, voters give up their political power. Through the act of voting, citizens forfeit their ability to be part of the collective. The leaders, once elected, grasp the power to make decisions, and with that, voters mostly lose their abilities to be part of a group. The group can and will speak up, for example when unpopular policies are proposed. Yet, it is also obvious that in modern democracies, the group is mostly powerless and easily distracted. In expressions of power such as the Women's Marches following the election of Trump, Black Lives Matter, the Occupy movement, or Greta Thunberg and other young advocates who protest against the lack of action of governments against climate change, the results are far from immediate. Even when millions of people protest, the power lies in places such as Washington, D.C., The Hague, Brussels, London, Paris, or Berlin. In our system, power is centralized in governmental institutions and courts.

In comparing ourselves to ants, it should be acknowledged that being part of a human society is complex and that humans and human societies are in many ways more complex than ants. Culture, intellectual abilities, planning, property, monetary exchange, laws, and ethical reflections are unique to human societies insofar as they are written down and enforced by systems of law. Yet, ants have their own complexities such as task allocations that we could only perform through systems that require writing, reading, and math. Even more, we can wonder if some of our systems perhaps create the obstacles to a society that is self-governing without a (central) government. We envision anarchy as dangerous and quickly start to project *Lord of the Flies* scenarios in which the rule of the strongest is forcefully and violently enacted. Obviously, we need not refer to literature or fiction, since we have plenty of historical examples of violence. Yet, the root of that violence is not human nature. The roots of violence, stinginess, as well as lack of cooperation and empathy, lie in the societies we live in. Policies, laws, and socioeconomic structures generate competition. The result is pettiness at best; greed, fear, bigotry, and hatred at its worst. Those structures that drive us apart also create humans who believe they cannot function without those same laws, policies, and economic structures. We cannot even imagine what it would be like to live without them. It is argued that we need laws to avoid exploitation and protect citizens. Yet our system of law mostly protects those who have power. Following Rousseau (and Marx), as well as some contemporary anarchist and communitarian movements, it can be suggested that the "social contract" is benefiting only the wealthy, making them powerful at the cost of the 99 percent. As already mentioned, within the context of human history, contracts have not been around that long, nor has money. Different aboriginal communities lived for tens of thousands of years without contracts and (as, among others, David Graeber points out) in gift economies. It is in fact rather curious that we are the only creatures who need written laws and contracts, or at least believe that we cannot possibly live without them.

Philosophers such as Immanuel Kant suggest that the ability to create and live by laws indicates our superiority over other animals. Kant also implies that those societies that live under laws and contracts are superior to those that do not. Contrary to Kant, we can wonder if our need for laws (or the perceived need for laws) can be an indication of our own weakness. Other species manage to collaborate and function well without them. Have we been led to believe in those needs to such a degree that we cannot even envision the possibility of life without laws and government? Against the popular Enlightenment story that witnessed progress all around us, overcoming "primitive" societies, we should reconsider aboriginal communities that can exist without contracts and laws as possibly superior.

In the following, I engage with these questions by first of all discussing the anarchist philosophy of Peter (Pyotr) Kropotkin. As a geographer who initially worked in the harsh environment of Siberia, he argues that animals do not primarily fight but have to collaborate in order to survive in adverse conditions. Through a reinterpretation of Darwin that challenges the so-called social Darwinists, he suggests that the social instinct that stimulates mutual aid is the most important one. He takes these lessons from the animal world as a basis for his anarchism, in which mutual aid leads to a reenvisioning of all human relationships.

I use Kropotkin's insights to analyze the ant, a species that is sometimes called anarchistic. Because of their decentralized decision-making and problem-solving skills, they form a very interesting political model. Certainly, as already mentioned, ant colonies are far from an ideal society to strive for as humans. Perhaps, we are even *too much* like ants. The latter is in particular suggested by anarchist writer Edward Abbey, whose novel, *The Monkey Wrench Gang*, is analyzed in the last part of the chapter.

A Scientific Ethics: Kropotkin

For Kropotkin, one of the main strategies to solve the injustice of poverty in a world full of wealth consists in the toppling of decentralized governance. Interestingly, his political ideas were informed by his early career as a scientist and geographer. With a background in Darwinism and his field studies in animal behavior in different regions, he argues that collaboration is the most potent force of any species. The scientific foundation for his political and ethical ideas is that cooperation and solidarity can be found in all animals. All living beings, even single-celled organisms, need to cooperate, and this need to cooperate determines evolution. Even for the most solitary beings, at some point in their lives cooperation occurs. For us humans, as living beings that depend on one another, our social capacities are a necessity. Kropotkin argues in a Darwinian fashion that our ethical capacities and social justice are part of our evolutionary development.

I will focus here primarily on *Mutual Aid,* his first book, and *Ethics: Origin and Development,* Kropotkin's last and unfinished work. In both works, he explores similar ideas on cooperation, yet his last work is supplemented by a history of ethics in which he analyzes the tradition of ethical thinking in the Western canon, with a few references to other traditions. His main idea in this work is that ethics overall has had the tendency to relate to metaphysical explanations when it comes to the origin of feelings of duty or morality, more broadly speaking. As opposed to religious metaphysics, Kropotkin discusses Darwin's natural or organic ethics, which claims that in all animals we find some sense of ethics and justice.

Kropotkin argues against other Darwinian scientists, such as T. H. Huxley, who emphasizes the struggle for existence and sees competition as the driving force for evolution.[3] Whereas Huxley paints a picture of animal life as a continuous fight, Kropotkin emphasizes spontaneous cooperation as the key aspect of life. He deems Huxley's ideas as a "grotesque distortion of Darwin"[4] because, as Kropotkin puts it, Huxley presents nature "as an immense battlefield and an extermination of the weak ones by the strongest, the swiftest, and the cunningest: evil was the only lesson which man could get from nature."[5] The image we are presented with is a very familiar one: the animal kingdom is cruel. Even our closest predecessors, the Neanderthals, are pictured as skull-smashing savages, a picture that recently has been challenged by new archaeological findings (as discussed in the introduction to this book). In many Darwinists, we find a strong opposition between the human and non-human realms, the latter full of violence, the former civilized. Those who follow this conviction will, according to Kropotkin, conclude that the source of good is "some other, extra-natural, or super-natural influence which inspires man with conceptions of 'supreme good,' and guides human development towards a higher goal."[6] For Kropotkin, such an appeal to a metaphysical realm is completely opposite to the theory of evolution.

Through a reading of parts of *The Descent of Man*, Kropotkin argues that Darwin, in fact, regards mutual aid as a more significant fact than the struggle for survival. In his reading of Darwin, he suggests that "warfare in Nature is chiefly *limited to struggle between different species*, but that *within each species*, and within the groups of different species which we find living together, the practice of *mutual aid is the rule*, and therefore this last aspect of animal life plays a far greater part than warfare in the economy of Nature."[7] The term "economy of Nature" is an interesting choice, considering that Kropotkin argues that political economy is to blame for the selfish and individualistic character of human actions. He, thus, seems to oppose the economy of capitalism with that of nature (or Nature).[8] In his economy of nature, it is not the struggle and warfare that we find in capitalism, but cooperation or mutual aid that rules, especially within a species and within groups of species that depend on one another. For Kropotkin, mutual aid "represents the best weapon in the great struggle for life which continually has to be carried on in Nature against climate, inundations, storms, frost, and the like, and continually requires new adaptations to the ever-changing conditions of existence."[9] Only in groups and through cooperation can animals survive and thrive.

Kropotkin, arguably, provides a somewhat one-sided story by emphasizing cooperation over struggle. He is certainly not oblivious to the struggles and violence we find in nature, but since others (such as Hobbes, Spencer, and Huxley) have so much emphasized these struggles, he argues that it is his task now to show "animal and human life under a quite different aspect."[10] As such, he seeks to provide a better interpretation of Darwin. He admits that, following Darwin, self-preservation does play an important role and can trigger "the purely egoistic instinct." Yet his point is that mutual sympathy is "*more permanently* at work."[11] When Darwin explains why we humans are "the most dominant animal that has ever appeared on the earth" he cites that, aside from intellectual capacities and corporeal structure, our "social habits" lead us to aid and defend one another.[12] Criticizing Mill, who states that human social instincts are not natural but acquired, Darwin suggests: "It can hardly be disputed that the social feelings are instinctive or innate in the lower animals; and why should they not be so in man?"[13] Social feelings are necessary for animals who need one another's aid, and we find all kinds of social animals living together, "even distinct species."[14] Humans inherited innate social instincts from other animals. We are, thus, in this regard, not essentially different from other animals.

Darwin seems a bit more careful in avoiding the suggestion that feelings in humans and other animals are similar in nature. Like most biologists, he does not want to raise the suspicion of anthropomorphism when discussing animal feelings.[15] He describes "services" that different animals provide to one another, from warnings against danger to ridding one another of parasites or thorns. Some animals hunt and fish together or defend one another. Nevertheless, he sometimes ascribes feelings to animals, for example in describing mutual affection in horses and dogs as well as their misery when "separated from their companions." While he does not use words such as "altruism," he acknowledges feelings such as "sympathy" and "pity" when speaking of "sympathizing with the pains and pleasures of others."[16] Meanwhile, he expresses some doubts and observes that feelings of pity and sympathy seem absent when animals leave wounded animals behind. Thus, he does not altogether deny the existence of such feelings in animals, yet suggests that in some cases, the instinct to "follow the troop" takes over, which he also finds in the human animal (discussed in the previous chapter in terms of Steinbeck's phalanx). In short, Darwin makes a few speculations about feelings and animals and explicitly states these are speculations. He also indicates that some examples, such as a blind pelican "well fed for a long time by its companions" are too specific instances to be driven by a special instinct.[17] Thus, Darwin suggests a more general feeling such as sympathy must be at play.

When Kropotkin uses ethical language to describe the non-human world he seems less concerned with anthropomorphizing the animal world. One could say that the fight-or-flight life is anthropomorphizing in the sense that we imagine the animal world as one similar to our world full of injustices (which we sometimes use to justify our injustices). Kropotkin argues that in the human realm we, indeed, find a plethora of negative feelings towards one another, which can be regarded as a complete transformation of the social feelings, such as empathy (or sympathy), into negative ones. Especially private property, political governance, and ethics that appeal to the metaphysical realm are culprits. While we find cooperation at every level of the animal world, we humans are overwhelmed by struggles and injustices, which are often not even recognized as injustices. Metaphysical explanations, for example, through a God that acts in ways we cannot grasp, pave the way for accepting all kinds of injustice such as the fact that some people are born more privileged than others. Kropotkin suggests that we shift responsibilities to a supernatural realm, and argues that religion is not the origin, but the destruction of ethics and justice. In the example of privileges, within the mindset of metaphysical ethics we need not solve the injustice that a combination of our birthplace, gender, and ethnicity largely determines our future. Moreover, these metaphysical explanations suppress our (natural) feelings of guilt when we witness injustices. In other words, poverty is not even seen as an injustice, and we fail to recognize Kropotkin's often repeated insight that all wealth is the result of the exploitation of the poor. Thus, instead of accepting things as they are, we should refute the current reality by recognizing that the lives we live are enabled through the poverty of others. The money and the resources we own are accumulated at the expense of the poor, who today often reside in developing countries. They are mining "our" resources, forging "our" steel, and building and making "our" cars, clothes, and gadgets after already having lost their natural resources, their natural means of sustenance, and with that their culture. Our food is grown and prepared and our buildings are constructed and cleaned by undocumented workers whom we need but do not want. Likewise, other species are exploited, often with the result of extinction or torture. We seem to have successfully suppressed our natural feelings of guilt and empathy. Making (tax-deductible) donations or buying carbon offsets provide us with enough satisfaction to justify the unjust and keep living the way we are. Government, laws, and law enforcement protect this unjust justification, without which the wealthy would have long lost their power (and wealth).

Kropotkin certainly acknowledges that the (non-human) animal world is not without injustices. Some animals are exploited. Yet, he argues that senses of justice can be found. For example, individual "misbehaving" animals that engage in activities that benefit themselves at the cost of others are often punished. He uses, among other things, the example of birds in a colony who collectively attack a young bird "which has stolen some straw from another bird's nest."[18]

Thus, for Kropotkin, the animal world is not defined in terms of selfishness (even while it can occur), but in terms of mutual aid. We human animals are, in our social and ethical capacities, not very different from other animals. We can be selfish, just like other animals, yet for Kropotkin, the problem of selfishness in the human world and the scale at which it is expressed is rooted in a social context in which private property drives our decisions, emotions, and behaviors. One could say that the social and legal context that states that something is mine triggers negative instincts. As Ryley in his work on Kropotkin puts it: "Private property dispossesses the people of their *collective*, not individual, property. What [in medieval times] guaranteed their independence and liberty was not personal possession but rights of access to communal land and productive forces via the village commons and the city guilds."[19] According to Garret Hardin, the (in)famous tragedy of the commons is inherent to human nature. Others have argued that it occurs within the context of capitalism (and actually it turns out that Hardin's example of the commons in England was heavily regulated). Selfish behavior at the expense of the community or society might be attributed to a system that runs on competition and greed, thus, triggering negative, selfish instincts. Following a similar thought, Ryley agrees with Kropotkin that communal land outside of capitalism will instigate selfless behavior, not unlike the altruistic behavior we find in animals. The problem, then, would not lie in the commons, but rather in the mindset of growth that is pervasive in a capitalist context. Indigenous cultures tend to blame the lack of checks and balances in the current world. For example, aboriginal scholar Yunkaporta draws upon the image of the emu (or simply Emu) as the cause of narcissism (in other cosmologies we find representation of greed and cunning in figures such as Raven and Coyote). Yunkaporta speaks about Emu as "a troublemaker who brings into being the most destructive idea in existence: I am greater than you; you are less than me."[20] We all have some narcissism in us, and if it remains unchecked it leads to destructive behavior, such as colonialism, slavery, racism, sexism, or speciesism. It silences other humans, non-humans, and whole societies. Thus, the Emu mentality "needs massive checks and balances to contain the damage it can do."[21] In today's socially fragmented world in which greed is encouraged, narcissism, or the Emu in us, is fed truckloads of fertilizer.

It is interesting how animals seem to have better checks and balances than we humans have. For Kropotkin, the animal world is based on collaboration and shared property. Again, following Darwin, he argues that in mutual sympathy we can find "the rudiments of the moral conscience."[22] The ground for morality is located outside of the human realm as he argues that a sense of justice and equity is found in many social animals. Accordingly, he suggests that nature is not amoral and that, in fact, "the very ideas of bad and good, and man's abstractions concerning 'the supreme good' have been borrowed from Nature. They are reflections in the mind of man of what he saw in animal life and in the course of his social life, and due to it these impressions were developed into *general* conceptions of right and wrong."[23] Here, we find human reflection and consciousness of morality on the one hand and animal actions of justice and equity on the other. If non-human animals do not reflect on actions, this does not mean that principles of morality cannot be found there. In fact, Kropotkin argues, these animal immediate actions form the very basis for our own principles.

Principles are often (if not always) arbitrary. Kropotkin refutes the principles that are based on some metaphysical realm; he, instead, steers us back to nature. It might be tempting to oppose relative human values to an absoluteness of nature, yet Kropotkin carefully avoids such language, which would bring us back to the realm of metaphysics. His approach, instead, is to regard ethics and justice as evolutionary developments. Ethics and justice are ideas that, in the history of Western philosophy, have always been interpreted as human qualities, considered to come from a divine realm and/or from (pure) reason, or in some cases from feelings. For Kropotkin, however, justice and ethics are biological, organic, and originate in the animal realm.

Despite the strong emphasis that our foundation of ethics is shared with other animals, Kropotkin does make an important distinction between human and non-human animals when it comes to morality. As opposed to ethics, he defines morality as the study, teaching, and reflection on ethics and states this as an activity we only find in humans. Yet, it is, for him, a mistake to regard morality as the origin of ethics. The study, reflection, and teaching of ethics are secondary to ethics, and the latter is possible because of mutual aid (found in all forms of life) and justice (found in many animals). While we often think of human morality as the highest form, for Kropotkin, it is the least important as he writes, "the third [morality], developed later than the others, is an unstable feeling and the least imperative of the three."[24] It is exactly in morality that we find excuses to act unjustly. Thus, interestingly, religion and metaphysics are not the ground for ethics, but ruin ethics, while nature is the (stable) origin of ethics. As he argues, for all animals, a "certain degree of identification of the individual with the interest of the group to which it belongs . . . manifests itself even among the lowest animals."[25] Along these lines, he calls the unity of mutual aid, justice, and morality "an *organic necessity*" and "a *universal law of organic evolution.*"[26] This suggests that we humans organically developed morality and that it is a natural capacity. Yet, that capacity is disrupted through capital and private property. For a group, mutual aid is a necessary condition for survival (assisting in fulfilling "the need for food, shelter, or sleep") and the necessary condition of evolution. Without these instincts, "the group, the race, the species dies out and disappears."[27]

These insights form Kropotkin's basis for a scientific ethics, in which religious and/or metaphysical grounds are replaced by evolutionary grounds. In Kropotkin's reading of Darwin, social animals love society, experience misery when left alone, engage continually in social intercourse, provide mutual warnings, and assist one another in hunting and self-defense.[28] He notes that "Darwin remarks that although man, such as he now exists, has but few social instincts, he nevertheless is a sociable being who must have retained from an extremely remote period some degree of instinctive love and sympathy for his fellows."[29] This suggests that in our relatively isolated contemporary human existence, we are assisted by feelings that are much older. Kropotkin, through Darwin, argues that while differences between social animals such as insects and human animals obviously exist, "*other essential features* point to a community of origin."[30] The common origin is "the social instinct . . . out of which all moralities originate."[31] He recognizes here the difficulty of the rather broad concept of "instinct" and distinguishes "the social instinct proper" from the "parental, filial, brotherly instincts as well as several other instincts and faculties, such as mutual sympathy, on one side, and reason, experience, and a tendency to imitation on the other."[32] Kropotkin points out that Darwin was carefully considering the hierarchy and relationship between the different instincts. In some places, he suggests that the parental and filial instincts probably form the ground for the other instincts, whereas, in other places, he suggests that the social instinct is a separate and more fundamental instinct. Sometimes Kropotkin seems to embrace the latter. Yet, he ultimately balances the different instincts, suggesting that while the social instinct is the stronger one, the other instincts have developed along with it.[33]

While acknowledging that nature itself is full of inequality and struggle, Kropotkin resists that these inequalities should be an excuse to rid ourselves of worries over equity, justice, or brotherhood. This is exactly the problem when we turn it into "a holy duty" to merely take care of the poor by sharing "'what can be shared' without parting with one's privileged position."[34] This is the hypocrisy we are all living in today and the great injustice Kropotkin was fighting against in his time. Moreover, this hypocrisy is going against nature by neglecting what he defines as the aim of ethics: "To create such an atmosphere in society as would produce in the great number, entirely by impulse, those actions which best lead to welfare of all and the fullest happiness of every separate being."[35] This is a natural principle for him, which creates a situation in which everyone can thrive. While this might sound utilitarian, the principle is not a rational "product of development" as it is in Mill, but an innate natural principle, an instinct that is found in all social animals.[36]

While *Ethics* traces the outlines of a scientific foundation of ethics, *Mutual Aid* provides a criticism of human political systems in which we fail to recognize the significance of cooperation and instead emphasize the struggle for survival. Kropotkin vehemently argues against top-down leadership. It is first of all a mistake to think that leaders are responsible for progress (as he argues in the preface to *Mutual Aid*). Leaders create conflict and war, often against the protest of the people. He published this work in 1914 at the outbreak of the First World War, a massive escalating conflict, in which the masses "nowhere had a voice."[37] All progress, he states, is the result of the "creative, constructive genius of the mass of the people . . . whenever a nation has to live through a difficult moment of its history."[38] This idea of struggle and progress through collaboration parallels with the situation of the animals he studied in the harsh conditions of Siberia. In terms of his political argument, this insight forms the first step towards his argument for decentralized governance, in which the leaders are replaced by a mass of people who provide the collective and constructive genius that leads a society out of difficult times and towards progress.

Popular belief suggests that if we let the people rule, nothing but selfishness will flourish. Thus, it is suggested that we will need leaders, who will serve the collective interest. We have seen how Kropotkin argues that many animals are engaged in ethical relationships. We humans share both the ethical and selfish/survival traits, yet we seem to often emphasize the latter. Instead of regarding human nature itself as predominantly selfish, according to Kropotkin, our political and leadership systems should be blamed. More precisely this means that in democracy as it currently functions people become selfish because there is no longer a collective, no mutual aid, and no feeling of responsibility. Individualism has created a false sense of independence, in which we now think we do not need to cooperate if we have the financial means to buy our food, goods, and support.

In the previous chapter, I discussed how Steinbeck explains our tendencies partially through the phalanx, in which we are always pulled towards group behavior. A collective can turn negative. For Kropotkin, the negative dynamic is mostly discussed as a turn away from the collective. This raises a straightforward (and rhetorical) question: what is the collective interest without the collective? Kropotkin indicates that human societies often nourish what he calls the "egoistic, individualistic instincts."[39] As already indicated, part of the problem of human ethical theory as identified by Kropotkin is that ethics fails to identify the scientific origin of duty, appealing instead to forces outside of nature. By moving outside of nature, to the metaphysical, ethics itself becomes something else than what it naturally is.

In *Ethics*, Kropotkin writes that ethics "aims at *the development of social habits and the weakening of the narrowly personal habits.*"[40] As we have seen, he does not consider ethics as a descriptive discipline, nor is it only prescriptive in the sense of what we should do. Ethics should not only tell us what to do, but also what to be. It tells us who we are or who we should be, recreating us into a new state of being in which we will leave the path of selfishness and move to a more altruistic state. It is clear to him that it is our society as well as our economic and political system that needs to transform, which will likewise create a new ethic: one that is more natural and emphasizes cooperation over anything else. The natural and scientific background to this is that we, by nature, already possess altruism. It often conflicts with selfish tendencies, but the task of ethics is to prevent selfish tendencies from dominating and to encourage our social/altruistic instinct.[41]

Anarchistic Ants

I am now turning to one of the social insects, the ant, a species sometimes called anarchistic because of its decentralized decision-making and problem-solving. I turn here to the biology of ants in order to get a sense of their behavior as a colony and a species. They certainly cooperate, yet we can wonder if they portray any ethical tendencies. My questions here include to what degree we act like ants and if perhaps our ant behavior leads to some of our problems.

We have seen that for Kropotkin, human progress should be attributed to the mass of people, not the leaders. The same can be said about social insects. In their study of ants, Laurant Keller and Élisabeth Gordon marvel at the tremendous success of ants: "These tiny creatures have not only managed to set foot on all five continents but have overrun them and thoroughly colonized them."[42] They state the reason for their success as "sociality." We might immediately notice a similarity here between ants and humans in the sense that we are colonizers, following our urge—in Steinbeck's words—to "western." Yet, in the case of humans, we cannot call our colonization "a fine ecological achievement" as Keller and Gordon describe ants who clean up the forest as "ecosystem engineers."[43] We humans might try to engineer ecosystems, yet almost always with destructive consequences. Ants have been around much longer than humans (around 100 to 130 million years as opposed to a mere 200,000 years for humans). They live in a strictly hierarchical society without government and, thus, are sometimes called "anarchist socialists" (Wheeler) or Marxist socialists (Wilson and Hölldobler).[44] From a perspective of freedom and human rights, the highly hierarchical structure we find in an ant colony is far from desirable, and it is obvious, as E. O. Wilson states in the prologue to his novel *Anthill*, that there are "of course vast differences between ants and men. Nevertheless, in fundamental ways their cycles are similar."[45] Following this, he provides a warning we can find in the life cycle of the ant colony: "The colonies grow and struggle and sometimes they triumph over their neighbors. Then they die, always."[46] Along similar lines he writes about humans: "For each careless step we take, our species will ultimately pay an unwelcome price—always."[47] The cycles of ants and humans "are similar" he writes, "there is something genetic about this convergence. Because of it, ants are a metaphor for us, and we for them."[48] Yet, the convergence of human and ant cycles is not merely a metaphor. The relationship is, as he states, genetic. In his novel, Wilson explores this idea by following an ant colony along with a human family. Ant colonies die when the queen dies, yet if successful, her genes will continue in her offspring through the forming of other colonies. Likewise, human offspring can form their own family while the old family eventually dies. The novel includes a matriarch aunt, resembling the ant queen, and Wilson draws many other parallels between human and ant families. Perhaps most notably, he describes the colony from the perspective of the ants, providing insights into the collective mind of the colony, the superorganism. Similar to what we see in Kropotkin, in De Waal, and in Steinbeck and Ricketts (as well as biologists, such as Allee and Ritter, who influenced them), two main tendencies can be triggered in animals: a more altruistic (or, more broadly, cooperative) or a combative one. For Steinbeck it was the phalanx that pulled us in a particular direction. Similarly, ants are pulled by the collective mind of the colony. Wilson's warning indicates that both ants and humans die collectively if careless steps are taken. The ant colony will die and so will the human colony. For humans living as a colony on a global scale, carelessness is a threat to the species itself.

Biologist Deborah Gordon is specifically interested in how ant colonies can work together without a central power that makes decisions. Although they live as a collective, decisions are made at the level of each and every individual through interactions with the group and with their environment. She describes ant collaboration in terms of a "task allocation" which is "the process that results in certain workers engaged in specific tasks, in numbers appropriate to the current situation."[49] While the needs of the colony are complex and while it is difficult to imagine how a colony functions without central control, "each worker need make only simple decisions . . . simple behavior in individuals can lead to predictable patterns in the behavior of groups. It should be possible to explain task allocation in a similar way, as the consequence of simple decisions by individuals."[50] Gordon's research has shown that a colony adjusts to changing circumstances. When foragers bring in less food, fewer (not more, as we might expect) foragers go out for food, to preserve energy. When the nest maintenance needs extra attention (because Gordon placed some toothpicks at the entrance), more workers became engaged in this task. In addition, in these kinds of situations, different activities are influenced. For example, in the situation in which fewer ants go out foraging, more activity is witnessed at nest maintenance. The dynamics of these changes are complex, with some ants remaining inactive (instead of switching tasks—since certain tasks are only performed by a certain class). According to Gordon, within this complexity of nuanced factors, we witness that simple decisions by individual ants lead to successful task allocation, energy preservation, nest maintenance, and so forth. It is described as a process far from exact: "The process results in more or less the right number of ants engaged in the appropriate task, often enough for the colony to carry on."[51] Gordon compares ant task allocation to human activities, such as allocating the right number of firefighters to a fire, or having the right number of firefighters on the payroll without wasting the city budget, while prepared for calamities. Echoing Steinbeck, we could suggest that we are ant-like in making sure the group "carries on."

Laurent Keller and Élisabeth Gordon point to Wheeler's observation that resemblances between ants and humans were already recognized by aboriginals.[52] As exemplified earlier in chapter 1 on salmon, aboriginal cultures often recognize kinship relations between animals and humans. The recognition of these relationships leads to a sense of respect for non-human societies. With that said, ants should not be romanticized, and as suggested in the following section, perhaps we should fear our own ant-like capacities. The division of labor in ants, in which many are sacrificed for the good of the colony, is problematic. Even more, it represents exactly what is wrong with many human societies. Aside from slavery and indentured labor, we can wonder how people who work two decades to pay back student loans obtained for an education required for a job are in any essential way different from ants that work for the greater good of the colony.[53] Although ants do not have student loans, they are part of a system, the collective mind of the colony, or the superorganism. I will assume they are not aware of what the common good might be, but as I will discuss with Abbey in the next section, and as suggested in the introduction to this book, we humans fail to agree on what the common good is. If we do agree, we find a rather perverse sense of the common good: gross national product, also known as growth for the sake of growth. We might be fairly similar to ants in following this demand (or urge) to grow.

As indicated by Wilson, colonies always fail, and in that regard, we also might be much like ants. As empires rise to power and expand, they seem invincible, yet as Rousseau already warned us, they always fail. Likewise, species often fail. The ants are successful ecological engineers and have lived for a long time. An ecologically destructive ant-like engineer, such as the human species, is unlikely to come even close to that success.

Perhaps our similarities with ants, our kinship, are hard to accept. As Wilson suggests, we can first and foremost learn who we are by thinking about how our cycles are fundamentally similar. While Kropotkin discusses animals that work together in large or small collectives and display ethical behavior, Wilson warns us against the destructive aspects. We have seen with the phalanx that groups can be negative and even incredibly dangerous.[54] In human contexts we often attempt to solve these problems by implementing certain principles that cannot be violated (such as "no individual or group shall in any way be treated differently or discriminated against based on their gender, race, sexual orientation, religion, nationality, legal status, or species"). Instead of stating principles or formulating laws, I suggest inspiring and encouraging new ways of thinking and being, based on a return to the simple insight that we are dependent on other living, as well as nonliving, beings and share the same building blocks. In this recognition of ourselves as part of the larger world, we can cultivate different kinds of affection, perhaps even affections that lie beyond juxtaposed emotions, such as those of love and hate. Empathy, sympathy, or compassion could play a significant role in this. We have to work towards societies that encourage emotions that stimulate the natural drive to cooperate instead of our destructive warlike tendencies.

Human Ants

I now turn to the anarchistic politics of Edward Abbey through whom we will find different ways to reflect back on ants and our destructive tendencies. Abbey encouraged the sabotage (or ecotage) of the machinery used for deforestation, road building, mining, and other practices that destroy ecosystems. I will start by prefacing this section by clarifying that ecotage, or radical environmentalism, is not a route I would encourage anyone to choose. Besides the dangers, including endangering others, this form of activism seems rather counterproductive, often generating more carbon emissions since whatever is destroyed will be replaced. There is no attempt at dialogue, and the result is anger and opposition toward environmentalists. Ecotage is aimed at the tools of destruction, not at the mindset that builds these tools. The sabotage of Edward Abbey's "Monkey Wrench Gang" is problematic as a strategy and at best provides only a brief solution. The industry of the workers who operate the machinery is redirected to fixing or replacing the machines. It might delay the completion of a road by a few months, but it will not stop the process. Radical environmental movements such as the Earth Liberation Front (ELF) have reversed their tactics and have advised to not burn down more properties since it merely creates greenhouse gas emissions after which whatever is burned down is rebuilt.[55] In other words, ecotage does not work. What we need instead is a change in our collective mindset. Yet, I discuss Edward Abbey exactly because he, as a gadfly, makes us wonder what else we can do. I argue that the destruction of the machinery as discussed in his work is ultimately asking us to change who we are.

Edward Abbey was an inspiration for the radical environmental movement and was on the FBI Watch List ever since he was an undergraduate philosophy and English major.[56] A philosopher at heart, he used fiction and irony as a way to express his ideas. He was a gadfly, "corrupting" those who tried to save the last pieces of American wilderness with radical methods. While one, indeed, could argue that he was in some ways a Socrates (and as a writer, a Plato) of his time, we are immediately confronted with a stark difference. While Socrates was law-abiding (and Martin Luther King Jr., who compared himself to Socrates, broke unjust laws via civil disobedience), Abbey argued that circumstances can entitle one to break the law. With that, their views of authority and government starkly differ, which is made evident in *The Republic*, where Plato famously describes the ideal state as led by the "philosopher king" while Abbey is extremely pessimistic about the possibility of any kind of government to work well. It is, arguably, not entirely clear how serious we should take Plato's and Socrates's suggestions: were they perhaps merely trying to criticize the existing democracy in Athens, full of influence by the wealthy, led by the sons of the wealthy who were trained by sophists to speak well, without any true knowledge? Although their criticism of the Athenian state is to be taken seriously, it is not so clear if we should take their suggestions literally, or if they perhaps, as good gadflies, wanted to stir things up.

We find similar problems in interpreting Abbey. A novel such as *The Monkey Wrench Gang*—which will be the central text this section—is a work of fiction and thus does not necessarily express Abbey's own ideas.

The "anarchist" novel is in many ways extremely humorous, and within that context, it might sometimes be hard to take anything that is said seriously. Nevertheless, the seriousness of the novel should not be underestimated since it became a call for action to disrupt the destruction of the American wilderness and inspired groups such as Earth First! In addition, underlying the hilarious character's adventures, we find a serious philosophical contemplation on issues such as the destruction of the American wilderness, responsibility, and government. An important background is that as a philosophy MA student, Abbey completed a thesis on anarchism and the morality of violence. In his detailed reflection in his thesis, he argues that violence is to be used only as a last resort and should only be directed at the destruction of machines. *The Monkey Wrench Gang* also seems in line with nonfiction writings such as Abbey's foreword ("Forward!") to Foreman's *Ecodefense*. In acknowledging these difficulties of interpreting Abbey, I do not promise a "true reading"—if there ever was such a thing—of his work. My reading can be regarded as a generous one, often giving him the benefit of the doubt, and possibly reflecting my hopes more than his true intentions. Nevertheless, I will always provide textual evidence to support my (generous) interpretation of Abbey.

For the reader unfamiliar with this novel: *The Monkey Wrench Gang* describes the adventures of a group of four dissidents who want to save part of the American wilderness by attacking the machinery that destroys it. Their activities consist of sabotaging heavy machinery such as bulldozers and a coal train, pulling up survey stakes, destroying bridges, or burning down billboards. Throughout the story, the gang often reflects on their activities, what they should do and should not do, why they should (not) do it, and what methods they allow themselves to use. Meanwhile law enforcement—mostly driven by personal conflict and greed—is slowly closing in on them.

Abbey uses an eclectic mix of characters to successfully bring across a message of anarchy. The potential of anarchism, along with its problems, seems to be expressed exactly by the haphazard gang consisting of Doc Sarvis (a widowed surgeon whose hobby consists of the destruction of billboards), Bonnie Abzug (Doc's assistant and lover who lives and meditates in her self-built geodesic dome—much hated and often ridiculed by Doc), Smith (a Mormon river guide who is "seldom seen" by his three wives), and Hayduke (a psychopathic and traumatized gun-loving Vietnam veteran). Their discussions, first of all, radically question "the common good." They are opposing the common good of economic growth, measured by the GNP. That common good is promoted by the government and destroys another common good—the American wilderness. It is exactly the intention of the gang to target the machinery that destroys the American wilderness, which is a full-on attack on the ideals of the American lifestyle of consumerism. Politicians build roads and infrastructure for an envisioned future, and for Abbey, the mass is just manipulated by whatever government commands them to do. We find again the group at work. For Kropotkin, Steinbeck, and Wilson, the group has its own mind and urges. In Abbey, the group is ultimately shaped around the idea of government as a powerful institution planning a future not necessarily wanted by the people but is instead driven by the interests of corporations. One could say that this is the problem in contemporary democracies and societies in which the only legal obligation of a corporation consists in creating profits for the shareholders. Why groups of people (whether we call them "a herd" or "a phalanx") who are largely victims of these policies and the resulting practices are not rebelling can be explained by the dynamics of groups, as we found in Steinbeck. In a group, one is taken by feelings of the collective, and these feelings plow everything else out of the way. Thus, we become convinced that anything but the current reality is possible. We are told that universal health care, ending global warming, providing equal education to all, or raising the minimum wage are all impossible. In addition, we are facing a very loose relationship with facts, in which for example climate change is blatantly denied. In the "alternative facts" world, it is even delusional to want a society without bigotry, hatred, cruelty, with equal opportunities, and lower carbon emissions because our "problem" does not exist or is exaggerated.

Going back to Abbey, he opposed the reality of a democracy run by corporate forces. As mentioned, the need to oppose the destructive forces of capitalism is not only expressed in Abbey's fiction. In the excerpt—"Forward!"—to Foreman's *Ecodefense: A Field Guide to Monkey Wrenching*, he writes:

> If a stranger batters your door down with an axe, threatens your family and yourself with deadly weapons, and proceeds to loot your home of whatever he wants, he is committing what is universally recognized—by law and morality—as a crime. In such a situation the householder has both the right and the obligation to defend himself, his family, and his property by whatever means are necessary. This right and this obligation is universally recognized, justified and even praised by all civilized human communities. Self-defense against attack is one of the

basic laws not only of human society but of life itself, not only of human life but of all life.

The American wilderness, what little remains, is now undergoing exactly such an assault.[57]

His argument is suggesting that we indeed have the right, and even an obligation, to defend the American wilderness. The analogy he offers between one's household and the American wilderness is not without problems. Abbey does not simply refer to the property as the house you pay a mortgage on—complicated enough in its own right—but he ties wilderness to the self-defense of life itself as a basic law.[58] Yet, the wilderness is not our home and to many even the opposite of home. Our homes might be built from the materials extracted from the wilderness, but we do not live in the wilderness. We live in cities, towns, villages, or suburbs. As our lives become more urban and wilderness becomes scarcer, the argument that the wilderness is our true home becomes less convincing. It is the machine of the capitalist consumer society that keeps furthering this division, and it is ultimately capitalism that we should fight, while Abbey's Monkey Wrench Gang is merely sabotaging the tools that destroy the American wilderness. The larger fight should aim for a return to the idea that wilderness is a common good, of which we become a part as a keystone species.

In using the argument of self-defense, Abbey grounds the right to ecotage in a natural law to sustain oneself. Ants, bees, and wasps will systematically attack an intruder; trees will strive for light and water, and procreate in ingenious ways. Regardless of whether we call this a will, a striving, an urge, an instinct, or a conatus, this basic law of nature is found in all life. It is this law that Abbey sees as the link to our right to defend the American wilderness: if we lose the last pieces of wilderness, if we let companies pollute our waterways and drinking water, and let them release toxins in the air, our own life is threatened. Ecotage, in that sense, should, for Abbey, be regarded as a basic right to self-defense. While in the United States environmentalists who have resorted to radical means of activism (such as burning down destructive businesses) have been tried as domestic terrorists, Abbey paints the opposite picture: the corporations and the governments that support them are the terrorists violently threatening our home and family.

For Abbey, we are faced with an ethical demand to stop mining, the destruction of forests, and the building of roads, bridges, and dams. The need for access to a seemingly unlimited amount of electricity, wood, paper, and the convenience of driving are all false productions of the common good. Hayduke, the veteran, argues that if we do not sabotage the destruction, we approve of it. When the others express their doubts about the use of explosives, he states (and lies, for he loves explosives) in an ironic mood:

> "I don't like it either . . . I'd a hell of a lot rather forget the whole thing and go fly fishing down on West Horse Creek. Let's forget Black Mesa. Let the coal company tear it up. Who cares if five years from now you can't see fifteen miles across the Grand Canyon because the air is so fucked up by these motherfucking new power plants. I'd rather be picking columbines up in the mountains above Telluride anyhow. Why the hell should we worry about it?"[59]

Hayduke here presents, in a way, our current predicament in which we keep postponing true solutions to the problem of climate change and extinction. We might choose to enjoy what is left of the wilderness before it disappears altogether, especially since the fight seems impossible.

Abbey (the gadfly), thus, makes us wonder: what, if anything, should or could we do? If we cannot change the mindset that destroys, should we destroy the tools of destruction? If not this, what else can we do in such a desperate situation? We are not only defending the last pieces of wilderness, we are defending the air we breathe, the water we drink, the food we eat, and the places where we and all other creatures live. How does one stop these maniacal, ant-like creatures with machines that mine and harvest the land and sea, every last bit of it?

In a democracy we can vote, protest, write, or resort to civil disobedience. Abbey recognizes the urgency of the situation, as well as the fact that people do not come to their senses. Thus, he has no faith in democracy and government at all. He suggests resorting to radical and violent methods. His approach is clear: nothing will stop the destruction unless we take matters into our own hands.

Abbey's willingness to use radical and destructive methods is rooted in his deep suspicions about groups. He considers group behavior to be a disaster, bringing out the stupidity of people. He expresses this, for example, when the Monkey Wrench Gang attempts to escape the law enforcement group that is closing in on them. They decide to send their pursuers in the wrong direction by walking backward, printing footsteps in the sand. Yet, they wonder if their pursuers will be stupid enough to fall for such a simple trick. Through the character of Smith, Abbey provides a damning and striking observation about groups making collective decisions: "One man alone can be pretty dumb sometimes, but for real bona fide stupidity, there ain't nothing can beat teamwork."[60] We have all experienced how groups can act stupidly, from groups of teenagers (or even adults) collectively taking up smoking, to masses of adults who listen to and vote for a demagogue, or lines of people waiting to pay for parking at machines, collectively missing the vacant machines behind them. It seems fair to suggest that within the context of Abbey's anti-government approach, we can read his comments on group dynamics as a reflection on democracy, the massive group of individuals that massively makes poor decisions, being tricked by incredibly simple ruses that no individual would fall for. Thus, "real bona fide stupidity" turns into leaders who fail us on every level, who trick us into believing they will represent us and fight for our interests and not those of corporations or of their own. We vote for individuals whom we would not even lend twenty dollars to if they personally asked us since we know we will never receive it back. Yet, as a collective, we give them the power to run our country. The psychology of the group includes the fear of individuals diverting from the group. In the chapter on Steinbeck and Ricketts, I have discussed the more positive sides of group being, as well as its dangers. Kropotkin and the biologists who inspired Steinbeck and Ricketts suggest that cooperation among all animals is the key to the success of life. Abbey provides a very negative assessment of group being, and for him the only solution is to escape the group (whereas for Steinbeck and Kropotkin such an escape seems impossible). Generally speaking, doing something else than the herd is risky, since it might make one look stupid. Thinkers such as Nietzsche and Sartre show how we are often afraid to take responsibility. By staying with the group, no individual can be blamed, or at least we tend to think so. In addition, individuals often rely on the false idea that the group as a whole knows more, and thus they do not want to question that larger intelligence. Perhaps, this shows again we are part of a collective mind similar to ants.

 Can we envision politics without "the bona fide stupidity" of a group (aka democracy) and even more, without any government? Abbey is highly suspicious of any form of government, and this is expressed on a few different levels in the novel. One way to look at this is through the functioning of "the gang" itself. The four function together, initially, by a somewhat democratic model. During their deliberations, it is typically Hayduke, the veteran, who is the minority. Yet, as their tactics tend to become more violent because of their use of explosives, Bonnie starts to side with him, eventually drawing the other two men in. It is around this point that their decision-making process changes. Hayduke wants to vote (even while he seems to be in the minority), but Doc (who might have won the vote) does not want to vote. A page later, he explains: "I don't believe in majority rule. You know that. I am against all forms of government, including good government. I hold with the consensus of the community here. Whatever it may be. Wherever it may lead."[61] It is perhaps a hilarious statement to say that one is against all government, including good government, but the humor should not obscure its depth. The question becomes who or what determines good government or good politics? Who determines "good"? If "good government" is allowing corporations to gut what is left of the American wilderness, we should, in Abbey's mind, be against it. Likewise, if the Monkey Wrench Gang itself governs well, Abbey, or at least Doc, would still be against it. "Good" in this instance is also drawing on the stupidity of the group (the men being drawn to Bonnie, possibly for the wrong reasons).

The statement brings out a tension between "the consensus of the community" (the Monkey Wrench Gang) and "the stupidity of the group." As we saw in the description of the bona fide stupidity, the consensus of the group can lead to disaster. Likewise, the destruction of the American wilderness can be regarded as the result of the consensus. Moreover, the accord of the Monkey Wrench Gang is based on a "dissensus" with the larger community.[62] In a sense, they find themselves in a situation in which they have to make decisions without regarding themselves as a government. Their rule is to disrupt and work against the machine of destruction. They oppose growth and power and ultimately governance: "Who's in charge here? We're all in charge here, Bonnie says. Nobody's in charge here, says Doc."[63] The last thing Doc wants is a democracy, which would provide a false sense of everyone being in charge, of cooperation, while it is in fact based on a false sense of group feeling. While explicitly against voting and democracy, Abbey seems to support consensus, which is not to be confused with voting, yet it remains unclear how the consensus will avoid the stupidity of the group.

Abbey disrupts the common view of the American lifestyle by making some striking and discomforting observations about all of us. Since what does a government do? What do our politics accomplish? Doc says:

> "All this fantastic effort—giant machines, road networks, strip mines, conveyor belts, pipelines, slurry lines, loading towers,

154 | Ecopolitics

> railway and electric train, hundred-million-dollar coal-burning power plant; ten thousand miles of high-tension towers and high-voltage power lines; the devastation of the landscape, the destruction of Indian homes and Indian grazing lands, Indian shrines and Indian burial grounds; the poisoning of the last big clean-air reservoir in the forty-eight contiguous United States, the exhaustion of precious water supplies—all that ball-breaking labor and all that backbreaking expense and all that heartbreaking insult to land and sky and human heart, for what? All that for what? Why, to light the lamps of Phoenix suburbs not yet built, to run the air conditioners of San Diego and Los Angeles, to illuminate shopping-center parking lots at two in the morning, to power aluminum plants, magnesium plants, vinyl chloride factories and copper smelters, to charge the neon tubing that makes the meaning (all the meaning there is) of Las Vegas, Albuquerque, Tucson, Salt Lake City, the amalgamated *metropoli* of Southern California, to keep alive that phosphorescent putrefying glory (all the glory there is left) called Down Town, Night Time, Wonderville, U.S.A."[64]

Abbey presents here one of the main problems of capitalism, which is always pointlessly seeking to grow. It can only flourish by selling unwanted and unneeded products and services. The ridiculous problem of overproduction was already discussed by Marx who argues that although capitalism and industrialization bring efficiency, their results are the opposite of a more comfortable and happier life.

In the previous sections of this chapter, we saw that ants function in an anarchistic way and could possibly (but cautiously) be compared to human societies in the sense that they follow the same cycles (E. O. Wilson) and engage in similar forms of task allocation (D. Gordon). Abbey considers ants to be a representation of the forces that destroy our natural environment. He compares human activity to that of ants that keep on working. It is Doc who expresses his hatred of ants and their colonies after he steps onto an ant nest and is bit:

> "The anthill . . . is sign, symbol and symptom of what we are about here, stumbling through the gloaming like so many stumblebums. I mean it is the model in microcosm of what we must find a way to oppose and halt. The anthill, like the Fulle-

rian foam fungus, is the mark of social disease. Anthills abound where overgrazing prevails. The plastic dome follows the plague of runaway industrialism, prefigures technological tyranny and reveals the true quality of our lives, which sinks in inverse ratio to the growth of the Gross National Product."[65]

Perhaps Abbey here appeals to a Cartesian image of the animal as a machine since he draws a parallel between the anthill and technological tyranny. Seeing a coal mining operation doing its business, Smith ("Seldom Seen") states " 'It's a mechanical animal.' 'Now you've got it.' Doc agreed. 'We're not dealing with human beings. We're up against the megamachine. A megalomaniac megamachine."[66] Besides the mechanical animal, Abbey also uses organic images, for example, when Doc speaks of "A planetary industrialism . . . growing like a cancer. Growth for the sake of growth. Power for the sake of power."[67] Interestingly, Abbey presents us with negative images of (mechanical) animals and organisms to paint a picture of "what we are up against." Besides a non-romantic view of nature, more importantly, this implies that technology and industrialism itself are organic and natural. In this mechanical animal that grows like a tumor, the behavior of the group is regarded as a natural process that we should fight, and for Abbey, it is, seemingly, another justification to use violence.

Abbey seems to be specifically suspicious of spheres, which represent the ideal of the engineer, opposing wilderness. He (without using any of the characters) writes: "The engineer's dream is a model of perfect sphericity, the planet Earth with all irregularities removed, highways merely painted on a surface smooth as glass. Of course, the engineers still have a long way to go but they are patient tireless little fellows; they keep hustling on, like termites in a termitarium."[68] Social insects, such as ants and termites, keep working and growing like a fungus, and while many biologists can find appreciation for their work, Abbey fails to find anything positive in their industry.

Is it perhaps our problem that we are too much like ants or termites? Are the negative outcomes, or our need to grow, rooted in an ant-like or termite-like urge? While building new roads that perhaps result in the ability to move a little faster from A to B, making the world a little smaller, it is ultimately useless and destructive. We know all too well how this works in heavily populated areas. If there is too much traffic or a bottleneck, we add a lane, metered lights, more entrances, or a loop around the bottleneck, after which traffic gets stuck in another location. If traffic flows improve, it will invite more cars, and eventually, traffic will be the same and more communities, green spaces, or farmlands need to be uprooted to create more asphalt. In rural areas, roads and bridges are in the service of the companies that provide energy and natural resources, aiding in accelerating the speed of deforestation and destroying whatever is left of the habitats of non-human animals.

Here, one could object that today in many cities we find a reverse movement in terms of greening cities, creating pedestrian areas, bicycle paths, lake, and river parks, and so forth. These are welcome developments, in which our ant-like industry is used for regreening and in some cases, even rewilding. Yet, the greening of cities is often driven by and driving a gentrification process. The neoliberal agenda is using the "regreening" efforts to sell cities and apartments. It will keep us on the same path of consumption and greed, and oppose a true collaborative society. In that regard, it will not be sufficient to reverse the path we are on. As Uri Gordon points out, a problem created by capitalism is not going to be solved by capitalism, since we will still run out of resources.[69] Along similar lines, he points out that the results of climate change, such as wildfires and flooding, should not be regarded as management problems, but as social problems.[70] As long as we keep tearing down forests, emitting toxins in the air and waterways, and destroying any wilderness that is left, a "greening" of cities is merely symbolic and a further distraction from the problem. A different approach is needed and possible.

How are we to overcome these social problems? If we want to maneuver ourselves outside of the neoliberal or capitalist framework, this will be the key question that needs to be answered. If we accept that we have ant-like capacities and tendencies, we can ask how we can create the social circumstances in which our energies lead to more positive activities. How, in Steinbeck's words, can we create a more positive phalanx or make sure we are the right material for one? We need to establish a way of thinking that refuses the growth for the sake of growth doctrine. A more radical change, a social change, is necessary to stop the process.

Is such a change possible? Can we become less ant-like? In the conclusion of this chapter, I will return to the more theoretical, anarchistic approach of Kropotkin in order to bring the different threads of this chapter together.

Conclusion

I started this chapter with the question of what we could learn from ant societies—their political anarchistic system. It seems now that we, as industrious beings, are perhaps too much like ants. Within the context of capitalism, our productivity, and with that the destruction of habitats of both human and non-human animals, has become destructive to the health of our planet. Our social instincts have been mostly suppressed, or used for production, while the selfish one is encouraged.

What are the lessons from this study of ants? Anarchism as we find it in ants certainly does not seem to provide an ideal model. It is often argued that anarchism will never work, certainly not beyond small groups and not long term. The reasons provided for failure typically lie in the realm of our tendency to either act on selfish grounds or to let our "animal" instincts take over. Thus, it is argued that without leadership no one is protected, and we end up at the mercy of one another. As mentioned at the outset of this chapter, considering our violent histories such warnings are not without reason. Within that context, I want to raise the following question: why do humans, as opposed to some other animals, fail to function without a top-down hierarchical system of organization? We have seen how ants function successfully in a decentralized, anarchistic model of cooperation. From that example, I will now propose two opposite directions. The first proposes that we should perhaps become more like ants (or some other social insect) in the sense that we can move towards better collaboration and better collective decision-making. For Kropotkin, the group is not the issue, it is the context in which we function. In fact, for him we should return to the group, sharing property and become more communal in our existence, perhaps more like ants. Some existing structures in our current society are anarchistic in nature. From public libraries (free sharing of knowledge), to crowdsourced software, to DIY music scenes in which concerts, tours, and labels are run without the exchange of money, contracts, or lawyers. All these show the potentially positive results of our group being. In chapter 4, I discussed Ricketts's idea that the tidepool is an unmasked replica of our own society and that (for Steinbeck and Ricketts) we are, like all other animals, driven towards group being. Also for them this is not necessarily negative, but it is a force to reckon with.

With those ideas in mind, I suggest a second opposite possibility, namely that we are too similar to ants in the sense that we simply follow the will of the group, even while in some cases, this might be plain stupidity or even suicidal. We have seen how the division of labor of ants leads to inequality, and in that regard Kropotkin would not want us to become antlike. Following the Darwinist route, we could even suggest that our tendency towards creating and, moreover, accepting societies with great inequalities might be rooted in the genes we share with ants. Different from ants, we function through management, centralized governments, and laws. All of this might, as Kropotkin suggests, make things worse for our ant-like existence. It creates further divisions and environmental destruction on such a scale that it can not only wipe out a group, but has already wiped out countless species, and will eventually wipe out our own.

Perhaps, we can suggest, with Nietzsche, that we have to step beyond our ant-like being and become something entirely different.[71] Being attracted to the herd is exactly the problem for Nietzsche since we do not become who we are. We, instead, are everyone else. Abbey's comparison of the work of humans to that of ants, can—in a Nietzschean way—be understood as our animal nature that makes us act in certain ways. It makes us dig, move, build, etc. It also makes us move towards the group, and it is here we find a tremendous difference between Abbey and Kropotkin: for the latter, we need to move to a collaborative model whereas for Abbey (as for Nietzsche) we should exactly not be like animals, but overcome this drive.

Yet, returning to Steinbeck's phalanx (chapter 4), we should also acknowledge that group being is an essential part of who we are and that we cannot simply stop being ants. Even more, in Kropotkin's natural ethics it is in fact a retreat out of our solitary existence back into a communal existence. It is not the natural ant-like capacities that generate our problems. The problem is instead the kind of group we are a part of: a capitalist, democratic society, combined with a metaphysically grounded ethics that justifies the unjust.

Taking into account that we are drawn towards groups, and that we need groups that make us into better beings, I propose a return to the original intention of democracy, in a decentralized manner. I am not suggesting the abolishment of government (as in some forms of anarchism) or moving towards a libertarian form in which government becomes smaller (as in some other typically right-leaning forms of anarchism). Rather, government becomes bigger, exactly by decentralizing. The government becomes the mass of all people, non-human animals, life, and that which makes life possible. Government becomes all the living relationships that tie us to one another and to the earth that is our home.

We are facing two important questions in this regard: (1) How will decentralized politics solve and/or avoid our problems of ant-like colonization and overconsumption? and (2) How can we move towards such a new system of governing? The most basic answer lies in a different mentality, a different kind of humanity, in which ethics is restored, in which sympathy or empathy is encouraged, and in which we experience ourselves as an integral part of a greater unity without which we could not exist. This simple realization acknowledges that it is not the uncertainty of a decentralized government that should scare us. What should really scare us is the current path we are on, in which we are separated from and opposed to the rest of the world.

If we follow Kropotkin, it seems that we do not need to invent this new form of politics. Mass self-governance to which all members of a community contribute (without endless meetings) seems daunting, yet the problem is not that we do not want to collaborate or that we are incapable of doing so. As mentioned earlier, many aboriginal societies functioned on the basis of anarchist structures. The problem is that the current system makes us believe any alternatives are unrealistic while our social circumstances force us to fight one another and dig in to promote our own interests. Within that fight and focus on individual interests, the alternatives remain unrealistic. Once we change this, and with that the political, social, and economic circumstances in which we live, "the impossible" becomes the only possible way forward.

It is then time to become something else, to move to a more natural existence in which ethics is truly ethical. It is not merely a rethinking of our political systems and how we function as a political unity. It is moreover a rethinking and reinvention of what it can mean to be political animals and thus a rethinking of who we are. To put it differently, our whole being: who we are, what we are, how we think, and how we are affected or related to one another is brought into question.

Conclusion

Ecopolitics as a Decentralized Basis for a New Future

Echoing Marx and Engels's specter of the *Communist Manifesto*, I suggest that there is another ghostly existence haunting us today. It is not a single specter and is not situated only on the left. It is a specter generated by climate change, unequal distribution of wealth, systemic racism, refugees, and a failed politics of representation, all brought onto a collision course through social media. Refugees are approaching Europe in great numbers; in cities, homeless encampments are common sights; the world is literally on fire; world powers are shifting; no job is secure; student loan debts are immense; demagogues get elected; protests from the left and right turn violent; and conspiracies are generated and quickly find followers. Social media spews out more disinformation than all collective news outlets can keep up with. A global pandemic has laid bare the problems of inequality, distrust in government and science, and lack of solidarity. It is a disorganized series of specters, often poorly informed, yet fueled by a feeling that things are not well. Arguably we need something like Marx's call for a unity of all workers. We already see success in the unified protests against police brutality through the global Black Lives Matter movement. Likewise, the Occupy movement, the Dakota Access Pipeline protests, Women Marches, the Thirty Meter Telescope protests, and the MeToo movement (to name a few) address long-standing injustices. While they have not led to a true revolt, they are signs that unrest is brewing and that we want change. Marx and Engels suggest that capitalism creates gravediggers, and it may very well be that refugees, homeless people, the poor, those in debt, those with underpaid jobs, the unemployed, Indigenous communities, the descendants of slaves, along with those suffering from the results of climate chaos, will be the gravediggers of capitalism in the form of a collective resistance to greed. If we can stay away from the new opium for the people, "smart" technology that takes over our communication and interaction with others, or steer this technology in new and useful directions, change might be upon us. We also need to recognize that the different problems the respective groups are facing (such as racism, environmental destruction, and sexism) are interrelated and caused by the same greed, narcissism, and individualism.

In the previous chapters I have argued that different animal societies exist as political units. They are political in the sense that they cooperate. More importantly, my claim is that human political societies are not radically different from these other communities. We collaborate in a variety of ways. We use some ant strategies, salmon tactics, monkey politics, are attracted to group being, sometimes with the addition of some rat empathy, and as a group we move like an amoeba.

We typically associate "politics" with power centralized in city halls, state capitals, or the seat of the government. Capitol Hill, the White House, the House of Commons, Downing Street, or Brussels have become the household names for politics. We find here the display of power, wealth, and/or the "dictatorship of democracy" in which only a few wield all the power. This leads us to the typical criticism that our votes have been transformed into a show of manipulation leading to decisions that are mostly determined by the industries that sponsor the parties and individuals "in power." Furthermore, I suggest that the displays of power occurring in places such as Washington, DC, are not worthy of the name politics and certainly not of *dēmokratia,* the power of the people. Through individualization, in which money and the appearance of having money has become the measure of everything including power, we have effectively stopped being political. Monetary exchange has impoverished all interaction. Community and collaboration towards the common good is a foreign idea. What we now call politics is indeed centered around money. A politician's rise to power and the measurement of their success is determined by it. One can be a pathological liar who disregards the constitution of one's country, obstructs justice, spreads hate through bullying and racist messages, makes disparaging remarks about women, gets accused of sexual assault, makes enormous consequential foreign policy blunders, considers a global pandemic that kills millions of people a hoax, threatens democracy itself in all possible ways, and against all evidence, still claim to have won reelection. Presumably Mr. Trump knows better himself, but for a considerable number of people, he speaks (or is) the truth. How can we deny reality around election results, climate change, or our own health? Politics as we today know it is in fact anti-political. It does not want participation or community, or only creates polarizing and destructive communities. It only further pulls us in the delusions that the corporate world successfully creates *for* us. In a polarized world, it seems that the aim to successfully live together as citizens has failed. Things, indeed, are not well. The Trump presidency itself (as well as the election of demagogues in Europe) is a symptom of our failures as a human society.

Significant percentages of people either don't bother to vote or vote with little enthusiasm. Around us, we hear pleas to not "politicize" certain issues, and we know better than to bring up our so-called "political views" with a perfect stranger. What we call "politics" within the context of capitalism is equivalent to power and extraordinary wealth in the hands of a few who serve in industries and the corporate world. Elections are run and determined by money and social media, not by policy choices. Elections themselves could be regarded as a problem because "political involvement" for the majority of people is reduced to the act of voting. Thus, we leave politics mostly to a few so-called "representatives" who fight over trivial issues, without our participation. In many countries, we find that the largest constituency does not consist of those who vote for a particular party: the largest group consists of people who do not vote at all.

If it is the case that humans are political by nature (and as I argue not unlike other animals), then how can we manage to be apolitical? It could be suggested that we humans did not give birth to the political, but have killed it. Against our natural tendency to collaborate, we have individualized. Yet, collaboration is not all gone. Even within these politically challenging times, we still find collaboration. While the messages are very different, the basic urge to join a Black Lives Matter (BLM) protest is presumably not different from the drive to join a "Liberate Michigan" or "Stop the Steal" event. The underlying urge, as we find it in Steinbeck's phalanx, is one that drives us towards groups, solidarity, and collaboration. We consider it a free decision (and a right) to join a protest or not, but to what degree does one freely choose to sympathize with this cause? How far can one shape one's life and worldview while rejecting other ones? Personally, I can provide a list of arguments to join the BLM movement while I fail to discover any rationality in, for example, the "stop the steal" conspiracies floated on social media. Others, who are attracted to these conspiracies will quickly dismiss my arguments and think in a negative way about my ideological ideas indeed as a conspiracy. They will suggest that I am the one who is irrational, for example in prioritizing the environment over jobs or non-human animals over humans. Or, they might find some of my values conflict with the position of their religious leaders. While calling out the inconsistencies or even craziness of the position of the other, it is tempting to disregard the basis of our own beliefs. Our beliefs are indeed beliefs, or (as Hume calls them) habits, rooted in feelings, not in reason.

What is human political life compared to that of an ant, a rat, a salmon, the critters in the tidepool, or a chimpanzee? We are living in a reality in which we have grown to be apolitical creatures that fail to interact, participate, or engage with one another. Moreover, we fail to observe the effects of our actions. Yet, no one is immune to destructive action. Going back to the destruction of the salmon population: it will come back to us. Likewise, at the human level, politics determines large aspects of our lives and how our communities take shape, from health care to infrastructure, public transportation, schools, social security, food, jobs, the price of gas, water and air quality, the protection of wildlife, civil and women's rights, and more generally safety and quality of life. It is an understatement to say that those who cannot vote are highly impacted by those who can. Since no one can be elected without monetary support, those who have money do matter, always. This dictatorship of wealth is built on the backs of those who cannot vote, on suppressed votes, or misguided votes. This is nothing new. The USA has been built by slaves and on land obtained through genocide, intimidation, and a legal system written by those who Charles Mills appropriately calls "the beneficiaries." In the past some could not vote because of their race or gender. Today many cannot vote because of the lack of an address, documentation, time, or means of transportation.

Politics at its best makes an attempt to work through racial tensions, provide health care, and curb pollution and carbon emissions. At its worst it fools the public and provides tax cuts to the wealthy, while denying climate change altogether. Even "politics at its best" is a far shot from doing enough. Governments are dysfunctional and fail to protect the most vulnerable, or attack those without health care, wealth, steady jobs, documentation, etc. In the phalanx that drives such politics we find a lack of sympathy or empathy for the vulnerable.[1]

Some offer the convenient neoliberal approach. They say we can create "green cities" by creating better transportation systems, clean rivers, reforest, and so forth. While I am supportive of greening, I am against regarding this to be *the* solution if the reigning economic discourse remains in charge. Neoliberalism clearly suggests that any radical revision of politics, and who we are both as individuals and as societies, is indeed too radical and unrealistic, while the neoliberal approach is realistic because it is already materializing by "investing in the future." The strategy suggests that we cannot only improve, but turn things around by making relatively small adjustments, by consuming greener, having greener transportation, less waste, more recycling, and so forth. I suggest we need to rid ourselves of the economic language of investing and consuming. This might be radical indeed, but the only feasible way to steer us in a different direction, away from the radical destruction of everything. And in fact, if we let go of the neoliberal approach our imagination might start to work once again.

The neoliberal approach will let capitalism run its course and function itself as the gravedigger, not of itself, at least not directly, but of the human species. Thus, while Nietzsche's madman exclaims, "You and I have killed Him [God]," we face here the situation in which a god—capitalism—kills us, leaving no one to exclaim anything, at least not in a human language.[2] The remaining species will first breathe a big sigh of relief and then laugh, in Nietzschean fashion, for centuries, while all our ridiculous efforts slowly deteriorate, overgrow, and return to the earth. Ants in particular will laugh. Some of their colonies can expand rapidly and unsustainably just like ours, but their colonies always fail without failing the species as a whole. Perhaps the end of humanity is the most likely (and possibly the best) outcome. All we need to do is keep ignoring the blatant signs that we are on a course to destroy the very possibility of living on this planet. Will perhaps a few survive the apocalypse? Who? The wealthy? How will they survive without those who actually labor? Will the instinct to collaborate finally be awakened? Perhaps it is more likely that some small tribe might survive. One that lives above water and not robbed of their sources of food, clean air, and water.

Some suggest the Anthropocene might not be so bad. I hope they are right. We can find some positive change in which our attitude towards nature has shifted. Environmental philosophy and literature is flourishing bringing Indigenous, Western, and comparative perspectives together on the shelf of any serious bookstore. Yet, the challenges we face should not be underestimated and cannot be tackled if we remain thinking, feeling, and acting in a discourse that has profits as its ultimate goal. If we remain greedy, stingy, and only measure efficiency and profits, we will remain on the same path.

The poet Robinson Jeffers, who had an important influence on Steinbeck and Ricketts, writes, "Humanity is / the start of the race; I say /

Humanity is the mould to break away from, the crust to break / through, the coal to break into fire, / The atom to be split."[3] I argue, indeed, that we have to break outside of humanity, outside of our limited species. We can do this, because the other-than-human is already deep inside us. Our tendencies and the acts that follow from those tendencies are shared with other species. Some of these tendencies we try to hide. I suggest we explore these tendencies, especially the political collaborative ones, in order to rethink our own political world. Ants, we have seen, are the ultimate example of a decentralized organization. We could and should object that we are not ants, yet we often seem to behave like them. It could be suggested that humans, like chimps, seem to thrive in hierarchy. Yet as Bookchin points out, our observations of these hierarchical structures might mostly lie in the eye of the beholder, as we use "terms borrowed from human social hierarchies."[4] We have come to believe that hierarchy is the only way in which a successful society can function well. Thus, we observe the same in other species, often failing to notice the much more subtler structures that make a society function. As De Waal noticed, what makes a chimpanzee colony a peaceful one, despite the display of power and the apparent hierarchy, is empathy. The weakest members of a chimp colony play a significant role. The alpha male needs alliances as well as the support of the colony, which he can only obtain by caring for its members in empathic ways. It is exactly empathy that is lacking in our society today. Empathy for people with a different skin color, gender, ethnicity, or religion (or all of the above) is often lacking. The same is true for those who are refugees, undocumented, poor, addicts, homeless, mentally ill, or of a different class. We have mostly incapacitated our feelings for others, human and non-human, especially for the victims of our actions. If we opened up ourselves to these human others (our victims), our actions would radically change. Indeed, as Stenger suggests, we need to make our decisions in the presence of our victims and open our feelings to them.

How to do this? Going back to our polarized world, we should first of all recognize our feelings and those of others. If we all simply hold on to our ideas we will remain stuck. We could acknowledge that while the other viewpoint might be wrong, the intentions are sincere and real. With the idea of the phalanx, the group is leading, yet might be led astray by politicians who play smartly with the feelings of the group. A leader who senses unrest and strong sentiments can play into this. Thus, while the anti-masker or climate change doubter might be sincere, it is the politician who is insincere and plays with the sentiments of potential voters. Politicians make the most bizarre claims and are often completely inconsistent, yet remain in power as long as they can satisfy their so-called base. This is one of the culprits of representative democracy in which voters need to be misled. Extreme polarization is the result. And yet, beyond the polarization and extreme distrust, we all hold common values: the future of our children or grandchildren, for example. With such a simple shared value we can start a conversation and again create groups that support one another. Likewise, we share kinship as human animals. I have argued that our drive to be part of a group is deeply rooted. We need to learn how to become part of the right groups. Those groups should not identify themselves based on political affiliation, ethnicity, race, or gender. They should unite by deterritorial strategies (following the rats) in becoming entirely different beings. Collectively these groups can generate more positive feelings and behaviors, both internally and externally.

For now, we humans cannot even remotely agree on what the common good is or should be. The decision-making that we witness in what is called human politics can rarely be said to aim for a common good. Ecopolitics is a collection of different goods, not one. It cultivates the feelings that aim for solidarity and sympathy, from which we can create a more empathic society. Revisioning what politics is and rethinking our collective are an important start for this.

We have no interest in "politics" and prefer to watch sports. In our daily lives we seem to have succeeded at creating a life of noninteraction, of nonparticipation, and of a lack of engagement. We have become individualistic creatures without any true individualism as we all act, think, and feel in the same way: we drive alone, or if we end up taking public transportation, mostly in urban areas, we plug in our earphones and are glued to the screens of our phones, glancing with annoyance at the two people who are actually trying to have a conversation. While traditionally music and dance have been communal forms of expression, ever since the Walkman, the ways in which we listen to music have become individual endeavors. At work, we sit behind our screens communicating "virtually" with some distant other human being. At the store, we check out our groceries ourselves. We sometimes use the register with a real person, with whom we exchange a few pleasantries unless we are distracted by our phones. The Covid-19 pandemic has generated even more "contactless" consumption. A QR code replaces a waiter. After a few swipes and clicks, our coffee or dinner is served or ready to be picked up. At work, decision-making is done in a hierarchical fashion. We might collectively contribute our thoughts on how cuts can be made, but the agenda is set by budgets that come from the top, driven by a system in which money is the ultimate goal.

Perhaps we are doomed as a species. But I would not have written this book if I had given up all hope. We can and should become more like salmon who are supporting their ecosystems as valuable members. Similar to chimpanzees, we can and should care for the weaker members, and quickly take power away from those who do not. Our rat-like capacities can challenge all boundaries, and make us collaborate with our fellows, emphasizing our ant-like urge. We need the right circumstances for such a politics. As we are facing multiple crises caused by humans (environmental collapse, racial injustice, and enormous differences in wealth distribution, to name a few), the need to collaborate is pressing. We are social creatures and we need others around us. The Covid-19 pandemic pointed out the tremendous contradiction of living in a world disconnected from others while relying on those others. We are cooperating behind a veil of independence which is dismantled when we find that we are utterly dependent on grocery store workers, health-care workers, delivery drivers, educators, co-workers, and random strangers. Others we hardly noticed before are all of a sudden presented to us as an essential part of our life.

How should we then work together in order to encourage solidarity and community—a general feeling that we are connected? We can genuinely wonder if more collective decision-making could ever work. Can we, like many other animal communities, organize without a central organization? Can we collectively make decisions and assess the different risks involved, so that it is more likely that we follow the regulations that resulted from the process we took part in? Despite our feelings of disconnectedness and isolation, we are utterly connected; we simply need to recognize it. We can approach this insight through other species, as I have suggested throughout this book.

From Lifeboat Ethics to Cruise Ship Decadence

Politics as the conscious or unconscious cooperation towards a common goal emphasizes the need to constantly cooperate. The Covid-19 pandemic has brought the awareness that while others can make us sick, they moreover provide food, goods, and social contact. Similar to other non-human animals, we cannot survive without some form of cooperation with the members of our own species. I have suggested to consider that there might be a certain wisdom in non-human cooperation, a wisdom that can perhaps inform our own practices, for example in the way we function in organizational structures.

The human city, or *polis*, typically functions on the basis of laws, framed through a language of rights. We see that rights might conflict with other rights, or that privileges are considered to be basic rights, even while only available to a limited group and at the cost of living standards and the health of others. In many instances, we notice that not laws and rights but structures of feelings form the true ground for our communities.[5]

One thing we learned from rats and chimpanzees is that the circumstances determine behavior based on feelings. While they can feel empathy, privilege and entitlement lead to closing off others. Likewise, our capitalist system is driven by feelings generated through the ideas of competition. Social Darwinist evolutionary theories emphasize survival of the fittest and forget that collaboration is an essential part of our nature. Like that of chimpanzees and rats, our behavior is not set in stone. We can become more collaborative and show more solidarity by encouraging feelings such as empathy.

Can ecopolitics as a politics based on our animal urges still guarantee freedom? Some political philosophers suggest that a society needs rules and should provide the basic necessities to all so that its members can pursue freedom, while in the typical libertarian approach, any government involvement is regarded to be treading on one's freedom. The ecopolitical approach is different in that it does, first of all, suggest that freedom should not be confused with choice and that today freedom is "exercised" in what Nietzsche would call the "herd mentality." In chapter 5, I have discussed anarchism as a way of organization that does not involve a leader or a central government, yet does not exclude the possibility of rules and structures. We have seen that in non-human societies, even some that can be regarded as anarchistic, members of that society cannot just do whatever they want. They are tied to structures and need to support the colony, the pack, the flock, the herd, or whatever name we give to their group, which in return supports them. Their interconnectedness is juxtaposed to our so-called individualism that tends to ignore our interconnected and intertwined relationships with one another. Nevertheless, the support of others and the structures of our societies provide the conditions for the possibility of our way of living. Relating ourselves back to non-human societies is a way to emphasize and understand the interconnected world we live in and to reenvision our way of living. This will liberate us from the idea that the current situation is the only one possible, and it will free us up to "the impossible." This in itself can be seen as anarchistic. We no longer see ourselves as ruler, but place ourselves in a much larger structure in which no one rules. No individual, no singular species, and no single system determines what to do and what is possible. It is, instead, the collective of living relationships that determines how we should live and what we should do.

I propose to reenvision politics in the human realm by stepping beyond the definition of political involvement as limited to those who partake on a daily basis in such processes. Instead, our daily activities involve all kinds of political choices. Even when we are walking on the street we negotiate with others, mostly without speaking. This idea that our daily lives are full of politics, and are political, in the sense that we collaborate, is essential in reimagining the political. If we keep holding on to the idea that politics is the business of career politicians and that political power is centralized in governments, we are limiting our potential as political beings. On the other hand, if even a walk through the park is considered political, we decentralize politics and can indeed be political activists even in our walking. The choice of the example of walking is not an arbitrary one. We can think of political marches, but even on a more basic level, how we move our body while walking can be political. Gender norms can be followed or challenged, for example, by subverting expectations. How safe we feel on a walk depends on, among other things, our race, gender, neighborhood, and time of the day. Whom we are walking with can be an issue for others. Walking can also be a religious or contemplative activity.

We have seen that different non-human communities' political structures exist, from nonhierarchical to complex and changing hierarchies, sometimes including personalities and empathy. The structures are indeed different depending on the species, yet with all kinds of resemblances. I have shown throughout this book that in studying animal communities we find structures that we can call political. These animal communities provide mirrors that reflect our own behavior, feelings, and possibilities. Yet, we know still so little about non-human communities: the complexity of social insects keeps surprising us; we have still not answered how salmon find their way back to their place of birth; we are not anywhere close to fully grasping the complexity of the chimpanzee colony; and even the tidepool consisting of relatively "simple" organisms constitutes a mysterious "city."

When we relate human political crises to natural disasters we find that our actions have both human and non-human victims. We also often encounter an immediate relationship between depleted natural environments and political instability. Throughout this book I have argued to consider non-human victims as political in their own right. We can take the comparison a step further by suggesting that our attacks on ecosystems destabilize the politics of ecosystems, which have repercussions in the human realm. In the non-human realm we find the tremendous influence of human presence either leaving no habitat for animals or radically changing animal migration patterns. The result is the Sixth Great Extinction. In the human realm, we find mass migration and the extinction of cultures. Foreign military presence across the globe changes local political dynamics and often creates powerful dictators. Even well-intentioned development work in the Third World can have unintended consequences, changing political relationships.[6] Human destructive presence in a forest or other ecosystem equally generates "dictatorships" of certain species, or we simply ourselves become dictators as a species.[7] The latter is fairly obviously the case, as we are the most dominant species on the planet. The global scale of our activities is the problem since (1) it creates a seemingly endless supply of resources, while (2) we do not witness the victims of our actions, and (3) it makes us able to expand at a scale that no other species can. It is true that ants also colonized all continents, but their colonies live and die in a limited territory. Even the most aggressive supercolonies remain within the range of a few miles at the very most. In the non-human and the human realms, a dictatorship always fails.[8]

We have seen that when an important species such as salmon disappears, human and non-human communities struggle. Industrial societies have become incredibly skillful at justifying pretty much anything as long as economic interests are met (if money indeed has become a god, this is arguably a metaphysical goal). Yet, as the situation around salmon makes clear: we are facing reality. Our assault on salmon is not just destroying their population, it is likewise an assault on other species that rely on them, including the human. By destabilizing natural ecosystems, we also destabilize social ecologies, such as human communities that rely on fishing.

By living as a species on a global scale, we typically do not know what and who have been involved in the creation of our consumer goods, as well as our food. In the case of refugees we are still able to convince ourselves that these people are just opportunity seekers; that they are not victims, or if they are victims, they are not our victims but of some evil regime we have had absolutely no control over. We can bomb the evil regime, kill the dictator, bring them democracy, and then be genuinely surprised that despite the heroism of our soldiers (whom we nonetheless fail to support), these "other people" do not change for the better. We can withdraw and conclude that it must really be their constitution, which was expected all along. Never mind that it is *we* who first encouraged, funded, and provided weapons to terrorist groups or the "evil" leaders.[9]

As we are facing climate change and run up against all kinds of limits, overpopulation is often indicated as the problem. Hardin's "lifeboat ethics" is typically followed here. At the center of the debate is the issue of overpopulation, which is a sensitive yet important one. However, the way Hardin presents the issue is problematic, first of all because his so-called lifeboat is not a lifeboat at all. The boat is not getting too full so that it will sink (which is his justification to keep others out so that we do not drown collectively). It is a luxury ship, as suggested by Tommy Orange in his novel *There There*. Orange takes up the issue of the lifeboat from the perspective of Native Americans who have never been allowed on the boat. Native Americans and the ancestors of slaves are the ones floating around in a lifeboat, while others sail on a luxury ship. The "lifeboat," as we find it in Hardin's analogy, is a luxury ship built by slaves and made possible by genocide. The ship is now (1) claimed to be the fruit of "our" labor, is (2) an environmental disaster, and (3) leaves nothing for those floating in the ocean. There would have been plenty of resources for all, if those aboard stayed away from what Orange describes as the "hors d'oeuvres" and "fluffy pillows." Floating on the seven seas, those aboard do not have to see the victims of their actions, those who are left behind, have lost their land, and are traumatized culturally and personally.[10]

Many of us are aboard the luxury ship. Maybe we are not on the upper deck, but still we live quite comfortable lives. In order to stay on the ship, we serve those on the upper deck, instead of helping those drowning in the sea. Beyond the US and the Western industrial world, we are facing a global lifeboat situation in which our luxury ship has generated a tremendous wave that shipwrecks the rest of the world. Securing the oil that energizes our ship involves destabilizing a large part of the world. Securing natural resources and mining has likewise fueled dictatorships and military escalations, along with destroying the traditional living conditions for huge parts of the global human population. We, of course, help out by donating to organizations that fight hunger and build hospitals and schools. Kropotkin argues that such donations are a justification of the unjust. In a global world this also includes an imperialistic attitude, at least present in the background. We think we know how to solve *their* problems, yet when those solutions fail, we blame those who "really do not want to be helped." We look down from our ship, and as Orange says, we judge: "It's too bad those people are lazy, and not as smart as we are up here, we who have built these strong, large stylish boats ourselves."[11] While Orange refers specifically to the situation of Native Americans, the same is true on a global scale. Children in the Third World make our clothing while our kids are educated in the art of making money. Somehow, we still think that the people in "developing countries" are lazy.

Towards Sympathy

How does ecopolitics address the lack of sympathy (or empathy) for others? How do we move towards a world in which we care about and for others, and feel solidarity? How can we open up our receptibility (or sensibility) to one another and move towards genuine being with one another and true exposure to others? The interesting aspect is that we are all collectively separating ourselves, thus collectively individualizing. Following Jeffers, this also provides the opening to break open the crust, the human shell that is in fact very thin.[12]

In the chimpanzee colony, empathy (or sympathy, yet *empathy* is the word used by De Waal) plays a significant role to guarantee mutual aid. It is clear that a leader who neglects the weaker members will fail. In other species, less complex emotions or feelings play a role to ensure the basic need to cooperate. To live is to cooperate, one could say. Yet, among rats and chimpanzees we have seen that empathy is not always guiding. Likewise, the need to cooperate can sometimes be overruled. Kropotkin certainly acknowledges the drive to survive, yet argues that instead of struggle and survival of the fittest, cooperation or mutual aid is the most basic drive. It can be selective and overruled in some circumstances. Kropotkin shows that cooperation is less common when the circumstances do not require it, for example when there is plenty of food, which seems to instigate a greed that is similar to the passengers on the luxury ship described by Orange. We have seen that rats can feel empathy, yet, in some cases they exclude outsiders without apparently any empathy, as we witness in the Indian temple rats. De Waal witnessed some extreme violence, unusual for chimpanzees. For these animals empathy can be put aside or is overruled by other feelings when the circumstances dictate it. For example, in zoo situations unusual aggression can occur around feeding times.

Sympathy or empathy can be regarded as one of the feelings inherited from other animals, although the working of empathy is not the same in rats as it is in humans. Within the context of a large brain and a global world, the feeling will function in different ways than it does in rats. In fact, even among human beings the feeling is not the same. It needs to be nourished, first of all, and studies have shown that feelings of empathy are less prevalent among those who are in a comfortable position. Without suffering oneself, it becomes more difficult to sympathize with the suffering of others. Genetic and epigenetic factors, along with upbringing and education, social status, and personal experiences, are some of the factors that determine the level of empathy an individual will experience. In addition, within the context of Kropotkin's distinction between ethics and morality as the study of ethics (and the mistaken metaphysical grounds), we find that through theorizing and studying we can create excuses for wrongdoing, an ability most animals lack. In short, the context of intellectual capacities that produce and follow theories, social structures, and other emotions will transform the feeling of empathy.

Emotions have evolved significantly, although it is assumed that certain primal emotions, especially fear, along with anger, disgust, sadness, and enjoyment are very old. Needless to say, fear is a helpful emotion for survival. Social emotions, such as pride, and filial emotions are regarded as separate from these primal emotions and are typically associated with social mammals. Yet, here a question emerges: what kind of emotion draws social insects or other pre-mammal species towards cooperation? Or are they driven by something else than an emotion or feeling? Scientists do not rule out that the actions of insects are driven by emotions. Yet, they are hesitant about whether animals such as insects feel those emotions. Neuroscience, thus, distinguishes between feelings and emotions, in which the latter is immediately associated with an action (run!), while a feeling is much more conscious (that was scary!). Similar to the salmon discussed in chapter 1, we find here again a mechanistic view of the emotional lives of animals. The Cartesian view of an animal as a complex automata is still kept alive. The argument seems to suggest that they might be beings with emotions, but those emotions are not experienced as a feeling. Thus, it is said that the ant fears but does not feel it. This begs the question: what exactly does it fear then? Could an emotion work without feeling it? Isn't feeling the essence of an emotion?

We can again find some answers in Darwin, who in *The Expression of Emotions in Man and Animals* suggests that insects express anger, terror, jealousy, and love. Some contemporary experiments have taken up Darwin's suggestion in a study that found that bees can be more or less optimistic.[13] We can also relate back to the chaos that emerges when the queen of an ant colony dies. When the scent of the queen disappears, the colony collapses. Would an ant at that point feel lost (even terrified), or would it only act? Again, it seems that emotions cannot lead to actions if the animal could not actually feel them.

As discussed in chapter 3, before Darwin, David Hume argued for the importance of sympathy for political societies. We could suggest that society and language provide the context in which sympathy (or empathy) can be either experienced or suppressed in particular situations. Returning to Orange's description of the luxury ship, the circumstances leave no opening to feelings of empathy for those drowning in the ocean. It is "too bad" they drown because of their own laziness and lack of intelligence. When, in his parable, someone aboard the ship objects "but your father gave you this yacht, and these are his servants who brought the hors d'oeuvres," the person is "tossed overboard by a group of hired thugs."[14] If our history lessons, stereotyping, and the narratives that circulate justify our own situation by forgetting and erasing the tragedies that have made that position possible in the first place, we create a society in which empathy cannot flourish, at least not for the victims who have built our society and serve us. Likewise, if our language is so poor that we cannot even envision alternatives to our current way of living, or in which substance abuse is always tied to an "abuser" (as opposed to a victim), we set up a language in which empathy is suppressed. Following Hume's thoughts, the idea that triggers our passions today is blaming the individual, not feeling with them. Thus, we are angry at the drug addict, whom we blame for their own demise. The narrative that suggests that they are destroying their own lives, oppresses the narrative that their lives have been destroyed by others, and the non-supportive or oppressive structures of society. In this regard, we are lacking the ideas that can trigger sympathy. We cannot feel with the person who is acting against themselves. Within the narratives of our society we cannot comprehend such "irrational behavior."

In chapter 5, I discussed how Kropotkin found that the same species of animals in the harsh environments of Siberia displayed a different behavior than those in Western Europe. Cattle in the cold can only survive by working together. In the affluent conditions of Western Europe, with milder temperatures and overall an abundance of food, such mutual aid is less at work. Thus, the Siberia cattle indeed displayed much more mutual aid than their Western European counterparts. Translating this to our own situation, we see that in situations of affluence individualism and selfishness often flourish, while in certain harsh situations humans do indeed work together.

Collaboration, for example, occurs among groups of people fleeing violence or a disaster. Steinbeck's *The Grapes of Wrath* documents such collaboration. While his work is fictional, it is based on actual events, and Steinbeck worked extensively in a camp that housed immigrants to California. Similar to Steinbeck's migrants, we can today find similar mutual aid among immigrants to Europe and North America. While some profit from the circumstances of refugees and illegal immigrants, very few would make it without mutual aid. In such situations, differences can often be put aside: race, ethnicity, gender, or nationality does not matter when fleeing from the same threat or towards a common goal.[15] A lesson can be learned from this.

In translating empathy from the rat and chimpanzee world to our own, we can identify similarities: the circumstances dictate our feelings, as do the circumstances of other empathic animals. As the cows grazing in wealth feel little need for mutual aid, the rats living in wealth feel no empathy towards outsiders who might bring a threat to their own situation. We also seem to be able to easily exclude others from our feelings of empathy. It often seems we only care about the superficial, about status and class, while seemingly experiencing little to no empathy for others, especially not for those who fall in a different class than ourselves. As discussed in chapter 3, De Waal describes how the corporate culture at Enron led to a corporation in which selfishness was cultivated and flourished until the company fell apart because of it. Important lessons can be drawn from that example when we think about our own communities, and the global industrial world that seems to thrive on greed and selfishness. Just like Enron, a world without empathy will ultimately fail.

The affluent are often failing to feel empathy for immigrants and refugees. If we are indeed like rats, it could be that wealth is to blame. The lack of empathy could also be a survival strategy. With news streaming from all parts of the globe, one could not survive the mourning of all the victims of military coups, wars, terrorist attacks, hurricanes, wildfires, contagious diseases, and so forth. Fatalities are expressed as abstract numbers: "Hurricane y claimed x deaths." "X people died in last night's terrorist attack in y." "The pandemic has claimed x millions of people." Research has shown how we empathize more with those closer to home, literally and metaphorically, than those far away. A friend across the street who is of my own age and loses his wife is in many ways closer to home than an Afghan woman who falls victim to the Taliban. As I am working out this example, I realize that even while both are imaginary my description of the Afghan woman, as well as my imagination, is a lot less vivid (and accurate) than that of the friend. We cannot mourn or fear the whole world.

We can object that communities without empathy towards outsiders (and even without empathy within the community) can exist for extended periods of time. As long as such a community has wealth they can stay within such a position, just like the temple rats (who are supported by a different species, humans). That we can be like rats is probably not surprising. Without the temple, rats behave deterritorially, crossing all borders and boundaries, obliterating them along the way. In the temple everything changes as wealth generates greed. Can we be less like the temple rat and more deterritorial creatures if we let go of our wealth? Can we be more like chimpanzees who have to be empathic in order to rule? Chimpanzee colonies, at least in a natural setting, do not allow a position of privilege. Leaders need to take care of all parts of the colony and show empathy. If they abuse the weaker members, the structure of the group dynamics is such that support will quickly disappear and their leadership role will be undermined.

Stengers speaks of coexisting with the beings (human and non-human) we share our *oikos* with. Similarly, Haraway emphasizes a notion of kinship. In order to move towards such a coexisting and kinship, I suggest opening up towards the feelings of others, by developing new discourses and practices, through which we relate in new ways to other species and the natural world. In the discussion of salmon, I discussed the Tlingit story of the salmon boy. Such a narrative suggests that all life is in essence the same and that communities of salmon suffer in similar ways human communities suffer. This is one way to express our kinship. As Kimmerer argues in *Braiding Sweetgrass,* our scientific discourses are always lacking in terms of kinship. The most common conception is that humans and nature are opposed to one another, failing to recognize any kinship.

We can connect with fellow humans all around us. In the realm of empathy/sympathy within the human realm, we need exposure outside of our own privileged position (and recognize it as privileged). If we are educated, live, and work within the environment of our own class we will, indeed, only understand the struggles, thinking, and morality of our own class. When it comes to non-human entities we encounter similar issues. For if our education and discourses exclude us from non-human species, we will also fail to experience empathy/sympathy, and overall we will fail to coexist with them, just as with humans.

We could say that children are the future. They are smart and sensitive, and it does not take much to connect to the non-human world as well as to the members of the human world who fall outside of one's class and status. It might be our natural tendency to protect our children, but we can only truly protect them by exposing them to all that is wrong on our planet, from homelessness and racism to climate change. My students are often angry, for example, at politicians and previous generations, who left a mess for them. We all should be angry and not leave the mess for our children but become (with) them. This will involve unsettling experiences for us, associated with feelings of guilt. As we found in Kropotkin, in our ethical system we can be perfectly comfortable with injustices, since we have built in mechanisms to take care of guilt. We can trick ourselves into believing we are compassionate humans by serving a meal at a homeless center or by donating money to a charity. These band-aids are indeed just band-aids which work for the small wounds on our feelings of guilt, but fail to stop the bleeding of the gaping wound that we should feel in a confrontation with the homeless, refugees, victims of domestic violence, people displaced because of climate change–induced natural disasters, depleted natural environments, species that go extinct, or animals in factory farming. It might seem that this is a rather random list, but they are all related to what I consider the sickness of our society. We can say that senses of justice in our society have become very exclusive, only applying to certain people as well as to certain animals (mostly our pets), indeed those of one's own status and/or class. Certainly, this is often aligned with race, religion, gender, and so forth. As mentioned, it is difficult to feel empathy for a person in a situation one cannot imagine, one that does not relate to one's own experience of the world. With the addition of increasing individualism we are on a path to feel no empathy at all.

We have seen how Kropotkin argues that animals do have a sense of justice. As he noted, society has implemented structures in which cooperation is replaced by individualism and a sense of justice is oppressed. Kropotkin suggested countering these structures through a decentralization of government, thereby restructuring society around cooperation. As Kropotkin and Deleuze's Hume suggest, society is crucial in shaping the individuals who make up that society. If we assume that society is created by selfish, entitled, and self-centered human beings, the structures set up to regulate those tendencies will in fact create the circumstances in which exactly those tendencies become emphasized. This is the case today and we need to break out of the cycle we inherited.

New Discourses, New Stories, New Ways of Being

Current scientific discourses, even while often still full of notions of purity when it comes to restoration and preservation, bring new discourses. An often-discussed project is that of the Oostvaarders Plassen, a nature preserve (in my homeland, the Netherlands) created by humans attempting to mimic a prehuman ecosystem. It is interesting because of the obvious contradictions. In the original conception of the project, humans were not interfering, although recently radical changes have been made. The whole project could in that regard inform us that the human-nature separation is problematic, especially in an age we call the Anthropocene.

A more recent and very different approach has been made with the construction of a number of islands in what is now the Marker Meer, a lake that used to be de Zuiderzee, before two dams disconnected it from the sea. This particular part was intended to be reclaimed in order to create more land, but was ultimately deemed unnecessary and not desired. A lake remains that today, because of the buildup of silt, has little life left in it. This is a failure of human engineering and complex politics that included decades of protesting and lobbying by a variety of interest groups. Some stakeholders lost, others won, yet the victim is life in the lake. Recognizing this failure, humans have taken responsibility by creating islands (using some of the silt in the lake), which are filtering the water and providing a basis for plants, birds, fish, snails, frogs, insects, and microbes to flourish. Even five years after the start of the project it is already a tremendous success. More than 2,500 species of animals and plants have been counted so far. The islands are smartly engineered, with water inlets on the west side to let in water during storms. The islands filter the water from silt, which is feeding the plants. The islands are explicitly built as a nature reserve. In previous decades, bird populations in the Netherlands have declined tremendously. Agriculture, urbanization, and housing needed for the continuous growth of the population have left little spaces for wildlife. These new islands provide a nesting opportunity as well as a resting place for migrating birds. A ferry shuttles people to the island. The small settlement allows people to dock their boats, to camp, to have a coffee or a grilled cheese sandwich. A few tiny houses can be rented for a few nights.[16] When walking around the main island, or sleeping in a tent among the continuous cacophony of thousands of birds, it is hard to imagine that this has all been established by humans in just a few years. In fact it is not just humans, but a collaboration of humans, water, silt and sand, wind, seeds, insects, birds, and fish (to name a few). Being here, and building these islands, *is* coexisting and a recognition of kinship with our victims. The islands are functional and provide an opportunity for humans to connect with other species, to be in an ecosystem planned and engineered to some degree by humans and in which we can collaborate with the non-human world. We can watch birds and fish or take pictures and upload them to a shared database used by researchers. While visitors are only allowed to stay for up to three nights, the lessons for coexisting long term are multiple. They include sustainable architecture, creating space for non-human species, and engineering with nature. I am not suggesting that technology and engineering alone will get us out of the crisis (the islands are in fact low-tech). However, these islands show us that it is possible to connect to nature in a different way and that we can build and engineer *with* nature.

One does not need to go into the wilderness to find the wild. Even in the city we can generate new ways of relating to the natural environment. During my sabbatical in 2021 I spent time in Amsterdam, where I lived twenty-two years earlier. During the time I lived in the US, the canals have undergone a tremendous transformation. They still look the same, but as opposed to the 1990s, the water is now clean enough to swim in, and I witnessed people and birds fishing. On warm days it is a true blessing for the human inhabitants of the city to be able to take a swim. With a kayak I discovered a flourishing non-human existence. Besides pigeons nesting under bridges, coots are building nests of all kinds of materials, loons are fishing, geese and ducks, as well as swans, are raising families on the canals and the Amstel River.

As part of our new discourses, our relationship to nature should be retold in a different way. The current political discourse needs to be retold in order to include the non-human. The destruction of natural environments and people is the result of oppressive politics in the human realm. Both are made possible because those in power believe they have a mandate in the form of a social contract. Destroyed environments now themselves have become oppressive and deadly to many species.[17] If we would indeed be rational beings we could have prevented this. The fact that we did not is another indication that we are less rational, and instead of reason, we follow our feelings. The main strategy that we are left with then is to change our feelings, or at least make sure we relate our feelings in a different way, so that we are attracted to the right group and are guided by positive passions. So far, we keep relying on technological solutions that deal with symptoms as opposed to true problems, and we fail to change our behavior. Designs that move towards a collaboration with nature are a step in the right direction. We can only start working on those designs by changing our relationship to nature, that is, by conceiving ourselves differently. One of the important first steps we have to make is to recognize that we are less rational and more biological, that is, driven by nonrational forces that somehow provide us with a trust in the mass-movement of our societies. Steinbeck, as discussed in chapter 4 uses the idea of the phalanx as a natural tendency to be part of a group and to collectively move in a particular direction, physically or otherwise. He sees us humans as "the material" for a phalanx. We do not choose which phalanx we are going to be a part of insofar as the phalanx just needs particular materials. What we can shape, though, is ourselves by becoming "the right material." If we combine this with the argument for empathy, to be more open to others by understanding ourselves differently, can we then rethink—or relearn by feeling differently—who we are? Deleuze, following Hume, suggests we are habitual beings, yet which habits we take up is not determined. It is possible to challenge and change old habits and institutions. As we can witness with the institution of same-sex marriage, it takes continuous effort and will often be challenged, yet it is not impossible. Following the thoughts of both Steinbeck and Deleuze, we see here that a successful transformation can only occur if we become "the right material." This, I suggest, can only occur through an actual engagement with the world, with others (human and non-human), including those who do not think alike.

In order to become better material, I have suggested that like rats we need to deterritorialize, become the other, recognize the other in ourselves, move beyond our individualism, and decentralize ourselves. More concretely, this means that we can start with engaging with the world directly. At the risk of being called a Luddite, I suggest we limit the time we spend behind screens and/or attached to gadgets. Our world today demands that we can whip out a smartphone in seconds and that we are constantly connected and available to our jobs, family, and friends. We have become predictable and are enslaved to algorithms. In relation to deterritorializing and decentralization, the algorithm does exactly the opposite: it is a tool that centralizes power—those who invest in the system can easily manipulate us, and we are the material that is quickly molded into something else.

Instead of algorithms, we need societies that are based on community. I do not merely think about a community of humans, but also a community of all living things. Such a construction can begin even on an afternoon hike, which connects us with those non-human and human others. It will not be enough to discourage and break down hierarchies and to decentralize power, but it is a lot more productive than spending an afternoon at the mercy of algorithms. The latter is exactly the opposite of freedom, even (or especially) when the messages it generates suggest that our freedom is at stake.

Language, or rather discourse, plays a significant role in the possibility to decentralize power and to have people think for themselves. Yet, the construction of new discourses itself needs to be a decentralized and collective endeavor. We need to create songs, poems, stories, and words that express ourselves as new beings who no longer thrive on the idea that the economy must keep growing and that success can only be measured in terms of GNP. The existence of the economic discourse is not in itself a problem. Efficiency has its place and, moreover, alternative economies (from Marxist to gift economies) exist. Yet, when a discourse dominates others in terms of its (short-term) goals, enormous problems ensue.

Lyotard discusses that which cannot be represented and shows us the limits of the possibility of a participatory democracy based on communicability. We find "a wrong" in the case that the injustice one experiences cannot be expressed in the terms of the oppressing regime. The injustices Native Americans continue to experience is an example of such a wrong. The land that was once their place is legally owned by corporations, institutions, governments, and individuals. Besides a few exceptions, legal challenges are only rarely successful. Lyotard's philosophy first and foremost wants us to recognize that such injustices exist precisely in the legal system itself. Furthermore, he wants us to grow more sensitive so that an inability to express an injustice in the regular discourses does not mean it does not exist. In the example of Native Americans, this means we need to step beyond legal discourses and become more sensitive towards their situation. As *There There* by Orange shows, literature can be an important medium in this regard, in this case by bringing the oppression of Native Americans into the present. We find a need to expand beyond existing discourses, yet such an expansion is only possible if we develop our sensibility.

This is arguably somewhat different from Hume and Deleuze who argue that habits and ideas can be changed. Yet the habits and ideas we need to change according to Deleuze are nevertheless rooted in a different kind of sensibility. Hume's philosophy is grounded in the idea that we are indeed beings of passion, much more so than beings of reason. Lyotard emphasizes a kind of sensibility that can even conflict with reason and with existing ideas. Contemporary thinkers, such as Rancière and Esposito, have been critical of Lyotard because in their interpretation, his philosophy only indicates the incommensurability between different discourses, leaving us in an impasse on what to do about the victims. Using slightly different dialectical philosophies (involving among others the third person) of becoming, they both propose an ethics beyond the I/Thou relationship, moving towards recognition of the third person "them." Rancière encourages a politics as activism on behalf of "Them," those that have been excluded, through a multiplication or doubling of persons in which we step beyond "I and Thou" by engaging in a dialogue on behalf of a third party, "Them." Esposito speaks of the impersonal (sometimes expressed as the third person) in which the oppressed, the victim who cannot be named, is named. Deleuze, as we have seen in the discussion of rats, is a philosopher of becoming and, not surprisingly, is discussed by Esposito. For the latter becoming animal means to return to our natural alteration.[18]

As discussed by Russell, both Rancière and Esposito attempt to deal with Lyotard's "wrong" by trying to give expression to that which by definition cannot be expressed.[19] We can wonder if they do not, in some way, underestimate the severity of the conflict Lyotard brings to the fore. The proposed solution to break out of the I-Thou dialectic in which one (or I) act(s) on behalf of them, might be too simplistic. Even more, the move could possibly result in even another wrong, when we assume we can represent the position of the suppressed group. We should not end in Wittgenstein's "Whereof one cannot speak, thereof one must be silent" which is explicitly not what Lyotard had in mind (and to be fair: Wittgenstein himself also departed from this standpoint). Part of Lyotard's point is that silence in itself can have a significance. A victim often cannot speak, and a Lyotardian victim is robbed of the means to speak, either literally because of trauma, or metaphorically because the legal structures are set up against them. If I, as a white male, claim to fully understand the struggles of a woman of color, I will rightfully be criticized. I cannot speak for her. Lyotard's example in *Le Différend* of the Holocaust shows that because few survived and those who did survive are deeply traumatized and dealing with feelings of loss, guilt, and/or posttraumatic stress, very few firsthand accounts of the Holocaust exist. Because of the lack of direct testimony, denial of an event such as the Holocaust thus becomes possible. In order to give testimony to such a traumatic experience we need a sensibility towards silence, towards the victim who has lost the means to speak, literally or symbolically.

Lyotard does not only speak of an abyss that cannot be bridged. In his work on aesthetics, he emphasizes the possibility to experience the abyss between the knowable and that which lies beyond representation. The point is that that which cannot be communicated directly is not without significance. His interpretation of the Kantian sublime gives testimony to this. The sublime is, for Lyotard, a way to show the limitations of reason, to point to a realm that cannot be expressed in words. A personal or cultural trauma is an example of this.

Lyotard's critics point to the necessity to speak for the victims. We can, for example, join a protest and attest to the struggles of a particular group, but we are always at a distance, not them. By speaking for *them* in the third person, an absence is maintained. This can be compared with Hume's model of sympathy in which we find a direct confrontation while maintaining the authenticity of the other: My sympathy is sincere, yet I am not suffering their loss. I cannot imagine the unimaginable, yet I can feel with (*sum*) them.

Today, besides the denial of events, we can also see the opposite: events that never occurred are called into being. In the age of fake news, we witness the danger of sensibility and passion. Conspiracy theories bloom exactly because they play with the sensibility of people. A distrust in government and a feeling of being forgotten are the basic ingredients of a susceptible audience that will believe almost anything that targets the establishment and the promise of a savior. Conspiracies that the Holocaust did not occur are supplemented with conspiracies that 9/11 was staged, that democratic elections were rigged, or that high-ranking officials of the American Democratic party were involved in human trafficking and child molesting. While Lyotard and other poststructuralists ask us to become sensitive towards language as a construction in which truth itself is a (social) construct, in today's reality that insight has been perverted so that almost anything can be said, become a truth, and be believed. Philosophers must emphasize that skepticism is still a healthy attitude. Yet, how do we distinguish between doubting conspiracies such as Pizzagate or the Clinton Body Count and doubting a historic event such as the Holocaust? Or to reverse the question, what is the difference between being a Holocaust denier and a Pizzagate denier?

I would suggest listening to unheard stories. Listen to the ancestors of survivors, of slaves, of those who are oppressed currently. Listen to the world, human and non-human, around us. We can listen to climate scientists, biologists, and ecologists who witness the collapse of ecosystems.[20] If we listen to those who have lived here for generations, especially those who farm or fish, we will be able to witness drastic and subtle changes. Our elders are forgotten in nursing homes, unable to post anything on social media and thus their stories, knowledge, and wisdom is dying with them. Our cities tell stories, as do the landscapes throughout the world. Artists, poets, writers, along with geographers and biologists all need to be listened to.

Only through a collective interdisciplinary approach can we learn that the loss of homes through ever increasing severe weather events, wildfires, and rising sea levels implies that we no longer can deny climate change. In 2016, Hurricane Matthew brought widespread destruction and killed hundreds of people from Haiti to the United States. Meanwhile, the West Coast of the United States was blanketed in smoke because of wildfires. Whole neighborhoods burned down. After such an apocalyptic wildfire and hurricane season, one would expect a radical change of heart. Yet, the economic discourse suggested that Hurricane Matthew was exaggerated in order to "sell" climate change, while the forests on the West Coast just needed better management. While to many the evidence of climate change is overwhelming, many others need to hear more stories, and indeed this is one of the most important tasks in order to change course: tell stories!

I have argued elsewhere to get to know the places where we live.[21] Perhaps we can return to the places where we grew up. We can mourn what is lost, and hopefully celebrate what is gained and improved. Sometimes mourning and celebration will come together. One of the places where I grew up has lost a lot of agricultural lands to industry and has newly established nature reserves. I mourn the loss of the meadows with birds, grazing cows, and sheep. I enjoy walking and riding a bicycle through the reserves. The same town has lost its view over the lake. Instead of seeing the IJssel Lake virtually unobstructed, one now looks at close to a hundred enormous wind turbines. The aesthetic loss (as well as loss of fishing grounds) is a step towards carbon neutrality. Like many others, I feel conflicted about the changed landscape. Perhaps we should see it ultimately as a call to consume less energy.

I argue, thus, that instead of letting ourselves be informed through social media or radio hosts, we go out and first of all try to experience the world. We are attracted to groups; we cannot change that. We are creatures of habit; we cannot change that. What we can change is the groups to which we are attracted, as well as the habits that we take up. In order to do so, we can observe the natural world around us. If we are observing, climate change can be witnessed everywhere. Species disappear, weather patterns change, our water, heating, or cooling bills go up, streets are flooded, we have to preserve water, one develops asthma. We have seen with the Humean-Deleuzian theory that our feelings are grounded in ideas. Those ideas, again, are copies of impressions. How we associate different ideas is ultimately grounded in experience. If our experiences are limited or poor, then so are our ideas. I suggest we can enrich our impressions, and thus the association of ideas, if we let our landscapes tell stories. These can be rural or urban stories.[22]

One might suggest that we are too stuck in our ways, that we will follow our instinctual drive to grow like ants. Yet there is a powerful movement partially constituted by our children, the next generation which demands change. The fact that a Greta Thunberg can come on the scene is an indication of a different atmosphere, grounded in an understanding that we are on the wrong course and need radical change. If we can agree with this next generation that we want them to have a future, we have to change with them and become them. That change will be more difficult for us then for them, as we need to become children and become the future that is livable, necessarily departing our current way of being. In many ways we need to learn new discourses, those that redetermine what politics is, do not think in terms of economics, and instead draw us into a new group, a phalanx that we all should want to be a part of.

Education is often proposed as an answer if we think about reshaping a society. In addition we need to rethink the nature of our educational systems. While staying away from behaviorist models à la Skinner to recreate our children, we should let our (grand)children recreate us—they are still empathic beings, who care more about climate change than any other generation. As already discussed, education is not only an education of our students but mostly an education of ourselves. We need to create languages to express injustices, so that we can feel them. Our discourses are now set up to exclude such feelings. Generating new ideas through language is connecting us, is making us experience feelings of sadness, anger, shame, and so forth. These feelings speak for the wretched of the earth.

We need interfaith, interracial, and interethnic movements to cross the boundaries and to question these boundaries, both in school and in our communities. This is not to suggest that we should entirely rid ourselves of our background, if that were even possible. Identities are important and I am not suggesting we should let them go, but it is equally important to continue to ask who we are. We need to all ask how we got where we are as individuals, as families, as cities, states, and countries. What atrocities have been and are committed in order to bring prosperity to our communities, families, countries, etc.? Who suffered? Who suffers? We might then indeed want to know how we can transcend the boundaries of those aspects that constitute our identities.

What is threatening us is technology that individualizes and disconnects us from one another and the natural world. We need different programs to unplug or disconnect in order to connect. There is not a single solution for all. Some might benefit from a church group, others from school organized outings, music, friends, or a sports club. What matters most is that we commit to spending time with others, without technological distractions, and preferably outdoors. We do not need to sail around Cape Horn, climb Mount Everest, or hike the Alps. We should first of all ensure that access to safe outdoor spaces is accessible to all. It is a first priority to make sure that everyone is able to take a walk in a local park, go for a swim in a nearby lake, or take an urban walk. As long as we are able to open our senses and reconnect to the world, the location and nature of the environment is not that important, but it does need to be available.

What underlies our current being is a capitalistic system that generates ever-increasing differences in wealth. We are familiar with the 1% and 99%. It is a no-brainer to abolish this insanely unjust distribution of wealth. The wealthy claim their success is based on being true wise risk takers. Let's invite them to take risks and distribute their wealth evenly among the population, which in the USA would mean that all Americans would have a net worth of over half a million dollars. Before they act, I encourage an ecopolitical way of thinking that leads to less consumption and that can celebrate without the compulsive neoliberal fashion to shop. Instead of further solidifying us as consumers, we should become nonconsumers. Our economy is based on consumption, and the story is that if the economy goes down, we will hurt. We lose jobs, salaries go down, we will lose our health insurance, the value of our homes diminishes, and so forth. These are no small matters, but isn't this exactly the problem of our society that lacks empathy? If our government was truly concerned about this, they could bail us out, instead of bailing out financial institutions. Governments, such as the US federal government, do sometimes issue "stimulus checks" to individuals. As the name clearly suggests, this money "without strings" is not meant to help individuals (and if it does it is an unintended consequence) but to stimulate the economy. Instead of encouraging consumption we could invest in building hospitals and quality health care, education, public transportation, and green infrastructure. We would generate new jobs and move towards a more sustainable future. Instead of following a path in which we are at all costs protecting corporations, we should establish a new system of measuring success. If we ignore Wall Street and other stock markets and instead invest in something that is truly worthwhile, including helping others and protecting our natural environments, we will be on a path towards ecopolitics.

Ecopolitics

From the portraits of political societies in different kinds of animals, I have argued for a different way of understanding ourselves within a larger political network. A different understanding of ourselves as part of a political system consisting of all living beings will lead to different actions. By reconsidering the *polis* and by reconsidering who we are, we will indeed become different political agents who act and make decisions, not as individuals, but as collectives. Without falling into Nietzsche's herd mentality we need in fact to learn how to coexist with a much larger group by nourishing empathy for others so that our groups are no longer highly selective but more inclusive. We recognize the individual and social relationships that determine who we are, and in doing so we can let go of our false sense of individualism, generated through class and status. Instead of overcoming our animal instincts, we should embrace them as passions that are fed by ideas, ideally ecopolitical ideas, exactly in order to let senses of justice and ethics appear again. Within this new political reality, we will in fact think more, not less, for ourselves precisely by giving up the false sense of individualism that our societies provide us with. We have become so predictable that algorithms can determine our political inclination after we click a few "likes" on a social media platform. Perhaps we can be compared to the ants who follow a scent. Yet, we fail to recognize that the scent is the stench of our own rot. Along the way we have indeed gone up in a quite undesirable phalanx, one that diminishes empathy, solidarity, and care, and encourages greed and a false sense of individualism.

Ecopolitics considers the *oikos* as a shared good in which we together, with those beings with whom we share it, can build a world. There is not one common good, but a multiplicity of goods and some of those goods will conflict. There is no ecopolitics without conflict. Yet, in emphasizing the shared aspects of our world, ecopolitics attempts to avoid abuse and oppression.

Ecopolitics reminds us that the neoliberal or capitalistic mindset is not the only possible one, even while it tries to sell itself as such. Robin Wall Kimmerer, from a Native American perspective, claims that the settler mind of property institutes an economy in which short-term thinking based on exchanges that do not establish long-term and ongoing reciprocal relationships are the cause of our problems. As opposed to this economy, she proposes a gift economy in which there are gifts of the land and between humans. The gift economy is nothing new. Capitalism likes to encourage a narrative that makes us believe that prior to money, people were bartering. Among others, anthropologist David Graeber makes clear this is a false image. Prior to money, gift economies existed for a much longer period than our current systems have so far.[23]

It is hard for us to imagine today that these gift economies actually functioned. We typically tend to think that if everything is free, universal laziness would be the result, and we would all die. A lack of trust is an underlying cause: we don't trust the government, the government doesn't trust us, and we don't trust one another. Indigenous societies survived for extended periods partially because of the trust established by a gift economy. Kimmerer argues that a gift establishes a reciprocal relationship in which we return the favor. Therefore, it would be a mistake to think that a gift is something free. Gifts create a set of relationships in which reciprocity is key. Drawing on the wisdom of her Potawatomi teachers, she writes, "Whatever we have been given is supposed to be given away again."[24] This might seem surprising and sound too much like our own economy in which we pay for whatever we want, but the dynamic is crucially different on all levels. First of all, we do not buy what we want, but we are given whatever is given. We might not even want it, or it might be different from what we hoped for. In the monetary exchange, we end the relationship immediately by settling the bill. In the gift economy, long-term relationships are established precisely because gifts are not free. A gift for free is exactly our mistaken form of thinking about gifts. In the gift economy, we are obligated to give back somehow, maybe with a thank you, maybe with another present. Moreover, nothing is truly ours. We always will pass things on again. A gift can be a gift of the earth, or it can be a gift from another person. It can be a gift from someone who lived a long time ago, as Kimmerer exemplifies with the maple trees planted long before she was alive, yet providing her today with maple syrup. A gift such as maple syrup is not without responsibilities: it is first of all a lot of hard work to harvest.[25] The work we put in taking care of trees, or in planting them in the first place, thus might not even return to us directly, but is a gift for someone else, sometimes a stranger, sometimes a stranger who is not even born yet. It is a long-term economy in which planting today might be a gift for people several generations later. Realizing this makes us aware that we should not just take natural resources, we are part of a cycle of giving and being given, in which we always are supposed to give back. Animal communities function—presumably unknowingly—on this principle. Their societies function without money, yet with the economy of an ecosystem, consisting of a community of animals, plants, and inanimate beings. Salmon provide health and life to different ecosystems; ants clean the forest; rats and mice break down borders (and challenge our system of food production); chimpanzees (and rats) show the importance of empathy; the tidepool mirrors our social order and yet tells us to break the crust, to become something else than human.

Indeed, ecopolitics tells us to redefine politics, and with that, it redefines us. We break out of our shells in order to become animal and with that the animal becomes something else. Ecopolitics, thus, proposes that we change our ways in order to save the planet as a place where children not yet born can thrive. It is a gift to the future.

Obviously, we have enormous hurdles to overcome. At this point, before we are running out of natural resources, we have already run into the first severe effects of climate change. Rising sea levels, destructive hurricanes, unprecedented monsoons, droughts, extreme temperatures, extreme weather patterns, and devastating wildfires are already here. Ecopolitics, by drawing on the politics of other species, provides a sense of hope, and I suggest that if there is a viable option out of our predicament, it will have to come out of a new kind of society in which we care for one another and our natural environment. This involves a radical reversal. It will not be done through technological developments (although those could help), not by some policy changes, and not through some individual changes of habit: we will have to collectively rethink who we are and how we live together. We have to end the individualistic approach, reverse greed, and, moreover, social structures that generate individualism, egoism, and greed. This is the essence of ecopolitics: we place ourselves outside of ourselves, let go of our greedy selves, and reconstitute our society as part of a greater whole, the earth.

Postscript I: Program for a Borderless Ecopolitics

- **Deterritorialize and get rid of borders:** It used to be the case that scientists regarded ecosystems as fixed, unchanging, and with clear demarcations. Where one ecosystem ended another one started. We now know that ecosystems are anything but fixed. They change and influence one another, and the borders are porous at best. This is a first lesson of ecopolitics: deterritorialize. This way we become something else and with that our past is also changing. Like salmon, everything about our being becomes something else. Likewise, the artificial, political, borders need to be overcome. Rats and mice can show us the way.

- **Engage in mutual aid** and become beings that others need and can rely on. Live with others: symbiosis.
- **Go for a walk and make walks possible for everyone** so that they can connect with people, animals, and the environment. Leave the smartphone at home, or use technology for constructive ways of communication and sharing real experiences. Get to know the place(s) you inhabit.
- **Engage in conversations** with people you disagree with and find shared values.
- **Provide free higher education for all**. Education is not an indoctrination, it is a collective exchange of ideas, a dialogue in which we all learn, and in which we learn to connect to those who do not agree with us.
- **Experience the suffering of others**, human and non-human and feel empathy / sympathy, together with a new sensibility for that which cannot be represented.
- **Create and tell stories**: share scientific narratives, poems, fiction, philosophical reflections, photographs, or other creative expressions.
- **Experience kinship with both the human and other than human world**.
- In summary: become (in Steinbeck's words) the **right material** for a positive phalanx.

Postscript II: A Final Story

Together finally again in person (!) without masks (?!) at the Marconi Center on Tomales Bay, we write together for a whole weekend. Two and a half years into the pandemic, it is probably our weariness of being together in indoor spaces which makes us collectively decide to have our first meal outside. After dinner each participant of the writing retreat shares the project(s) they hope to complete here. I am one of the last people to share mine: finishing this book! The sun has set, a chill is in the air, daylight is about to disappear. While I list the different animal political communities I discuss in the book, two deer run up to the deck where we are seated. They probably are no longer used to sharing this space with humans, and they look as startled as we all do and quickly take off. One of my fellow writers comments, "They want to be in your book as well." Indeed, they do, and they made it onto the last page, into my last little story, as their politics, along with so many other animals, intersects with ours and thus they are part of the greater whole, of ecopolitics.

Notes

Introduction

1. Aristotle, *History of Animals* (Loeb Classical Library 437. Cambridge, MA: Harvard University Press, 1965), I.i, 15.

2. Bernard Charbonneau, *The Green Light: A Self-Criticism of the Ecological Movement* (London: Bloomsbury Academic, 2018).

3. See for example Marc Bekoff, *The Emotional Lives of Animals: A Leading Scientist Explores Animal Joy, Sorrow, and Empathy—and Why They Matter* (Novato, CA: New World Library, 2007).

4. Tyson Yunkaporta, *Sand Talk: How Indigenous Thinking Can Save the World* (New York: HarperOne, 2020), 109–10.

5. Jacques Rancière, *Dissensus: On Politics and Aesthetics* (London: Bloomsbury Academic, 2015), 29.

6. John Culliney and David Jones analyze the evolution of human cooperation starting from subatomic particles. See: John Culliney and David Jones, *The Fractal Self: Science, Philosophy, and the Evolution of Human Cooperation* (Honolulu: University of Hawai'i Press, 2017).

7. Since 2002 the Netherlands is home to the first political party that represents the interest of animals (Partij voor de Dieren / Party for the Animals). In 2021, the party had six seats in the house and three in the senate of the Dutch government as well as one member in the parliament of the EU. In other countries and states, different groups advocate for animal rights, for example leading to anti-crating laws. A party dedicated to non-human animals can work in parliamentary systems such as the one in the Netherlands or the EU. We should consider these seats and laws that protect animals as victories against the oppression of animals. Yet, by all means, it is not enough, first of all, because it is situated in the realm of human politics.

8. Gary Snyder, *A Place in Space: Ethics, Aesthetics, and Watersheds* (San Francisco: Counterpoint, 1995), 127.

9. Snyder, *A Place in Space*, 128.

10. Snyder, 128.

11. Elisa Aaltola, *Varieties of Empathy: Moral Psychology and Animal Ethics* (Lanham MD: Rowman & Littlefield, 2018), 207.

12. Bruno Latour, *Politics of Nature* (Cambridge, MA: Harvard University Press, 2004), 47.

13. Donna Haraway, *Staying with the Trouble: Making Kin in the Chthulucene* (Durham, NC: Duke University Press, 2016), 33.

14. Haraway, *Staying with the Trouble*, 58.

15. Snyder, *A Place in Space*, 76.

16. See for example my article: Gerard Kuperus, "Heterogeneity and Injustice: A Sketch for a Lyotardian Approach to Animal Ethics," *Trans-Humanities* 8, no. 3, October 2015, 149–68.

17. De Waal has used the term extensively. See Frans de Waal, *Mama's Last Hug: Animal Emotions and What They Tell Us about Ourselves* (New York: Norton, 2019).

18. Sam Mickey and Adam Robbert, "Cosmopolitics," in *Integral Ecologies: Nature, Culture, and Knowledge in the Planetary Era*, ed. Sam Mickey, Sean Kelly, and Adam Robbert (New York: SUNY Press, 2017), 234.

19. Isabelle Stengers, "The Cosmopolitical Proposal," in *Making Things Public*, ed. Bruno Latour and Peter Weibel (Cambridge, MA: MIT Press, 2005), 995.

20. Jacques Rancière, *Dissensus*, 27.

21. Rancière, *Dissensus*, 28.

22. Murray Bookchin, *The Ecology of Freedom: The Emergence and Dissolution of Hierarchy* (Palo Alto, CA: Cheshire Books, 1982), 23–24.

23. Bruno Latour, "How to Talk about the Body? The Normative Dimension of Science Studies" *Body & Society* 10, no. 2–3 (2004): 205–29, 210.

24. Baird Callicott, "Environmental Philosophy Is Environmental Activism: The Most Radical and Effective Kind," in *Environmental Philosophy and Environmental Activism*, ed. D. E. Marietta, and L. E. Embre, 19–36 (Lanham: Rowman & Littlefield, 1995).

25. Richard Nelson *Make Prayers to the Raven: A Koyukon View of the Northern Forest* (Chicago: University of Chicago Press), 1986.

26. Robin Wall Kimmerer, *Braiding Sweetgrass: Indigenous Wisdom, Scientific Knowledge, and the Teachings of Plants* (Minneapolis: Milkweed Editions, 2015), 31.

27. In principle, this could (and presumably should) be the idea around taxes. I am paying taxes in return for good education, health care, infrastructure, security, and so forth. Yet, in particular places like the US where privatized services have convinced the public that paying taxes is evil, most people think that taxation is the equivalent of the government stealing their money. Money is contributing to this alienating experience. If we instead regarded our labor and other contributions as a gift to our society from which we receive the gifts of health care, education, infrastructure, and so forth, we would feel very different about everything, including

(and perhaps most importantly) ourselves. To regard our society as an ecology of gifts (as opposed to an exchange economy) is indeed what ecopolitics wants.

28. *The Biggest Little Farm* is a beautiful documentary on sharing ecosystems, even with those "unwanted" critters who actually make it a better place. One of the lessons learned is that it is typically we and our lack of understanding who are the problem.

29. Kimmerer, *Braiding Sweetgrass*, 55.

30. Kimmerer, 55.

31. "They were people who were also a *res*, a thing." David Graeber, *Debt: The First 5000 Years* (New York: Melville House, 2011), 200.

32. Bookchin, *The Ecology of Freedom*, 23.

33. Bookchin, 22.

34. Bookchin, 25.

35. Bookchin, 41.

36. Bookchin, 18.

37. In the alternative music scene, a whole global anarchistic network of individuals and venues exists. Musicians provide visiting musicians a place to sleep and perform. They can count on someone else doing the same for them elsewhere. Other examples can be found in the academic world. While the capitalistic aspects of the neoliberal university often seem dominant these days, we find underlying structures in which the generosity of faculty, students, staff, and librarians results in all kinds of groups (some organized, others very loose) that promote, share, and give. The biggest threat to those groups is that the university administration will institutionalize such generosity and the resulting structures. A writing or reading group, a support group for new faculty, are sure to go extinct once the university gets involved and buys some external "supportive platform." It is the grounds-up approach that makes it work, and any top-down approach will kill it (which does not mean that the top should not support the people who do the grounds-up work).

Chapter One

1. Parts of this chapter have been published previously in the article "Listening to the Salmon: Latour's Gaia, Aboriginal Thinking, and the Earth Community," *Environmental Philosophy* 16, no. 2 (2019).

2. Kimmerer discusses even a "Council of Trees" describing pecan trees all fruiting at the same time. See: Robin Wall Kimmerer, *Braiding Sweetgrass: Indigenous Wisdom, Scientific Knowledge, and the Teachings of Plants* (Minneapolis: Milkweed Editions, 2015), 11 ff.

3. J. E. Morrow Jr., "Schooling Behavior in Fishes," *Quarterly Review of Biology* 23, no. 1:27–38 (1948): 28.

4. Morrow "Schooling Behavior in Fishes," 28.
5. Morrow, 30.
6. Shinnosuke Nakayama, Reiji Masuda, and Masaru Tanaka, "Onsets of Schooling Behavior and Social Transmission in Chub Mackerel Scomber Japonicus," *Behavioral Ecology and Sociobiology* 61, no. 9 (2007), 1388.
7. As discussed in chapter 5, Frans de Waal discusses in, among other books, *Chimpanzee Politics*, how leaders (the alpha males) always take up the task of protecting the weakest in the colony.
8. Bruno Latour, *Facing Gaia: Eight Lectures on the New Climatic Regime* (Hoboken, NJ: Wiley, 2017).
9. Bruno Latour, *We Have Never Been Modern* (Cambridge, MA: Harvard University Press, 1991).
10. Bruno Latour, "Pragmatogonies: A Mythical Account of How Humans and Nonhumans Swap Properties," *American Behavioral Scientist* 37, no. 6 (1994): 791–809.
11. Bruno Latour, *Politics of Nature: How to Bring the Sciences into Democracy* (Cambridge, MA: Harvard University Press, 2004).
12. Bruno Latour, *Facing Gaia*, 62.
13. Latour, 93.
14. Latour, 98.
15. Latour, 100.
16. Latour, 100.
17. Latour, 101.
18. Latour, 101.
19. Latour, 100.
20. Latour, 68.
21. David R. Montgomery, *King of Fish: The Thousand-Year Run of Salmon* (Boulder, CO: Westview Press, 2003), 16.
22. Latour, *Facing Gaia*, 110.
23. Latour, 142.
24. Latour, 142.
25. Latour, 284.
26. Latour, 282.
27. Although the term *Gaia* is part of one of these older cultures.
28. The Tlingit are doing relatively well, despite the continuous challenges that they have faced: Russian and American invaders, boarding schools, the prohibition to speak their language in those schools, tourism, commercial fishing, and governmental institutions without Tlingit representation, to name a few. Today their language is spoken fluently by fewer than ten people, yet attempts are made at reinvigorating the language. See my *Ecopolitical Homelessness* for a more detailed discussion of Tlingit culture and senses of being.

29. Needless to say, various versions of this story exist. I refer here mostly to Swanson's two versions "Moldy-end," one obtained in Sitka and one in Wrangell. The two versions are numbered 99 and 100. John Reed Swanton, *Tlingit Myths and Texts* (Washington, DC: Government Printing Office, 1909), 301–20.

30. I apologize for taking the story out of context. First of all, the story should be told (although versions—including the ones I use here—have been written down), and secondly it is a story that belongs to Tlingit territory. The story, as many other aboriginal stories, contains a thorough knowledge of place, such as the names of creeks, species of salmon, the time of the year they return to spawn, and so forth.

31. Gary Snyder, *Practice of the Wild* (San Francisco, CA: North Point Press, 1990), 112.

32. David Montgomery, King of Fish (Boulder, CO: Westview Press, 2003), viii.

33. At least this is true for the Pacific Salmon. The salmon in the Atlantic can survive their act of reproduction.

34. Latour, *Facing Gaia*, 80.

35. It is tempting to just recognize "Salmon Boy" and other stories as myths. We might still value myths and we might say that science is a myth, or is based on myths. We could call a natural law such as gravity a myth, or we could argue that it is based on the myth called "natural law." Yet, we could also reverse the argument: instead of "reducing" science to myth (and insulting as well as alienating our colleagues in the natural sciences) we could "upgrade" myth to science, which is in many ways a more interesting move. I owe this insight to Professor Alexandria Wilson, Native American scholar and a member of the Cree Tribe in Saskatchewan, who in a personal conversation insisted that we have it all wrong: Native American culture does not consist of myths but of science.

36. Gerard Kuperus, "An Ecology of the Future: Nietzsche and Ecological Restoration," in *Ontologies of Nature*, ed. Gerard Kuperus and Marjolein Oele (New York: Springer, 2017).

37. Cf. Richard Nelson, *Make Prayers to the Raven: A Koyukon View of the Northern Forest* (Chicago: University of Chicago Press, 1986).

38. Together with my students I had the privilege to listen to some of the Raven stories as told by Chuck Miller of the Sitka Clan of the Tlingit People. I was at first very surprised to how Chuck was personifying Raven, constantly making fun of him. He ridiculed how Raven walked, all the things he wanted, and how selfishly he behaved. Eventually, it dawned on me that the story tells us that we should not be like Raven, something that is lost when reading the story, without the humorous enactments of Raven.

39. Tyson Yunkaporta, *Sand Talk: How Indigenous Thinking Can Save the World* (New York: HarperOne, 2020), 26–27.

40. Friedrich Nietzsche, *The Gay Science: With a Prelude in Rhymes and an Appendix of Songs* (New York: Vintage Books, 1971).

Chapter Two

1. Peter Fimrite, "Exterminating Mice with Poison Would Protect Rare Seabirds on Farallons," *San Francisco Chronicle*, July 12, 2019.

2. Fimrite, "Exterminating Mice with Poison."

3. See also my "An Ecology of the Future: Nietzsche and Ecological Restoration," in *Ontologies of Nature*, ed. Gerard Kuperus and Marjolein Oele (New York: Springer, 2017).

4. Fimrite, "Exterminating Mice with Poison."

5. Parallels can be drawn with the Oostvaardersplassen in the Netherlands, where groups "advocated" for mammals (the "large grazers") to be fed, arguing that during harsh winters the (re)wild(ed) animals should not be left starving. The debate is complex, but as Jozef Keulartz has argued, feeding or killing actually creates more issues, since it disrupts natural cycles. For example, during a period of hunger the female animals will not ovulate, thus naturally reducing the growth of the population. The parallel with the mice on the Farallones is that in both cases we humans think that we can improve the existing situation. See Jozef Keulartz, *Dieren in ons Midden: Samenleven met dieren in het tijdperk van de mens* (Gorredijk: Noordboek, 2019).

6. Maanvi Sing, "Helicopters to Drop Poison on California's Farallon Islands amid 'Plague' of Mice," *The Guardian*, December 17, 2021.

7. Wildcare, "Stop the Farallon Islands Poison Drop," December 2021, https://discoverwildcare.org/rat-poison-rodenticides-farallon-islands/.

8. Leonard Lawlor, "Following the Rats: Becoming-Animal in Deleuze and Guattari," *SubStance* 37, no. 3 (2008): 171.

9. Leonard Lawlor, "Following the Rats, 175.

10. Lawlor, 176.

11. Lawlor, 177.

12. Lawlor, 170.

13. Lawlor, 184.

14. David Graeber, *Fragments of an Anarchist Anthropology* (Chicago: Prickly Paradigm Press, 2004), 78.

15. Graeber, *Fragments of an Anarchist Anthropology*, 78.

16. John Steinbeck, *Of Mice and Men* (New York: Penguin Books, 1993), 34.

17. Steinbeck, *Of Mice and Men*, 8–9.

18. Steinbeck, 13. The novella is full of animals and constantly relates humans with animals. One animal predominantly present, besides the mice and the dog, is the rabbit. The dream farm George and Lennie hope to own includes rabbits, which will be tended to by George. The rabbit represents the softness he likes so much, but it also seems that owning the rabbits involves some kind of transition from oppressed to oppressor. Rabbits are known to reproduce quickly, and so their future dream farm will have an abundance of these rabbits, as there is an abundance of farmworkers dominated by farm owners.

19. Robert Burns "To a Mouse, On Turning Her Up in Her Nest with the Plough," in *Collected Works* (http://www.robertburns.org/works/75.shtml), 1785. The contemporary English version is: "But little Mouse, you are not alone, / In proving foresight may be vain: / The best laid schemes of mice and men/ Go often askew, / And leave us nothing but grief and pain, / For promised joy!"

20. The reasons why George kills his friend are multiple. Even while it is the most dramatic moment, the shot is not unprecedented. Most of all, there are clear parallels between Lennie and the old, stinky, blind, and arthritic dog of Candy, the old man. The others living in the bunkhouse are fed up with the dog, especially with its smell. Crooks in a mean-spirited comment suggests to Lennie that George might leave him. If that happens, he suggests, "They'll tie you up with a collar, like a dog" (Steinbeck, *Of Mice and Men*, 70). Yet, Lennie is eventually not tied up like a dog, but shot like a dog. The dog is euthanized, killed by a gunshot, and the same happens to Lennie. Both were shot in the back of the head and did not see it coming.

21. John Steinbeck, *Of Mice and Men*, 71.

22. John Steinbeck, 75.

23. John Steinbeck, 72.

24. The idea of the "face of the other" and the "face-to-face" is most famously formulated in *Totality and Infinity*. Important to note is that Levinas speaks of the singular face, not of the massive face that I suggest here. Emmanuel Levinas, *Totality and Infinity: An Essay on Exteriority* (Pittsburgh, PA: Duquesne University Press, 1969).

25. According to the Bureau of Labor Statistics about 70 percent of businesses will fail within a decade after starting up. Of the 30 percent remaining only a small percentage turns into a booming business.

26. Vinciane Despret, "The Enigma of the Raven," *Angelaki* 20, no. 2 (2015): 63.

27. Vinciane Despret, "Thinking Like a Rat," *Angelaki* 20, no. 2 (2015): 126.

28. Despret, "Thinking Like a Rat," 127.

29. Despret, 127.

30. Despret, 127.

31. As discussed in the concluding chapter, studies on empathy have indicated that many humans who have never experienced poverty, racism, or forms of oppression have difficulty relating to those who are experiencing it. This suggests that in these situations empathy for the other is lacking, since one can literally not imagine oneself in the situation of the other.

Chapter Three

1. In the academic world today, we find this model at work as well in the form of adjunct labor, which constitutes a significant amount of the workforce in higher education. Adjuncts often teach more students than full-time professors,

have the last choice when it comes to teaching schedules, often have to work at multiple institutions, have virtually no job security, and get paid less. As a full-time colleague, one has to be careful to stay away from justifying this injustice, since it simply cannot be done.

2. In *Mama's Last Hug* De Waal writes about the danger of "anthropodenial" (the opposite of anthropomorphism) in which we fail to ever understand ourselves because we keep arguing for our special status as human beings. See: De Waal, *Mama's Last Hug: Animal Emotions and What They Tell Us about Ourselves* (New York: Norton, 2019), 61.

3. Frans De Waal, *Chimpanzee Politics: Power and Sex Among Apes* (Baltimore, MD: Johns Hopkins University Press, 1982), 3–4.

4. De Waal, *Chimpanzee Politics*, 5.

5. De Waal, 9.

6. De Waal, 9.

7. De Waal, 8.

8. De Waal, 9.

9. De Waal, 29.

10. De Waal, 41.

11. De Waal, 53.

12. De Waal, 78.

13. De Waal, 81.

14. De Waal, 103.

15. De Waal, 117 ff.

16. De Waal, 118.

17. De Waal, compare 137.

18. De Waal, 47.

19. De Waal, 54.

20. De Waal, 55.

21. Eric Michael Johnson, "Frans de Waal on Political Apes, Science Communication, and Building a Cooperative Society," *Scientific American*, July 11, 2011.

22. Frans de Waal, *The Age of Empathy: Nature's Lessons for a Kinder Society* (New York: Crown, 2009), 44.

23. De Waal, *The Age of Empathy*, 38 ff.

24. De Waal, 39.

25. Compare De Waal, 45 and 201 ff.

26. De Waal, *Chimpanzee Politics*, 10.

27. De Waal, *The Age of Empathy*, 75.

28. Jacqueline Taylor, *Reflecting Subjects: Passion, Sympathy, and Society in Hume's Philosophy* (Oxford: Oxford University Press, 2015), 39.

29. Hume, *Treatise* 2.1.11.3, quoted by Taylor, *Reflecting Subjects*, 41.

30. Gilles Deleuze, *Empiricism and Subjectivity* (New York: Columbia University Press, 1991), 44.

31. Deleuze, *Empiricism and Subjectivity*, 47.
32. Deleuze, 47.
33. Compare Taylor, *Reflecting Subjects*, 40–41.
34. De Waal, *The Age of Empathy*, 82–83.
35. De Waal, 42.
36. De Waal, 32.
37. De Waal, 33.
38. Johnson, "Frans de Waal on Political Apes, Science Communication, and Building a Cooperative Society."
39. Henry Rosemont, *Against Individualism* (Minneapolis: Lexington Books, 2016).
40. Rosemont, *Against Individualism*, 24 ff.
41. Rosemont, 18. He provides the examples of being immoral and being impolite (28). Being impolite is in the Western world seen as negative, but not in an immoral way. As a Western individual I might forget to say "please" or "thank you," yell at someone, or make some rude gesture. It might not be good, but it is not immoral. Yet, in a Confucian context rude actions might themselves be seen as immoral.
42. See Claire Clark and William Hoynes, "Images of Race and Nation after September 11," *Peace Review* 15, no. 4 (2003), and Eduardo Mendieta, "Patriotism and Anti-Americanism," *Peace Review* 15, no. 4 (2003).
43. It is Sen's point that such perceptions of differences are created. Moreover, he argues that by simply tying the identity of being a Muslim to the religious aspect, a dangerous situation is created in which religious leaders all of a sudden become powerful. Without the influence of the West these leaders had not necessarily been given any political power by their own community. Yet, Western politicians regard them as leaders, since in the limited idea of identity they are seen as the essence of the Muslim world. With that gesture the West actually gives these religious leaders power and enforces the religious aspect of Muslim identity. Amartya Sen, *Identity and Violence: The Illusion of Destiny* (New York: Norton, 2007).
44. The other part of Sen's argument is to focus on the shared part of our identities, first of all by recognizing that we are all human beings. The one essential feature that is more basic than a community is that we are human beings. In addition, we also find a shared intellectual history of Muslims and Christians. He names Maimonides who fled to a Muslim region in the twelfth century, mathematics that was developed in the Arab world, the influence of Ancient Greece (politics + philosophy) on both the Western and non-Western world, and the influence of non-Western traditions on Greece.
45. While Hobbes, Rousseau, and other social contract theorists describe a state of nature in which early humans did not cooperate or have much contact with one another, archaeologists have found evidence of the existence of the nuclear family in the early history of human life. Even Neanderthals, who lived for

thousands of years alongside early Homo sapiens, lived presumably as families. Yet, how important and how permanent such relations were, is unclear. Maybe groups of humans were living similar to chimpanzees, with alpha males. Or perhaps the organization even of the family was very loose. Of course, we are all familiar with the textbook example we studied in school: the image of a hunting and gathering man (possibly with others), a woman (possibly with other women) who takes care of the children and had other domestic responsibilities. The truth of the matter is that from the little archaeological evidence we have of these early human societies, we can deduct very little.

Chapter Four

1. Some parts of this chapter have been published in a very different context and format in Gerard Kuperus, "Westering and Breaking Through: Zen Buddhism on Cannery Row," in *Philosophy in the American West: A Geography of Thought*, ed. Josh Hayes, Gerard Kuperus, and Brian Treanor (London: Routledge, 2020).

2. Warder Clyde Allee, *Animal Aggregations: A Study in General Sociology* (Chicago: University of Chicago Press, 1978), 352.

3. John Steinbeck and Edward Ricketts, *The Log from the Sea of Cortez* (London: Penguin, 2001), 3. This book is a collaborative project with Ed Ricketts, Steinbeck's closest friend. Steinbeck did most of the writing, yet the work would not have been written without Ricketts, who not only has been described as the fountain of inspiration for Steinbeck, but parts of the books are taken verbatim from unpublished work written by Ricketts. Ricketts's logbook was also used extensively to draft the text (see Richard Astro, *John Steinbeck and Edward F. Ricketts: The Shaping of a Novelist* (Aberdeen, IA: Western Flyer Publishing, 1973), 14, 16, and 26). Lastly, and most importantly, Ricketts's insights in ecology and animal and human group behavior had a tremendous influence on Steinbeck. Although the publisher wanted to publish the book without Ricketts listed as the coauthor, Steinbeck insisted both their names should be listed. It is for that reason odd that the second edition (published after the death of Ricketts) was published with only Steinbeck listed as the author.

4. Steinbeck and Ricketts, *The Log from the Sea of Cortez*, 3.

5. Astro, *John Steinbeck and Edward F. Ricketts*, 29.

6. Steinbeck and Ricketts, *The Log from the Sea of Cortez*, 85.

7. Astro, *John Steinbeck and Edward F. Ricketts*, 11, 12. See also the letter from September 15, 1946, from Ricketts to Steinbeck in John Steinbeck, *Steinbeck: A Life in Letters* (New York: Penguin Books, 2014).

8. Allee, *Animal Aggregations*, 44, 66, and 70.

9. Allee, 176.

10. Allee, 177, see also 354.

11. Steinbeck and Ricketts, *The Log from the Sea of Cortez*, 165. Astro contrasts the non-teleological biology of Ricketts with the "organismal conception" of Ritter, which presumably made a big impression on Steinbeck when he took a marine biology course in 1923. It is, however, not evident which of Ritter's ideas made a lasting impression on Steinbeck. The quote I use here is also discussed by Astro, who points out that this section of the text does not appear in Ricketts's journal and, thus, can probably be attributed to Steinbeck (Astro, *John Steinbeck and Edward F. Ricketts*, 45). Astro argues that the ideas of Ritter and Allee are very different from one another, in which he contrasts Ritter's ideas of the whole being more than the sum of its parts with Allee's idea that organisms tend to cooperate. These are, indeed, different claims. For Astro, the ideas of Allee and Ritter are for, respectively, Ricketts and Steinbeck, leading to conflicting standpoints in which Ritter and Steinbeck follow a teleological path. Astro is mistaken here as he neglects the actual adoption of the ideas by Steinbeck and Ricketts. In fact, they take elements of both theories and merge them. Even the attribution of teleology to Ritter can be questioned because Ritter is thinking in the tradition of Darwin. While survival could be seen as a telos, it seems problematic to translate ideas of relationality and that a whole is more than the sum of its parts, into teleology.

12. Steinbeck and Ricketts, *The Log from the Sea of Cortez*, 240.

13. Steinbeck and Ricketts, 241.

14. Ricketts, *The Outer Shores*, quoted in Astro, *John Steinbeck and Edward F. Ricketts*, 11.

15. Ricketts, *The Outer Shores*, quoted in Astro, *John Steinbeck and Edward F. Ricketts*, 28.

16. Steinbeck and Ricketts, *The Log from the Sea of Cortez*, 216.

17. Steinbeck and Ricketts, 217.

18. Steinbeck and Ricketts, 217.

19. Quoted in: Astro, *John Steinbeck and Edward F. Ricketts*, 65.

20. Astro, *John Steinbeck and Edward F. Ricketts*, 64.

21. Steinbeck's unpublished essay on the phalanx, quoted in Astro, *John Steinbeck and Edward F. Ricketts*, 65.

22. Steinbeck's unpublished essay on the phalanx, quoted in Astro, *John Steinbeck and Edward F. Ricketts*, 65.

23. Steinbeck and Ricketts, *The Log from the Sea of Cortez*, 34.

24. Steinbeck and Ricketts, 32–33.

25. Steinbeck and Ricketts, 257.

26. Steinbeck and Ricketts, 257. Astro gives a lot of significance to the fact that Boodin is quoted, and he argues that the philosopher had a great influence on Steinbeck. Boodin's ideas clearly argue that the world is too organized to be the result of chance, and since Astro attributes the Boodin quote (and possible influence) to Steinbeck, it seems to constitute a problem here as Boodin's thinking is clearly inconsistent with Ricketts proposed non-teleological account of nature.

Nevertheless, even while Boodin is quoted here, the *Logbook* does not develop the idea of intelligent design.

27. Such feelings can be found throughout Steinbeck's work. For example, in *East of Eden*, Lee has a dark feeling the first time he meets the wife of Adam.

28. Steinbeck and Ricketts, *The Log from the Sea of Cortez*, 259.

29. Steinbeck and Ricketts, 257.

30. The danger of the phalanx can also be seen in the depletion of the land leading to the Great Dust Bowl, an event at the heart of *The Grapes of Wrath*, and mostly due to the use of agricultural methods that worked well on the East Coast and in western parts of Europe, but not in the American prairies. Turning the new into the known caused ecological and humanitarian disasters. The group here turned into a beast without a head and collectively makes stupid decisions. One farmer's deep plowing and causing erosion is not the problem. It is the collective plowing of virtually all farmers in an extended area which causes great calamity.

31. We can presumably attribute this romantic aspect of *The Grapes of Wrath* to Steinbeck's own urge to travel. *Travels with Charley* starts with a description of this longing in himself (and in many other people) to go places. He does balance this positive anticipation with a sense of gloom right before and at the start of the journey (which we also find in *The Log from the Sea of Cortez*: they take what appears to be the better part of a day to say goodbye to family and friends before leaving the dock).

32. Astro, *John Steinbeck and Edward F. Ricketts*, 72.

33. Steinbeck, "Letter to Albee," in *Steinbeck: A Life in Letters*, 79–80.

34. Steinbeck, 81.

35. Steinbeck, 80.

36. Steinbeck, 81.

37. It seems that close to half of the people we elect into office, from the local level to the federal level, are incompetent. No individual in their right mind would have made the mistake of giving any of the people whom we collectively support a chance to run our municipality, state, or nation. It is, then, these elected individuals we should blame for making poor decisions. It is our tendency to follow the group, which we need in order to survive. It might be true that we only truly trust a few individuals or that we can trust a community of a few hundred people, but beyond trust lies the field of group emotions, which can make millions of people act as one, diminishing their individuality as a soldier loses their individuality in the phalanx.

38. Steinbeck, "Letter to Albee," in *Steinbeck: A Life in Letters*, 81.

39. Steinbeck, 80.

40. Steinbeck, 123.

41. John Steinbeck, *The Red Pony* (London: Penguin Books, 2012), 129.

42. Benedictus de Spinoza. *The Ethics: Treatise on the Emendation of the Intellect* (Indianapolis: Hackett, 1992), 152.

43. Hasana Sharp, *Spinoza and the Politics of Renaturalization* (Chicago: University of Chicago Press, 2011), 34.

44. *Travels with Charley* is partially a travel journal sometimes presented as an ethnography, although scholars have raised suspicions about the authenticity of the conversations described, especially since a lot of the characters resemble those found in his novels.

45. John Steinbeck, *Travels with Charley: In Search of America* (New York: Penguin Books, 2017), 94.

46. Steinbeck, *The Red Pony*, 129.

47. Steinbeck, 129.

48. Steinbeck, 129.

49. Steinbeck, 129–30.

50. Allee, *Animal Aggregations*, 177.

51. Allee, 178.

52. On adaption to change he writes: "Biology teaches the inevitability of change, if it teaches anything. We must have some device in our system which will allow for needed changes, some means of making those compromises at which the English and the French are so proficient in their international affairs. In international as in legal circles, we must have some peaceful means of declaring a defunct nation bankrupt." Allee, *Animal Aggregations*, 197.

53. Likewise, in stories such as "The Pearl" it is made clear that modern technological societies are driven by greed and lack the ethical standards that determine less developed societies. Steinbeck's "ethics of hope" is at times Buddhist in nature. In *The Log from the Sea of Cortez*, he and Ricketts are not blaming the Japanese fishermen for destroying all life on the sea floor, but the problem is the system (or the phalanx) of which they are a part. After having spent some hours on a Japanese fishing vessel that dredged the bottom of the sea for shrimp (taking every living thing with it), they write: "We liked the people on this boat very much. They were good men, but they were caught in a large destructive machine, good men doing a bad thing. With their many and large boats, with their industry and efficiency, but most of all with their intense energy, these Japanese will obviously soon clean out the shrimps of the region. And it is not clear that a species thus attacked comes back. The disturbed balance often gives a new species ascendency and destroys forever the old relationship." Steinbeck and Ricketts, *The Log from the Sea of Cortez*, 249.

54. Peter Lisca, *The Wide World of John Steinbeck* (New York: Gordian Press, 1981), 107.

Chapter Five

1. The study estimated that about 20,000 trillion ants live on the earth. Patrick Schultheiss, Sabine S. Nooten, Runxi Wang, et al., "The Abundance, Biomass, and Distribution of Ants on Earth," *Proceedings of the National Academy of Sciences* 119, no. 40 (2022).

2. Murray Bookchin makes this point in his introduction to the *Ecology of Freedom* (Palo Alto, CA: Cheshire Books, 1982).

3. Peter Kropotkin, *Mutual Aid: A Factor of Evolution* (New York: New York University Press, 1972), 6.

4. Kropotkin, *Mutual Aid*, 7.

5. Peter Kropotkin, *Ethics: Origin and Development* (Montréal, New York : Black Rose Books, 1992), 12.

6. Kropotkin, *Ethics*, 13.

7. Kropotkin, 14.

8. He might also refer to the idea of ecology, the oikos of "the groups of different species which we find living together" (the word *ecology* was introduced by Ernst Haeckel in 1869).

9. Kropotkin, *Ethics*, 14.

10. Kropotkin, *Mutual Aid*, 23.

11. Kropotkin, *Mutual Aid*, 15.

12. Charles Darwin, *The Descent of Man and Selection in Relation to Sex* (Cambridge: Cambridge University Press, 2009), 136.

13. Darwin, *The Descent of Man*, 71.

14. Darwin, 74.

15. For example, Hölldobler and Wilson discussed below provide plenty of warnings about using a "value-laden word" when introducing the topic of altruism in ants. Bert Hölldobler and Edward Wilson, *The Ants* (Cambridge: Belknap Press:, 1990), 179.

16. Darwin, *The Descent of Man*, 76.

17. Darwin, 77.

18. Kropotkin, *Ethics*, 16.

19. Peter Ryley, *Making Another World Possible: Anarchism, Anti-capitalism and Ecology in Late 19th and Early 20th Century Britain* (London: Bloomsbury, 2013), 30.

20. Tyson Yunkaporta, *Sand Talk: How Indigenous Thinking Can Save the World* (New York: HarperOne, 2020), 26.

21. Yunkaporta, *Sand Talk*, 27.

22. Kropotkin, *Ethics* 15.

23. Kropotkin, 16–17.

24. Kropotkin, 31.

25. Kropotkin, 30.

26. Kropotkin, 30–31.

27. Kropotkin, 31.

28. Kropotkin, 34. The basis for the scientific approach is found in Darwin's *Descent of Man*. Kropotkin quotes Darwin's discussion of social instincts "which lead the animal to take pleasure in the society of its fellows, to feel a certain amount of sympathy with them, and to perform various services for them" (Kropotkin,

Ethics, 33; Darwin, *Descent of Man*, 72). The feeling of comradery and mutual sensibility leads to a "capability to be influenced by another's feelings" (Kropotkin, 33). Within the theory of evolution, such feelings are part of the species instead of being "acquired by each individual separately" (Kropotkin, 33). Evidence that such feelings exist in animals other than humans is by Darwin first of all identified in the social animals.

29. Kropotkin, *Ethics*, 35.
30. Kropotkin, 37.
31. Kropotkin, 37.
32. Kropotkin, 37.
33. Kropotkin suggests that the social aspect, mutual aid, or cooperation is found in all life. He admits that mutual aid can sometimes conflict with selfishness or with the care for offspring. He provides the example of birds leaving behind their young, which he explains as a social act: the attraction to the group is so strong that when the group leaves, even one's own offspring becomes secondary (Kropotkin, *Ethics*, 38). Thus, we find group cooperation, which is predominantly explained as cooperation among the same species, although he does refer to some cross-species cooperation, such as the adult robin redbreast that takes care of the offspring of a wren (Kropotkin, 20). The discussion of which of the different instincts is the strongest continues today in debates around kinship and group selection. Different theories suggest that animals seek to protect either *their offspring or the group*, even at the cost of sacrificing their own lives.
34. Kropotkin, *Ethics*, 26–27.
35. Kropotkin, 26.
36. Kropotkin, 240.
37. Kropotkin, *Mutual Aid*, 14.
38. Kropotkin, 14.
39. In the *Conquest of Bread*, for example, he mentions how jealousy will spring up when "it becomes a case of who is the most influential person on the board. The least inequality causes wranglings and recriminations. If the smallest advantage is given to any one, a tremendous hue and cry is raised—and not without reason" (Peter Kropotkin, *Conquest of Bread* [New York: Penguin Random House, 2015], 239). We are quite familiar with this. Politics from the local to the national level is often reduced to nothing but a game in which only the members of the political body, the politicians, matter. The constituents only matter in so far as they elect an official. This means that their so-called representatives, at least in appearance, have to act in their best interest, but in reality, the game is all about the politicians whose actions are determined by egoistic instincts and feelings of jealousy and anxiety about losing power, nourished by the political system itself. Very few politicians can truly listen to and represent the needs of their constituents. As we know all too well, the influence of corporations and their lobbyists even further exacerbates this issue.

40. Kropotkin, *Ethics*, 308.

41. In *Ethics*, within the context of discussing Herbert Spencer, Kropotkin reflects on the relationship between altruism and egoism. Spencer argues that altruism depends on egoism, since "egoistic pleasure" can be derived from altruistic acts. Kropotkin does not disagree with this idea but comments that with the development of morality in human and animal societies, we aim to move beyond egoism.

42. Laurent Keller and Élisabeth Gordon, *The Lives of Ants* (Oxford: Oxford University Press, 2010), 17.

43. Keller and Gordon, *The Lives of Ants*, 17.

44. See Keller and Gordon, 18.

45. Edward O. Wilson, *Anthill* (New York: W. W. Norton & Co, 2011), 15.

46. Wilson, *Anthill*, 15.

47. Wilson, 16.

48. Wilson, 15.

49. Deborah Gordon, *Ants at Work: How an Insect Society Is Organized* (New York: The Free Press, 2011), 117.

50. Gordon, *Ants at Work*, 118.

51. Gordon, 118.

52. See Keller and Gordon, *The Lives of Ants*, 1.

53. https://educationdata.org/average-time-to-repay-student-loans. Retrieved May 25, 2021.

54. Besides fascist movements, we can think about the mass movement of consumerism which is destroying the habitats of other species and that of our own species. We should, thus, be careful to frame any decentralized political system in such a way that it avoids populism and the oppression of minorities.

55. On their now defunct website, ELF pointed out that people *can* get hurt or killed in the use of radical tactics such as fire. It states that "torching sport utility vehicles, ski resorts, research labs and McMansions, releases huge amounts of toxic gasses into the atmosphere—creating far more greenhouse gasses than if they were left alone. The end result: everything is rebuilt, replaced or repaired. This DOUBLES the burden on the environment and taxpayers! An exercise in futility and self-defeat. Think about it." The statement was posted after a series of raids and the eventual prosecution of ELF members as domestic terrorists after a long and extensive FBI investigation. They warn: "Regardless of the frustration we all feel about the enormous perils facing our Mother Earth, engaging the perceived wrong-doers with threats, intimidation and destructive tactics will always fail. Fighting fire with fire will get you burned." http://earth-liberation-front.org/. Retrieved August 15, 2012.

56. In terms of his education, it is worthwhile to mention that Kropotkin was one of the thinkers discussed in Abbey's MA thesis, as an anarchist who rejected pacifism. Kropotkin arguably influenced Abbey in terms of approving violence. In Kropotkin's time, most anarchists regarded war as an expression of capitalism and

argued against the immorality of sending working-class soldiers to war. While initially sharing these sentiments, Kropotkin ultimately decided that the outcomes of a revolution, even a violent one, could justify it. In terms of capitalism, he speaks about a plague we need to overcome and the outcome of a revolution is the salvation of humanity (such language is interestingly coming from someone who refuses the metaphysical basis of ethics). Both Kropotkin and Abbey criticize government and capitalism's demand for growth, yet Abbey's version of anarchism is centered around environmental destruction, whereas Kropotkin is more focused on poverty. On Kropotkin's stance on war, see Ryley, *Making Another World Possible*.

57. Edward Abbey, "Forward!," in *Ecodefense: A Field Guide to Monkeywrenching* by Dave Foreman (Chico, CA: Abbzug Press, 2002), 3.

58. The appeal to law and morality seems to appeal to the "common" conception of law and morality, which is not necessarily the same as Abbey's notions. By referring to this common notion, he seems to write for a broader audience that might recognize self-defense as indeed a basic right.

59. Edward Abbey, *The Monkey Wrench Gang* (Philadelphia: Lippincott, 1975), 168.

60. Abbey, *The Monkey Wrench Gang*, 368.

61. Abbey, 170.

62. In the introductory chapter of this book, I discussed Rancière's claim that consensus is dangerous since it returns politics to the police. If dissensus, on the other hand, is some kind of difference society has with itself, this could be regarded as a helpful way to think about overcoming our ant-like existence.

63. Abbey, *The Monkey Wrench Gang*, 75.

64. Abbey, 173.

65. Abbey, 84. The disagreement with Buckminster Fuller, someone also concerned with the sustainability of our current model, might seem a bit surprising. Yet, Fuller was interested in cooperation and technological advancement. Doc (and Abbey) on the other hand, are interested in disruption and destruction of the colony, against "technological tyranny," the machine of industrialization, and are never impressed by any piece of technology. Fuller, at least in Abbey's eyes, was an engineer creating the ant colony. His geodesic dome, ridiculed by Doc, is, besides our ant-like activity, another symbol for those natural human processes we should fight. The dome presents a technological wonder in an organic shape, mimicking nature.

66. Abbey, *The Monkey Wrench Gang*, 167.

67. Abbey, 64.

68. Abbey, 80.

69. Uri Gordon, "Anarchism and Political Theory," PhD thesis, University of Oxford, 2007, 252.

70. Gordon, "Anarchism and Political Theory," 251.

71. Nietzsche mentions ants in aphorisms 49 and 206 of *Daybreak*. Friedrich Nietzsche, *Daybreak* (Cambridge: Cambridge University Press, 2012).

Conclusion

1. The encyclical *Laudato si'*, by Pope Francis, makes a very similar argument. For a discussion of *Laudato si'* in comparison, see my "Our Common Home and the True Dharma Eye: Dōgen and Laudato si' in the Anthropocene," in *Faith and Social Justice: Environmental and Economic Justice* (San Francisco: University of San Francisco Press, 2020).

2. Friedrich Nietzsche, *The Gay Science: With a Prelude in Rhymes and an Appendix of Songs* (New York: Vintage Books, 1971), §125.

3. Robinson Jeffers, "Roan Stallion," in *The Selected Poetry of Robinson Jeffers* (Stanford, CA: Stanford University Press, 2001), 125.

4. Murray Bookchin, *The Ecology of Freedom: The Emergence and Dissolution of Hierarchy* (Palo Alto, CA: Cheshire Books, 1982), 27.

5. For example, one might feel entitled to a particular habit, such as working in one's office. Yet, it turns out one is not protected by any right to do so, even while one might feel their right is violated when the access they used to have is revoked.

6. James Ferguson provides a famous and interesting analysis of this with a case study in Lesotho. Most development work is done without true cultural knowledge and often ends up further empowering the military, against the intentions of the project, which presented itself as nonpolitical in the first place. See James Ferguson, *The Anti-politics Machine: Development, Depoliticization, and Bureaucratic power in Lesotho* (Minneapolis: University of Minnesota Press, 1994).

7. As for the first, the case of the disappearance and reintroduction of the wolf in Yellowstone is well studied. The chapter on salmon discussed how different animals, plants, and trees are relying on this species.

8. Ironically, in the non-human realm we often target so-called predators, whom we regard as dictators who need to be dethroned, failing to recognize the important contributions they make to the health of an ecosystem. Bears, we have seen, are important members along with salmon. In many places bears are gone, and the negative effects are numerous.

9. Countries from the Middle East to South America have been targeted by the West, in particular the USA, in order to destabilize unwilling governments, often with many unintended consequences. Of all the natural resources, securing oil has played the most significant role in this regard. Klare's *Blood and Oil* provides an excellent discussion of American strategies around oil since World War II. See: Michael Klare, *Blood and Oil: The Dangers and Consequences of America's Growing Dependency on Imported Petroleum* (Hagerstown: McDougal, 2005).

10. Tommy Orange, *There There* (New York: Knopf, 2018), 137.

11. Orange, *There There*, 138.

12. Jeffers, "Roan Stallion."

13. Michael T. Mendl and Elizabeth S. Paul, "Bee Happy: Bumblebees Show Decision-Making That Reflects Emotion-like States," *Science* 353, no. 6307 (2016): 1499–1500.

14. Orange, *There There*, 138.

15. As the documentary, book, and TV series *Surprising Europe* makes clear, the motives of immigrants seeking opportunity is clear. They are often sent by their families, who collectively pay for their flights. The immigrant is now indebted to their family, not only because of family ties, but also because of financial obligations. Both the family and the immigrant have false expectations about making money and standards of living. Some immigrants who fail to make money for their families back in Africa shamefully disappear.

16. The settlement is entirely off the grid. The architecture is stunning. The first thing one sees of the island is the bird watchtower, a beautiful piece of architecture. The architecture of the island is explicitly not human-centered and won the 2021 Dutch Design Award.

17. While estimates vary, it is suggested by many that about a dozen species go extinct every day and that we are losing species at a rate of 1,000 times the "backdrop" rate (which would be the rate occurring under "normal" circumstances). While it is the case that great extinctions have happened before, the point is that we are the cause. The 2021 Climate Report (the IPCC Sixth Assessment Report) states the human cause without any ambiguity.

18. Roberto Esposito, *The Third Person* (Cambridge: Polity, 2012), 150.

19. Russell, M. S. "The Politics of the Third Person: Esposito's Third Person and Rancière's Disagreement," *Critical Horizons*, 15 no. 3 (2014): 211–230.

20. Scientists often have done themselves a disservice by presenting their findings as truths as opposed to theories that attempt to explain certain observed phenomena. Manipulation of data occurs in order to make the theories work. Prestige and grants are at stake. Yet, as Latour makes clear, a natural scientist tells a story as we do in the humanities and works with constructs just as much as the social scientist. Going back to the just mentioned distrust in politicians and government, the lack of trust in science provides in a world of climate change and pandemics a particularly dangerous situation.

21. Gerard Kuperus, *Ecopolitical Homelessness: Redefining Place in an Ensettled World* (New York: Routledge, 2016).

22. An example of urban stories in the landscape can be found in Amsterdam. As other old cities, this city is full of stories, some beautiful, some horrific. Plaques tell us of historical events, who or what was housed here when; ornamental stones in facades of houses sometimes show scenes of slavery; bronze tiles in the sidewalks provide names of the persons who lived here once and were deported and killed in places such as Treblinka, Sobibor, Auschwitz. Once we open up to this, the streets speak and tell stories.

23. See David Graeber, *Debt: The First 5000 Years* (New York: Melville House, 2011).

24. Robin Wall Kimmerer, *Braiding Sweetgrass: Indigenous Wisdom, Scientific Knowledge, and the Teachings of Plants* (Minneapolis: Milkweed Editions, 2015), 28.

25. Kimmerer, *Braiding Sweetgrass*, 69–70.

Bibliography

Aaltola, Elisa. *Varieties of Empathy: Moral Psychology and Animal Ethics.* Lanham, MD: Rowman & Littlefield, 2018.
Abbey, Edward. *The Monkey Wrench Gang.* Philadelphia: Lippincott, 1975.
Allee, Warder Clyde. *Animal Aggregations: A Study in General Sociology.* Chicago: University of Chicago Press, 1978.
Astro, Richard. *John Steinbeck and Edward F. Ricketts: The Shaping of a Novelist.* Aberdeen, IA: Western Flyer Publishing, 1973.
Amster, Randall. "Dark Tidings: Anarchist Politics in the Age of Collapse." In *Contemporary Anarchist Studies,* edited by Randall Amster et al. London: Routledge, 2009.
Aristotle. *History of Animals, Volume I: Books 1–3.* Translated by A. L. Peck. Loeb Classical Library 437. Cambridge, MA: Harvard University Press, 1965.
Bekoff, Marc. *The Emotional Lives of Animals: A Leading Scientist Explores Animal Joy, Sorrow, and Empathy—and Why They Matter.* Novato, CA: New World Library, 2007.
Bookchin, Murray. *The Ecology of Freedom: The Emergence and Dissolution of Hierarchy.* Palo Alto, CA: Cheshire Books, 1982.
Burns, Robert. "To a Mouse, On Turning Her Up in Her Nest with the Plough." In *Collected Works.* http://www.robertburns.org/works/75.shtml, 1785.
Callicott, Baird. "Environmental Philosophy Is Environmental Activism: The Most Radical and Effective Kind." In *Environmental Philosophy and Environmental Activism,* edited by D. E. Marietta and L. E. Embre, 19–36. Lanham, MD: Rowman & Littlefield, 1995.
Charbonneau, Bernard. *The Green Light: A Self-Criticism of the Ecological Movement.* London: Bloomsbury Academic, 2018.
Clark, Claire, and William Hoynes. "Images of Race and Nation after September 11." *Peace Review* 15, no. 4 (2003).
Culliney, John L., and David Jones. *The Fractal Self: Science, Philosophy, and the Evolution of Human Cooperation.* Honolulu: University of Hawai'i Press, 2017.
Darwin, Charles. *The Descent of Man and Selection in Relation to Sex.* Vol. 1. Cambridge: Cambridge University Press, 2009.

De Waal, Frans. *Chimpanzee Politics: Power and Sex among Apes*. Baltimore: Johns Hopkins University Press, 1982.

———. *The Age of Empathy: Nature's Lessons for a Kinder Society*. New York: Crown, 2009.

———. *Are We Smart Enough to Know How Smart Animals Are?* London: Faber and Faber, 2016.

———. *Mama's Last Hug: Animal Emotions and What They Tell Us about Ourselves*. New York: Norton, 2019.

Deleuze, Gilles. *Empiricism and Subjectivity*. New York: Columbia University Press, 1991.

Despret, Vinciane. "The Enigma of the Raven." *Angelaki* 20, no. 2 (2015): 57–76.

———. "Thinking Like a Rat." *Angelaki* 20, no. 2 (2015): 121–34.

Esposito, Roberto. *The Third Person*. Cambridge: Polity, 2012.

Ferguson, James. *The Anti-Politics Machine: Development, Depoliticization, and Bureaucratic Power in Lesotho*. Minneapolis: University of Minnesota Press, 1994.

Fimrite, Peter. "Exterminating Mice with Poison Would Protect Rare Seabirds on Farallons." *San Francisco Chronicle*, July 12, 2019.

Foreman, Dave. *Ecodefense: A Field Guide to Monkeywrenching*. Chico, CA: Abbzug Press, 2002.

Gordon, Deborah. *Ants at Work: How an Insect Society Is Organized*. New York: The Free Press, 2011.

Gordon, Uri. "Anarchism and Political Theory." PhD thesis, University of Oxford, 2007.

Graeber, David. *Fragments of an Anarchist Anthropology*. Chicago: Prickly Paradigm Press, 2004.

———. *Debt: The First 5000 Years*. New York: Melville House, 2011.

Haraway, Donna. *Staying with the Trouble: Making Kin in the Chthulucene*. Durham, NC: Duke University Press, 2016.

Hölldobler, Bert, and Edward Wilson. *The Ants*. Cambridge: Belknap Press, 1990.

Hume, David. *A Treatise of Human Nature*. Mineola: Dover, 2003.

Jeffers, Robinson. "Roan Stallion." In *The Selected Poetry of Robinson Jeffers*. Stanford, CA: Stanford University Press, 2001.

Johnson, Eric Michael. "Frans de Waal on Political Apes, Science Communication, and Building a Cooperative Society." *Scientific American*, July 11, 2011.

Keller, Laurent, and Élisabeth Gordon. *The Lives of Ants*. Oxford: Oxford University Press, 2010.

Keulartz, Jozef. *Dieren in ons Midden: Samenleven met dieren in het tijdperk van de mens*. Gorredijk: Noordboek, 2019.

Kimmerer, Robin Wall. *Braiding Sweetgrass: Indigenous Wisdom, Scientific Knowledge, and the Teachings of Plants*. Minneapolis: Milkweed Editions, 2015.

Klare, Michael. *Blood and Oil: The Dangers and Consequences of America's Growing Dependency on Imported Petroleum*. New York: Henry Holt, 2005.

Kropotkin, Peter. *Mutual Aid: A Factor of Evolution*. New York: New York University Press, 1972.

———. *Ethics: Origin and Development. The Collected Works of Peter Kropotkin, Vol. 8*. Montréal, New York: Black Rose Books, 1992.

———. *Conquest of Bread*. New York: Penguin Random House, 2015.

Kuperus, Gerard. "Heterogeneity and Injustice: A Sketch for a Lyotardian Approach to Animal Ethics." *Trans-Humanities* 8, no. 3 (October 2015): 149–68.

———. *Ecopolitical Homelessness: Redefining Place in an Unsettled World*. New York: Routledge, 2016.

———. "An Ecology of the Future: Nietzsche and Ecological Restoration." In *Ontologies of Nature*, edited by Gerard Kuperus and Marjolein Oele. New York: Springer, 2017.

———. "Listening to the Salmon: Latour's Gaia, Aboriginal Thinking, and the Earth Community," *Environmental Philosophy* 16, no. 2 (2019).

———. "Our Common Home and the True Dharma Eye: Dōgen and Laudato Si in the Anthropocene." In *Faith and Social Justice: Environmental and Economic Justice*. San Francisco: University of San Francisco Press, 2020.

———. "Westering and Breaking Through: Zen Buddhism on Cannery Row." In *Philosophy in the American West: A Geography of Thought*, edited by Josh Hayes, Gerard Kuperus, and Brian Treanor. London: Routledge, 2020.

Latour, Bruno. *We Have Never Been Modern*. Cambridge, MA: Harvard University Press, 1991.

———. "Pragmatogonies: A Mythical Account of How Humans and Nonhumans Swap Properties." *American Behavioral Scientist* 37, no. 6 (1994): 791–809.

———. "How to Talk about the Body? The Normative Dimension of Science Studies." *Body & Society* 10, no. 2–3 (2004): 205–29.

———. *Politics of Nature: How to Bring the Sciences into Democracy*. Cambridge, MA: Harvard University Press, 2004.

———. *Facing Gaia: Eight Lectures on the New Climatic Regime*. Hoboken, NJ: Wiley, 2017.

Lawlor, Leonard. "Following the Rats: Becoming-Animal in Deleuze and Guattari." *SubStance* 37, no. 3 (2008): 169–87.

Levinas, Emmanuel. *Totality and Infinity: An Essay on Exteriority*. Pittsburgh, PA: Duquesne University Press, 1969.

Lisca, Peter. *The Wide World of John Steinbeck*. New York: Gordian Press, 1981.

Lyotard, Jean-François. *The Differend: Phrases in Dispute*. Minneapolis: University of Minnesota Press, 1988.

Mendieta, Eduardo. "Patriotism and Anti-Americanism." *Peace Review* 15, no. 4 (2003).

Mendl, Michael T., and Elizabeth S. Paul. "Bee Happy: Bumblebees Show Decision-Making That Reflects Emotion-like States." *Science* 353, no. 6307 (2016), 1499–1500.

Mickey, Sam, and Adam Robbert. "Cosmopolitics." In *Integral Ecologies: Nature, Culture, and Knowledge in the Planetary Era,* edited by Sam Mickey, Sean Kelly, and Adam Robbert. Albany, NY: State University of New York Press, 2017.

Montgomery, David R. *King of Fish: The Thousand-Year Run of Salmon.* Boulder, CO: Westview Press, 2003.

Morrow, J. E., Jr. "Schooling Behavior in Fishes." *Quarterly Review of Biology* 23, no. 1 (1948): 27–38.

Nakayama, Shinnosuke, Reiji Masuda, and Masaru Tanaka. "Onsets of Schooling Behavior and Social Transmission in Chub Mackerel Scomber Japonicus." *Behavioral Ecology and Sociobiology* 61, no. 9 (2007): 1383–90.

Nelson, Richard. *Make Prayers to the Raven: A Koyukon View of the Northern Forest.* 1st ed. Chicago: University of Chicago Press, 1986.

Nietzsche, Friedrich. *The Gay Science: With a Prelude in Rhymes and an Appendix of Songs.* New York: Vintage Books, 1971.

———. *Daybreak.* Cambridge: Cambridge University Press, 2012.

Orange, Tommy. *There There.* New York: Knopf, 2018.

Pope Francis. *Laudato si': On Care for Our Common Home: Encyclical Letter.* Rome: Libreria Editrice Vaticana, 2015.

Rancière, Jacques. *Dissensus: On Politics and Aesthetics.* London: Bloomsbury Academic, 2015.

Rilke, Rainer Maria. "The Panther: In Jardin des Plantes, Paris." Translated by Stanley Appelbaum. In *Great Short Poems from Antiquity to the Twentieth Century.* Mineola, NY: Dover, 2011.

Rosemont, Henry. *Against Individualism.* Minneapolis: Lexington Books, 2016.

Russell, M. S. "The Politics of the Third Person: Esposito's Third Person and Rancière's Disagreement." *Critical Horizons* 15, no. 3 (2014): 211–30.

Ryley, Peter. *Making Another World Possible: Anarchism, Anti-capitalism and Ecology in Late 19th and Early 20th Century Britain.* London: Bloomsbury, 2013.

Schultheiss, Patrick, Sabine S. Nooten, Runxi Wang, et al. "The Abundance, Biomass, and Distribution of Ants on Earth." *Proceedings of the National Academy of Sciences* 119, no. 40 (2022).

Sen, Amartya. *Identity and Violence: The Illusion of Destiny.* New York: Norton, 2007.

Sharp, Hasana. *Spinoza and the Politics of Renaturalization.* Chicago: University of Chicago Press, 2011.

Sing, Maanvi. "Helicopters to Drop Poison on California's Farallon Islands amid 'Plague' of Mice." *The Guardian*, December 17, 2021, https://www.theguardian.com/us-news/2021/dec/17/california-farallon-islands-plague-mice-helicopter-poison.

Snyder, Gary. *Practice of the Wild.* San Francisco: North Point Press, 1990.

———. *A Place in Space: Ethics, Aesthetics, and Watersheds.* San Francisco: Counterpoint, 1995.

Spinoza, Baruch. *The Ethics: Treatise on the Emendation of the Intellect; Selected Letters.* Indianapolis: Hackett, 1992.

Stegner, Wallace. *Beyond the Hundredth Meridian: John Wesley Powell and the Second Opening of the West*. Boston: Houghton Mifflin, 1962.
Steinbeck, John. *Of Mice and Men*. New York: Penguin Books, 1993.
———. *The Grapes of Wrath*. Paramus, NJ: Globe Fearon, 1995.
———. *The Red Pony*. London: Penguin Books, 2012.
———. *Steinbeck: A Life in Letters*. New York: Penguin Books, 2014.
———. *Travels with Charley: In Search of America*, 2017.
Steinbeck, John, and Edward F. Ricketts. *The Log from the Sea of Cortez*. London: Penguin, 2001.
Stengers, Isabelle. "The Cosmopolitical Proposal." In *Making Things Public*, edited by Bruno Latour and Peter Weibel, 994–1003. Cambridge, MA: MIT Press, 2005.
———. *Cosmopolitics I*. Minneapolis: University of Minnesota Press, 2010.
———. *Cosmopolitics II*. Minneapolis: University of Minnesota Press, 2011.
Swanton, John Reed. *Tlingit Myths and Texts*. Washington, DC: Government Printing Office, 1909.
Taylor, Jacqueline. *Reflecting Subjects: Passion, Sympathy, and Society in Hume's Philosophy*. Oxford: Oxford University Press, 2015.
White, Lynn. "The Historical Roots of Our Ecologic Crisis." *Science*, 15, no. 3767 (1967): 1203–7.
Wildcare. "Stop the Farallon Islands Poison Drop." https://discoverwildcare.org/rat-poison-rodenticides-farallon-islands/. December 2021. Retrieved May 20, 2022.
Wilson, Edward O. "Is Humanity Suicidal?" *New York Times,* May 30, 1993.
———. *Anthill*. New York: W. W. Norton & Company, 2011.
Yunkaporta, Tyson. *Sand Talk: How Indigenous Thinking Can Save the World*. New York: HarperOne, 2020.

Index

Abbey, Edward, 134, 146–56
Abram, David, 14
Actor Network Theory (ANT): concept of, 9, 15–16, 115; salmon as political beings and, 39, 44–50, 53–54, 58–62
adjunct labor, 199n1
Aesop fables, 51
Against Individualism (Rosemont), 103–4
aggression. *See* conflict
Albee, George, 122–23
Allee, W. C.: *Anthill* (Wilson) and, 144; on collaboration and cooperation, 10, 114, 116, 127–28; phalanx theory (Steinbeck) and, 122–23; Steinbeck and Ricketts and, 114, 116, 117–18
alpha males, 31, 88–89, 91–96, 104–5, 166
"alternative facts," 149
amoebas, 123
Amsterdam, 180, 211n22
anarchism: Abbey and, 134, 146–56; ant colonies and, 31, 131–34, 143–45, 154–59, 166; ecopolitics and, 21–22, 169–70; Kropotkin and, 134–35, 159, 208n56
Animal Aggregations (Allee), 114, 117
ant colonies: collaboration and cooperation in, 5, 131–32, 144–45, 157; decision-making and anarchism in, 31, 131–34, 143–45, 154–59, 166; Wheeler on, 116
Anthill (Wilson), 13–14, 144, 146, 149, 154
Anthropocene: as global crisis, 15; as "postnatural period" (Latour), 49; potential positive change in, 165–68; salmon as political beings and, 38, 51–54, 171; Sixth Great Extinction and, 15, 38, 171
anthropodenial, 20, 200n2
anthropofabulation, 4, 47
anthropomorphism, 48–49, 137
arche, 44–46
"Argument of Phalanx" (Steinbeck), 118. *See also* phalanx theory (Steinbeck)
Aristotle: Actor Network Theory (Latour) and, 45–46; on animal societies as political, 2, 4–5, 6; on humans as political animals, 2, 109, 110; on *logos*, 2
Astro, Richard, 115–16, 118, 122, 123

bears, 18, 37–38, 46, 210n8
bees, 2, 118, 131–32, 174
behavioral ecology, 116
behaviorism, 186

219

Bergson, Henri, 100
Between Pacific Tides (Ricketts), 115
Beyond the Hundredth Meridian (Stegner), 125
Bible, 51
The Biggest Little Farm (documentary), 195n28
Black Lives Matter movement, 3, 133, 161–62
Blackfish (orca), 1
Boodin, John Elof, 120
Bookchin, Murray, 2, 23, 29–30, 31, 166
borders. *See* deterritorialization and decolonization
Braiding Sweetgrass (Kimmerer), 177
brown bears (grizzlies), 18, 37–38, 46
Buddhism, 3–4, 103
bullshit jobs, 107
Burns, Robert, 74–75, 76
Bush, George W., 108

Callicott, Baird, 25
capitalism: Abbey on, 149–51, 154; democracies and, 158; empathy and, 87–88, 97–98; failures of, 25, 187–88; U. Gordon on, 156; Kropotkin on, 136, 208n56; Machiavellian or Hobbesian politics and, 91–92; Marx and Engels on, 161–62; neoliberalism and, 164–65; politics and, 162–65; refugees and, 71–73; Ryley on, 139; social Darwinism and, 97–98; Waal on, 97–98, 107–8, 176
Capitalocene, 15
Catalina Islands, 66
Charbonneau, Bernard, 2–3
children, 173, 178, 186
chimpanzee politics: collaboration and cooperation and, 5, 88–90, 98–99, 110–11, 173; empathy and, 5, 10, 43, 88–90, 92, 96–99, 101–3, 104, 113, 166, 169, 173, 177; identity politics and, 106–9; mice and rats and, 90; personalities and self in, 93, 103–6; power and leadership in, 10, 31, 88–96, 102–3, 104–5; role of females in, 31, 95–96, 97
Chimpanzee Politics (Waal): Gingrich and, 88; on personalities and self, 93, 103–6; on power and leadership, 88–99, 107
Christianity, 6–7, 56, 103
Civil Rights movement, 3
classism, 129
climate change: failed human politics and, 11–12, 77, 149, 151, 161–62, 172; as global crisis, 15; migration and, 129–30; new discourses and, 185–86; protests and, 133; social problems and, 156
collaboration and cooperation: ant colonies and, 5, 131–32, 144–45, 157; benefits of, 5; chimpanzee politics and, 5, 88–90, 92, 98–99, 102, 110–11, 173; vs. conflict, 85; ecopolitics and, 24–25, 129, 175–76, 191; empathy and, 92, 98–99; as essential, 10–11, 91; neo-Darwinism on, 39, 114, 116, 117–18, 127–28; politics and, 8–9, 162, 168–69; salmon as political beings and, 5, 38–39, 40–50, 113, 117; social movements and, 163–64; Steinbeck and Ricketts on, 116–18; in tidepool communities, 128–29. *See also* mutual aid (Kropotkin)
collective unconscious, 119–20, 124
colonialism, 23
colonies, 131–32. *See also* ant colonies
colonization, 78, 110–11, 125, 143. *See also* deterritorialization and decolonization

Communist Manifesto (Marx and Engels), 161–62
competition: capitalism and, 97–98; chimpanzee politics and, 88–90; empathy and, 133; vs. mutual aid (Kropotkin), 3, 32, 85, 175–76; survival of the fittest and, 10–11, 97–98, 102, 117, 169, 173
conatus, 124
conflict: chimpanzee politics and, 89, 92–99, 102, 173; Kropotkin on, 142–43; roots of, 133; Steinbeck and Ricketts on, 85; survival of the fittest and, 10–11, 97–98, 102, 117, 169, 173
Confucianism, 103–5
Conquest of Bread (Kropotkin), 207n39
conspiracy theories, 120–21, 161, 163–64, 184
consumerism, 208n54
convergent evolution, 4
cooperation. *See* collaboration and cooperation
cosmopolitics, 17, 20. *See also* ecopolitics
Covid-19 pandemic, 161–62, 168–69
coyotes, 27–28
Critical Mass movement, 77–78
Cuyahoga River, 52

Dakota Access Pipeline protests, 3, 161–62
Darwin, Charles, 7, 55, 174–75
Darwin, George, 119
Darwinism: on groups, 41; Kropotkin and, 134, 135–41, 157–58; misinterpretations of, 56; on survival of the fittest, 10–11, 97–98, 102, 117, 169, 173. *See also* neo-Darwinism; social Darwinism
Dawkins, Richard, 98
De anima (Aristotle), 2

decision-making: ant colonies and, 14, 31, 131–34, 143–45, 154–59, 166; in bee colonies, 131–32; chimpanzee politics and, 93–96; elections and, 31, 60, 132–33; groups and, 5; in non-human societies, 31
decolonizing politics, 64–65, 78, 82–84
deer, 192
Deleuze, Gilles: on "becoming," 64, 68–73, 79, 82–83; on Hume, 100–101, 178, 181, 182–83, 185–86
democracies: Abbey on, 151–53; in Athens, 147; capitalism and, 158; ecopolitics and, 21–22; failures of, 12–14, 149; Kropotkin on, 142; Lyotard on, 182. *See also* elections
dēmokratia, 162
Dempster, Beth, 16
deontology, 103
Derrida, Jacques, 68
The Descent of Man (Darwin), 136, 205n28
Despret, Vinciane, 79–81, 84, 115
deterritorialization and decolonization, 64–65, 70–72, 82–84, 181, 190–91
differend, 18–19, 22, 23
Le Différend (Lyotard), 183–84
Dust Bowl, 73–74, 121, 122, 204n30

eagles, 18, 37–38, 46, 66
Earth First! 148
Earth Liberation Front (ELF), 147
Ecodefense (Foreman), 148, 149–50
ecopolitics: aims of, 24–30, 188–89; anarchism and, 21–22, 169–70; collaboration and cooperation and, 129, 175–76, 191; on common good as shared good, 21–24; context of, 15–19; Indigenous cultures and, 12–13; new discourses and, 179–82; *oikos* (home) and, 18–21,

ecopolitics *(continued)* 23–24, 27–28, 29, 33, 62, 177, 188; program for, 190–91; sympathy (empathy) and, 24–25, 26, 167–68, 173–78, 191
ecotage, 146–56
education and educational systems, 186, 191
elections: capitalism and, 162–64; decision-making and, 31, 60, 132–33; ecopolitics and, 21–22; polarization and, 166–67
Elton, Charles S., 29
emotions, 174–75
empathy: Aaltola on, 14; capitalism and, 87–88, 97–98; chimpanzee politics and, 5, 10, 43, 88–90, 92, 96–99, 101–3, 104, 113, 166, 169, 173, 177; collaboration and cooperation and, 88–90, 92, 98–99; competition and, 133; ecopolitics and, 24–25, 26, 167–68, 173–78, 191; in human societies, 87–88, 166–67, 199n31; Kropotkin on, 137–41; mice and rats and, 5, 43, 64, 65, 83–84, 85, 90, 113, 169, 173–74, 176, 177; new discourses and, 158–59; role of, 146; social Darwinism and, 105–6; Waal on, 88–90, 92, 96–99, 101–3. *See also* sympathy
Emu, 57–58, 139
Engels, Friedrich, 161–62
An Enquiry Concerning Human Understanding (Hume), 100
Enron, 97–98, 107, 176
environmental philosophy and literature, 15, 25, 165
Esposito, Roberto, 183
ethics, 19, 135, 137–41, 146, 158, 172, 174, 178. *See also* virtue ethics
Ethics (Kropotkin), 135, 141, 142–43, 208n41

euthanasia, 67
evolutionary theory. *See* Darwinism
The Expression of Emotions in Man and Animals (Darwin), 174–75

Facing Gaia (Latour), 39, 44–50, 53–54, 58–62
fake news, 184
Farallon Islands, 65–68
fascism, 23, 120, 123, 124, 129
Ferguson, James, 210n6
Foreman, Dave, 148, 149–50
Foucault, Michel, 2, 26, 106, 118
Francis, Pope, 56, 210n2
Freud, Sigmund, 95
Fuller, Buckminster, 209n65

Galilei, Galileo, 53
gender identity and gender roles, 69–70, 96
genocide, 7, 125, 164, 172
gift economy: concept of, 26, 134, 189–90; chimpanzee politics and, 102; salmon as political beings and, 37–38, 46, 54, 58
Gingrich, Newt, 88
glaucous-winged gulls, 66
globalization, 68, 77
Gordon, Deborah, 144–45, 154
Gordon, Élisabeth, 143
Gordon, Uri, 156
Graeber, David, 28, 72, 107, 134, 189
grammar of animacy, 50
The Grapes of Wrath (Steinbeck): collaboration and cooperation in, 176; on Dust Bowl, 74, 121, 122, 204n30; as hopeful, 75; phalanx theory (Steinbeck) and, 121–23, 204n30; undocumented workers and, 129
grizzlies (brown bears), 18, 37–38, 46
Grotius, Hugo, 6, 9

groups: Abbey on, 151–53; beginning of politics and, 9–11, 32–33, 109; chimpanzee politics and, 92–99; decision-making and, 5; Kropotkin on, 149, 152, 158. *See also* mutual aid (Kropotkin); power and, 77–78; salmon as political beings and, 40–50, 61–62, 117; Steinbeck and Ricketts on, 43, 113–18, 126, 129, 152, 157. *See also* phalanx theory (Steinbeck)
The Guardian (newspaper), 67
Guattari, Félix, 64, 68–73, 79, 82–83
Gulf of California (Sea of Cortez). See *The Log from the Sea of Cortez* (Steinbeck and Ricketts)

habitat, 39–40
habitat restoration projects, 52–53, 66
Haida culture, 1
Haraway, Donna, 13, 16–17, 21, 177
Hardin, Garret, 139, 172–73
Hawadax Island, 66
Hawaiʻi, 78
Heidegger, Martin, 39–40, 59, 118
Heinrich, Bernd, 80
herd culture, 41
herd mentality, 3, 118–19, 152, 158, 169, 188
higher education, 191
Hitler, Adolf, 120, 123
Hobbes, Thomas: on animal societies as not political, 6, 11; Kropotkin and, 136; on power and leadership, 91–92, 95, 107; social contract theory and, 6, 9, 10, 106, 110
Hölldobler, Bert, 143
homelessness, 11, 26, 127, 161–62
Homo sapiens, 110
human political societies: beginning of, 9–11, 32–33, 109; capitalism and, 162–65; collaboration and cooperation and, 168–69; failures of, 11–14, 25, 38, 77, 149, 151, 161–68, 171–72; non-human societies and, 1–14, 30–33, 109–11, 170–71
Hume, David: Deleuze on, 178, 181, 182–83, 185–86; on habits, 164; on sympathy, 99–101, 175, 184
Hurricane Matthew, 185
Husserl, Edmund, 14
Huxley, T. H., 135, 136

identity politics, 106–9
Indigenous cultures: colonialism and, 23; decolonizing politics and, 78; ecopolitical wisdom of, 12; environmental philosophy and, 15; gift economy and, 134, 189–90; on narcissism, 57–58, 139; orca (Blackfish) in, 1; as political, 6–7; salmon as political beings and, 38, 39, 49–51, 53, 54–59, 60–62, 84–85, 145. *See also* Tlingit culture
individualism, 3–4, 103, 167–68, 175–76
Italian fascism, 120, 123, 129

January 6, 2021, storming of the Capitol, 122
Japan, 120, 123
Jeffers, Robinson, 165–66, 173
Jung, Carl Gustav, 119, 123, 124
justice, 19, 135, 137–41, 146, 158, 172, 174, 178

Kafka, Franz, 64
Kant, Immanuel, 3, 22, 103, 134
Karni Devi Temple, 64, 82–83, 99, 177
Keller, Laurant, 143
Keulartz, Jozef, 198n5
killer whales (orcas), 1–2
Kimmerer, Robin Wall: on gift economy, 26, 37–38, 54, 102,

224 | Index

Kimmerer, Robin Wall *(continyued)* 188–89; on grammar of animacy, 50; on kinship, 177; on Potawatomi (language), 28–29
King, Martin Luther, Jr., 147
kinship, 16, 28, 38, 145, 167, 177, 191
Kropotkin, Peter (Pyotr): anarchism and, 134–35, 159, 208n56; *Anthill* (Wilson) and, 144; Darwinism and, 134, 135–41, 157–58; on groups, 149, 152, 158. *See also* mutual aid (Kropotkin); on justice and ethics, 19, 135, 137–41, 146, 158, 172, 174, 178; on morality, 135, 139–41, 174; on mutual aid, 3, 5, 8–9, 10, 32, 85, 96, 134, 135–39, 140–43, 152, 173, 175–76; on power, 2; on sympathy (empathy), 137–41; Waal and, 96, 102

language, 28–29, 39–40, 182, 186
Latour, Bruno: Actor Network Theory (ANT) and, 9, 15–16, 115; ecopolitics and, 21, 24; on natural science, 211n20; salmon as political beings and, 39, 44–50, 53–54, 58–62
Laudato si' (Pope Francis), 210n2
Lawlor, Len, 64, 68–72
"The Leader of the People" (Steinbeck), 126
leadership: chimpanzee politics and, 31, 88–96, 102–3; Hobbes on, 91–92, 95, 107; Kropotkin on, 142; Machiavelli on, 91–92; phalanx theory (Steinbeck) and, 123–24, 132–33, 166; Waal on, 88–96, 102–3, 104–5, 107
Leviathan (Hobbes), 6, 11
Levinas, Emmanuel, 78
lifeboat ethics, 172–73
Lisca, Peter, 128

Locke, John, 6
The Log from the Sea of Cortez (Steinbeck and Ricketts): *Anthill* (Wilson) and, 144; on collective unconscious, 119–20; on conflict, 85; on groups, 43, 113–18, 126, 129, 152, 157; phalanx theory (Steinbeck) and, 205n53; on technology, 128
logos, 2
Lovelock, James, 53–54
Lucretius, 120
Lyotard, Jean-François, 18–19, 22, 23, 101, 182–84

Machiavelli, Niccolò, 91–92, 95, 107
Mama's Last Hug (Waal), 200n2
Marker Meer, 179–80
Marx, Karl, 2, 3, 106, 133, 154, 161–62
Matthew (hurricane), 185
mētis, 79–80
MeToo movements, 3, 161–62
mice and rats: "becoming" (Deleuze and Guattari) and, 64, 68–73, 79, 82–83; chimpanzee politics and, 90; decolonizing politics and, 64–65, 78, 82–84; deterritorialization and, 64–65, 70–72, 82–84, 181; empathy and, 5, 43, 64, 65, 83–84, 85, 90, 113, 169, 173–74, 176, 177; as good pets and sacred animals, 64, 82–83; as pests, 63–68; salmon as political beings and, 84–85; in Steinbeck's fiction, 64, 73–77, 79, 84; territoriality at Karni Devi Temple of, 82–83, 99, 177
Mickey, Sam, 20
migration: climate change and, 129–30; compared to mice and rats, 65, 68–69, 71–73, 77, 83–84. *See also* deterritorialization and decolonization; Dust Bowl and,

73–74, 121, 122, 204n30; empathy and, 177–78; Steinbeck on, 125–27, 128. *See also* refugees
militarism, 120, 123, 129
Mill, John Stuart, 136, 141
Miller, Chuck, 197n38
Mills, Charles, 7, 106, 164
The Monkey Wrench Gang (Abbey), 134, 146–56
Montgomery, David, 47, 51
morality, 135, 139–41, 174
Morrow, James, 42
mutual aid (Kropotkin): vs. competition, 3, 32, 85, 175–76; Darwinism and, 135–39; as essential, 5, 10, 134, 140–43, 152, 173; ethics and justice and, 8–9; politics as, 8–9; Waal and, 96
Mutual Aid (Kropotkin), 135, 141–42

narcissism, 57–58, 139
Native American cultures: salmon as political beings and, 38, 39, 49–51, 53, 54–59, 60–62, 84–85, 145; *There There* (Orange) and, 172–73; violence, genocide, and injustice against, 7, 71, 164, 182. *See also* Indigenous cultures
Natsilane, 1
natura naturata, 124
nature/culture distinction, 46–47
Nazi Germany, 120, 123
Neanderthals, 10, 110, 135
Nelson, Richard, 25–26
neo-Darwinism: on collaboration and cooperation, 39, 114, 116, 117–18, 127–28; on conflict, 85; Waal and, 102. *See also* Allee, W. C.
neoliberalism, 164–65
Netherlands, 179–80, 193n7
Nietzsche, Friedrich: on Christianity, 56; Deleuze and Guattari and, 69–70; on God as dead, 165; on herd mentality, 3, 118–19, 152, 158, 169, 188; social contract theories and, 7
non-human societies: human political societies and, 1–14, 30–33, 170–71. *See also* ant colonies; chimpanzee politics; mice and rats; salmon as political beings; tidepool communities

Occupy movement, 133, 161–62
Of Mice and Men (Steinbeck), 74–77, 79, 84, 122
oikos (home), 18–21, 23–24, 27–28, 29, 33, 62, 177, 188
Oostvaarders Plassen, 179
oppression, 125, 129
Orange, Tommy, 172–73, 175, 182
orcas (killer whales), 1–2
organicism, 117
owls, 66, 67

Partij voor de Dieren (Party for the Animals), 193n7
Pateman, Carole, 7
"The Pearl" (Steinbeck), 205n53
phalanx theory (Steinbeck): ant colonies and, 144, 145; on dangers of groups, 146, 149; ecopolitics and, 191; *The Grapes of Wrath* (Steinbeck) and, 121–23, 204n30; on groups as essential, 158, 163, 181; Kropotkin and, 142; leadership and, 123–24, 132–33, 166; *The Log from the Sea of Cortez* (Steinbeck and Ricketts) and, 205n53; new discourses and, 156; politics and, 164; salmon as political beings and, 121; tidepool communities and, 114, 118–27, 129–30
phenomenology, 14
"The Philosophy of Breaking Through" (Ricketts), 123

plagues, 73, 76–77
Plato, 3, 147
poison (rodenticide), 66–67
polis, 2, 4–5, 12, 169, 188
politics: as mutual aid, 8–9; vs. society, 2–3, 5–8. See also ecopolitics; human political societies; non-human societies
Politics of Nature (Latour), 48
posthuman humanism, 13–14
Potawatomi (language), 28–29
power: chimpanzee politics and, 10, 31, 88–96, 92–96, 102–3, 104–5; democracies and, 132–33; groups and, 77–78; Hobbes on, 91–92, 95, 107; politics and, 2–3; Waal on, 88–96, 102–3, 104–5, 107

queens, 131–32

racism, 123, 125, 129, 161–62
radical environmental movements, 146–56
Rancière, Jacques, 10, 22–23, 183
rats. See mice and rats
Raven (Tlingit trickster), 55–58
ravens, 80
Rawls, John, 7, 9
The Red Pony (Steinbeck), 123–24
refugees: compared to mice and rats, 65, 68–69, 71–73, 77, 83–84. See also deterritorialization and decolonization; empathy and, 177–78; failed human politics and, 11–12, 25, 77, 161–62, 171–72
The Republic (Plato), 147
Ricketts, Ed: on amoebas, 123; on collaboration and cooperation, 10; Jeffers and, 165–66. See also *The Log from the Sea of Cortez* (Steinbeck and Ricketts)
Ritter, W. E., 114, 144

rivers and creeks, 52–53
Robbert, Adam, 20
rodenticide (poison), 66–67
Rosemont, Henry, 103–4
Rousseau, Jean-Jacques, 2, 6, 10, 83, 106, 110, 133
Russell, M. S., 183
Ryley, Peter, 138–39

salmon as political beings: Actor Network Theory (Latour) and, 39, 44–50, 53–54, 58–62; Anthropocene and, 38, 51–54, 171; collaboration and cooperation and, 5, 38–39, 40–50, 113, 117; disappearance of, 51–54; emotions and, 174; gift economy and, 37–38, 46, 54, 58; habitat and, 39–40; habitat restoration projects and, 52–53, 66; mice and rats and, 84–85; Native American philosophies and, 38, 39, 49–51, 53, 54–59, 60–62, 84–85, 145; *oikos* (home) and, 18; phalanx theory (Steinbeck) and, 121
"Salmon Boy" (Tlingit story), 50, 54–55, 58–59, 60–62, 177
San Francisco Chronicle (newspaper), 66
San Francisco—Still Wild At Heart (documentary), 27
Sartre, Jean-Paul, 152
science studies, 15
Sea of Cortez (Gulf of California). See *The Log from the Sea of Cortez* (Steinbeck and Ricketts)
selfish gene, 98
Sen, Amartya, 108
sensus communis (consensus), 22–23
Serres, Michel, 7
Sixth Great Extinction, 15, 38, 171
Skilling, Jeff, 98
slavery, 7, 28, 71, 172

Smith, Adam, 122
Snyder, Gary, 13, 14, 17–18, 19, 51
social behavior, 42
social contract theories: on beginning of politics, 10, 109; identity politics and, 106; mice and rats and, 83; new discourses and, 7–8, 180–81; on society and politics as human, 5, 10–11; on state of nature, 6–7, 110; subjection and passivity in, 9; wealthy and, 133–34
social Darwinism: capitalism and, 97–98; empathy and, 105–6; Kropotkin and, 134; Steinbeck and Ricketts and, 117; on survival of the fittest, 10–11, 97–98, 102, 117, 169, 173; Waal on, 105–6
social media, 27, 161–62
social transmission, 42
society: vs. politics, 2–3, 5–8
Socrates, 147
Spencer, Herbert, 97–98, 136, 208n41
Spinoza, Benedictus de, 118–19, 124
Stegner, Wallace, 125
Steinbeck, John: imagery of mice and, 64, 74–77, 79, 84; Jeffers and, 165–66; on migration, 125–27, 128; Nobel Prize acceptance speech by, 128. See also *The Log from the Sea of Cortez* (Steinbeck and Ricketts); phalanx theory (Steinbeck)
Stengers, Isabelle, 17, 20, 21, 22, 25
stimulus checks, 187–88
stories and storytelling, 191
Surprising Europe (documentary, book, and TV series), 211n15
survival of the fittest, 10–11, 97–98, 102, 117, 169, 173
symbiosis, 191
sympathy: ecopolitics and, 24–25, 26, 167–68, 173–78, 191; Hume on, 99–101, 184; Kropotkin on, 137–41; new discourses and, 158–59; role of, 146. *See also* empathy
sympoiesis, 16

taxation, 194n27
Taylor, Jacqueline, 99
technology: Abbey on, 155; Fuller on, 209n65; Steinbeck and Ricketts on, 128; uses and impact of, 27, 59–60, 81, 162, 180, 187, 191. *See also* social media
telos, 44–46
temp workers, 87–88, 107–8
terrorism, 72
There There (Orange), 172–73, 175, 182
"Thinking Like a Rat" (Despret), 79–81, 84, 115
Thirty Meter Telescope (TMT) protests, 78, 161–62
Thoreau, Henry David, 127
Thunberg, Greta, 133, 186
tidepool communities: collaboration and cooperation in, 128–29; phalanx theory (Steinbeck) and, 114, 118–27, 129–30; Steinbeck and Ricketts on, 113–18, 119–20, 157
tides, 57
Tlingit culture: orca (Blackfish) in, 1; salmon as political beings and, 38, 50–51, 53, 54–59, 60–62, 177; "Salmon Boy" story and, 50, 54–55, 58–59, 60–62, 177
"To a Mouse" (Burns), 74–75, 76
totalitarianism, 23, 120, 123, 124
Travels with Charley (Steinbeck), 125–27
trees, 18, 38, 46, 52–53
Trump, Donald, 162–63

Uexküll, Jakob von, 80
undocumented workers, 129

University of San Francisco, 27–28
utilitarianism, 103

"The Vigilante" (Steinbeck), 123
violence. *See* conflict
virtue ethics, 103
voting. *See* elections

Waal, Frans de: *Anthill* (Wilson) and, 144; on anthropodenial, 20, 200n2; on capitalism, 97–98, 107–8, 176; on collaboration and cooperation, 10; on empathy, 88–90, 92, 96–99, 101–3, 166, 173; on power and leadership, 88–96, 102–3, 104–5, 107; on role on females, 31, 95–96, 97
walking, 191

war. *See* conflict
westering, 125–27, 128
What Is Philosophy? (Deleuze and Guattari), 69–70
Wheeler, William, 114, 116, 143, 145
White, Lynn, 56
Wildcare, 67
Williams, Charles, 123
Wilson, Alexandria, 197n35
Wilson, E. O., 13–14, 144, 146, 149, 154
Wilson, Edward, 143
Women's Marches, 3, 133, 161–62

Yunkaporta, Tyson, 6–7, 57–58, 139

Zen Buddhism, 3–4, 103